PRAISE FOR
THE SALES PLAYBOOK FOR HYPE.   ____ GROWTH

"*Proof this works!* We hired Dan Larson as our coach to help us implement a sales coaching plan turnaround for one of our portfolio companies based on Jack Daly's proven systems. Dan helped us coach, train, and implement a plan to fix the culture problem. He helped create a focused sales strategy, install new sales-management and team models, and use robust processes for sales training using a clear Sales Process and better tools to improve results. All driven by our sales-management team. After two-plus months proving results in one sector, we rolled it out to our four other sectors in the company.

Our results: We removed weak, nonproductive, overpaid sales management that was standing in the way of growing and replaced them with more effective Sales Managers. We doubled topline revenue and continued growing at double-digit rates.

Our focus areas to implement success:

1. Effective sales management with the right leaders, in the right spots, with the right focus

2. Goal Achievement Plan implementation: setting goals back-to-front with a committed Action Plan

3. Focus on High Payoff Activities and Minimum Standards of Performance

4. Individual development plans, including one-on-one coaching for Managers with reps

5. Measuring, tracking, and accountability systems

6. Sales meetings, skills training, and sales-success tools

7. Energizing vision and building a winning culture

Jack's training and books cut right to what really works to grow sales results. Dan's coaching and what he's developed at Leverage Sales Coaching make it clear how to train, build, and implement it into a Sales Playbook that works. *Devour this book, and get busy using it!*"

GREG LINDBERG, CEO, Eli Global

"Building a playbook for your business is not an easy task but is necessary. *The Sales Playbook* is a great resource to guide and organize the creation of your business' plan to grow."

JACK CANFIELD, award-winning speaker; internationally recognized leader in personal-development and peak-performance strategies; author, *Chicken Soup for the Soul*® series

"Routine sets you free—and it's no different for building a world-class sales organization. Jack and Dan's book details in a very readable style exactly what you need to do, step-by-step, to identify your most high-potential activities and then build them into a winning playbook—the same thing the most consistently winning sports coaches, and their players, have done to be champions."

VERNE HARNISH, author, *Scaling Up (Rockefeller Habits 2.0)*; founder of the world-renowned Entrepreneurs' Organization (EO)

"Bottom line: If you are looking to improve performance, drive sales, and push your company into hyper growth, THIS is your playbook. Buy it, study it, execute on it."

DARREN HARDY, former Publisher & Editor *SUCCESS* magazine and *New York Times* bestselling author of *The Compound Effect*

"As a guy who has spent his lifetime in sports, I know that the best have a Playbook that drives best practices. The knowledge Jack and Dan have compiled in *The Sales Playbook* is a must-have for any business leader, with its systems and processes that are proven to grow most businesses."

DON YAEGER, nine-time *New York Times* best-selling author

"You can stop winging it! Most sales teams don't have a plan—they go out and work harder than they need to, achieving mediocre results because they are making things up as they go. You can stop that now! Read this book, create your 'Playbook,' and follow it! I know it works—I have built two companies from scratch that together employ over two thousand people. I did this in part because I have been using Jack's principles for over twenty years."

JASON REID, chairman, EmpireWorks

"This isn't a book to read. It's a book to use. *Playbook* shows us precisely how to put the winning Sales Process into action. It is a must-read (make that *must-use*) if you and your team want to achieve record sales!"

SHEP HYKEN, customer experience expert; *New York Times* best-selling author, *The Amazement Revolution*

"Jack Daly talks my language. When I read his books I understand every word because he's coming from the same core beliefs that guide me. He and Dan Larson have created a game-changing Sales Playbook for you. Consider this the first day of your new sales career at a higher level than before. *Use* this book, don't merely read it. Your life will change for the better."

JIM CATHCART, author, *Relationship Selling*, www.RelationshipSelling.com

"Jack taught me early in our friendship to 'model the masters.' Why reinvent the wheel when you can learn from those who have already created highly effective sales strategies? Jack is the best sales teacher I know—a master well worth following!"

BRIAN SCUDAMORE, founder and CEO, O2E Brands and 1-800-GOT-JUNK?

"Jack Daly has taught me that greatness does not choose you, you choose it. Greatness is determined by choices made every day, every hour. The ones that are extraordinary choose to be. *The Sales Playbook* gives your team the tools to choose greatness."

JOHN R. DIJULIUS III, author, *The Customer Service Revolution*

"Many sales books are long on great ideas, but short on how exactly to implement them. Thanks to Jack, we now have a practical, down-to-earth Playbook for getting the sales you want. Read it, use it, and see your revenue soar!"

CHRISTINE COMAFORD, neuroscience-based leadership and culture coach;
author, *SmartTribes: How Teams Become Brilliant Together*

"Jack Daly should write a Playbook for life, as no one does life better. As for Sales, Hyper, and Growth all in one sentence . . . they each equal Jack. I have heard, hired, and spoken for audiences worldwide and there is no greater sales trainer on the planet than Jack Daly. This Playbook is your ticket to sales success. Grab it the way Jack grabs life, and you will be a winner . . . ka-ching!"

MIKKI WILLIAMS, CSP, Speaker Hall of Fame; TEDx speaker; executive speech coach;
creator, Speakers School and Keynote Kamp

"This is a great gift to any organization with the courage to implement best-practices methodology. No successful company operates without a Playbook. I learned firsthand watching the amazing impact Jack Daly had by implementing a Sales Playbook into our organization."

MARK MOSES, founding partner and CEO, CEO Coaching International

"Very few companies are truly skilled at creating solid sales planning and coaching superstars. This book is a vivid 'how- to' manual, which will unequivocally ensure increased sales for companies of all sizes. Read this book now to maximize your valuable resources"

JAYNIE SMITH, author, *Creating Competitive Advantage*; CEO, Smart Advantage, Inc.

"*Hyper Sales Growth* is full of ideas and has had immense success as a best seller. The Playbook that Jack and Dan have created gives you a road map for developing the systems and processes to put their world-class ideas to work in your business."

RICHARD CARR, chair, Vistage

"A Sales Playbook is essential to the success of any amazingly successful sales team or company. Jack's newest book gives you step-by-step instructions to construct a proper Playbook while giving you interesting exercises to improve your team's performance. If you can't afford to hire Jack to come train your sales team, then buying this book is the next-smartest thing you can do to grow your sales. As someone who has grown sales from $1 to over $1 billion dollars, I strongly recommend Jack and *The Sales Playbook for Hyper Sales Growth.*"

RICH BALOT, founder and executive chairman, A Wireless

"Every business needs a Playbook . . . period. Jack and Dan have put together what I feel is one of the most important books for business today. Sales are the lifeblood of every business, and this book makes great sales available to everyone. There are no more excuses–take this book and go build your Playbook."

ANDY BAILEY, head coach, Petra Coach

"Jack and Dan are masters at the selling game, and following their Playbook is like getting an inside look into the 'secret sauce' of a championship team. These guys have lived the sales-trench warfare and deliver credible real-world examples that resonate with real salespeople. The Playbook kept our team focused on doing more of what works and less of what doesn't."

JOHN R. GROTE, VP of sales and marketing, Grote Industries

"I don't throw the word 'guru' around lightly. But Jack is the living embodiment of his own genius. He systematically aligns vision, goals, metrics, and tasks daily, weekly, monthly to help those around him accomplish more than they could on their own. Jack is a sales guru all right, and this book is a gift for anyone looking to create a better sales organization."

MICHAEL MADDOCK, CEO and founding partner, Maddock Douglas

"In addition to being a fantastic Xs and Os sales coach, Jack has shown over the years an impressive ability to adapt his lessons and tactics for a broad range of audiences. When we started working with Jack, our company was very small with just a handful of salespeople. Over twenty years later, we are a much different and larger company with hundreds of salespeople across dozens of countries. His messaging and guidance has evolved with us, which is very impressive to me. I can confidently say that any sales group, large or small, can learn a tremendous amount from Jack Daly."

LIZ ELTING, cofounder and co-CEO, TransPerfect

"A football team can have the best players and equipment, yet without the right coach, their genius won't show up on the field. Jack is an incredible coach who has a way of decoding the small actions in sales that deliver the highest outcomes. Anyone who is interested in increasing sales performance need only follow the instructions in this book."

CHRISTINA HARBRIDGE, mischief executive officer, Allegory, Inc.

"In my opinion, Jack Daly—a friend and mentor for more than twenty years—is hands down the best sales teacher on the planet. In today's world, many business owners are overworked, tired, and chasing to find the answer to their sales-growth problem. Well, they have found it. *The Sales Playbook* is a step-by-step blueprint for any company to use to increase sales, improve culture, and save a lot of time in the implementation process. This book provides the shortest path from point A to point B."

RICK SAPIO, CEO, Mutual Capital Alliance, Inc.

A couple of lessons that I have learned from Jack . . . you can smell culture the minute you walk into the door, how does your culture smell? After really paying attention to the smell of my sales team, I fired the entire group and recreated the team based on critical cultural criteria. We are now up over 50 percent on our close rates, and it's so much more fun to come to work! You don't grow sales; you grow your salespeople. Develop the Sales Process point-by-point based on the Best Practices of the top performers. You get what you measure: Are you measuring the results that you would like to produce?"

PATRICK CONDON, founder and CEO, Finished Basement Company

"I have known Jack for over twenty years through his speaking/teaching, guiding, and mentoring in Young Entrepreneurs' Organization and Young Presidents' Organization. I hired Jack to speak to our nationwide two hundred-person direct sales team, and his methods were key as we grew from $15M to $100M in sales in three fast years! Jack has a process—he cuts to the chase and makes one strive to achieve his or her personal best. And he leads by example in everything he achieves!"

JAMES F. KENEFICK, chairman, Better World Telecom

"*The Sales Playbook* is essential reading for CEOs, Sales Managers, salespeople, and others in any organization that plans to grow.

Jack has been a mentor and role model for over twelve years and is our go-to solution for building our sales organization. In those years, our sales have grown over four times, and profits have risen eight times. With this new tool, we can power our way higher in the next ten years. I plan to give copies to our customers so they can drive more sales for themselves and our company. Thank you, Jack!"

MICHAEL FANGER, president, Eastern Funding

"*The Sales Playbook* isn't a book to be read unless you have a highlighter and notepad handy. Jack Daly presents concepts that will enable your sales team to sell more and sell better. A must-read for executives!"

LEE B. SALZ, sales-management strategist; best-selling author, *Hire Right, Higher Profits*

"The last fourteen years, Medix has organically scaled from $0 to $170,000,000. For the last decade, it's been equally amazing to have a business mentor like Jack Daly. Through his books, presentations, and conversations, he has helped me bring vision, values, and culture into my organization. His strategy around people in the right seats with the right training is invaluable and is now in *The Sales Playbook for Hyper Sales Growth!* I'm a long-time Green Bay Packer fan and love Vince Lombardi. One thing Lombardi always had was a terrific Playbook. One thing that every sales organization needs for Hyper Sales Growth is Jack's new sales book, *The Sales Playbook*."

ANDREW D. LIMOURIS, president and CEO, Medix

"Jack simplifies the many complexities involved in running a sales force into simple measurable processes anyone can follow and implement. Jack will show you how to focus your time and attention on activities that will produce hyper results with your sales force. Jack is brilliant at making the complex simple and immediately implementable. Everything Jack does is focused on producing *hyper* results, and this book is no different. This is a must-read for anyone who is involved with building revenues."

BARRETT ERSEK, founder and CEO, Holganix

"If you want tremendous results for your sales team—*run,* don't walk—and get Jack's new book *The Sales Playbook for Hyper Sales Growth.*

Jack's amazing new book is exactly what every owner and Sales Manager needs to achieve Hyper Sales Growth! It walks you step-by-step on how to put systems in place for every facet of a winning sales team. This book will be a huge part of our winning sales program. Jack's done it again!"

JIM BENNETT, CEO, Worldwide Express

"Jack Daly isn't just an outstanding coach—he is the guru of growth. I have grown personally, and our company has grown exponentially from Jacks hands-on coaching. We wouldn't be where we are today without the systems and Playbooks he helped create. *The Sales Playbook for Hyper Sales Growth* is a must-read if you want to create the proper sales systems and processes in your business. The only thing better than the book is working with Jack!"

ERIK CHURCH, COO, Ordinary 2 Exceptional Brands

"Dan builds on the foundation of *Hyper Sales Growth* with the disciplines, planning, and Best Practices developed through years as a leading sales person and as the president and head coach of Leverage Sales Coaching. *Sales Playbook* brings it all together with proven systems and processes that demystify the art of sales and the path to true sales leadership–the ability to achieve repeatable successes."

BRAD VAN DAM, president and CEO, MARICH® Confectionery Company

"When business development is done right, there is no limit to what can be accomplished! What would happen for your business if every seller on your team, including your 'A' players, could sell more? If you want to know how to have your team follow your company's unique recipe for selling more in less time and with less effort, read this book. Jack Daly and Dan Larson nailed the key information and the path to success with *The Sales Playbook for Hyper Sales Growth*."

CARYN KOPP, chief door opener, Kopp Consulting, LLC

"Jack told the world how to accelerate sales growth two years ago with his book *Hyper Sales Growth*. Now his partner Dan Larson has detailed out the systems and processes to make it even easier to scale your business. Combine the books together and there can be no excuses!"

SCOTT DUFFY, founder and CEO, Content.Market; cohost, *Business & Burgers* podcast

"Having known Jack for years, I'm excited he put the Playbook into a book for entrepreneurs to be able to create a Sales Playbook in easy, concrete steps. Having done it himself in every company he was at, Jack is an expert at helping sales teams up their game by creating a concrete plan of action and an approach that is standardized across the company. Readers will be able to take this and create their own Sales Playbook that will launch the next chapter in their company's growth cycle."

JOHN BLY, CPA, founder, LBA Haynes Strand, PLLC; author, *Cracking the Code: An Entrepreneur's Guide to Growing Your Business thru M&A for Pennies on the Dollar*

"In a culture dominated by spin, Jack Daly continues to preach a stable, consistent, get-your-head-out-of-your ass-and-GET IT-DONE truth. The *Sales Playbook* cuts through all theories, 'what ifs,' and 'might works' and goes right to the 'how to.' The only question left is 'will you?'"

ARNIE S. MALHAM, founder and president, CJ Advertising, Legal Intake Professionals, and BetterBookClub; author, *Worth Getting Wrong*

"I first met Jack in 1999 when he spoke to my Vistage (CEO) group. I recognized his brilliance immediately. I have since had him speak at our annual national sales meeting multiple times, and each time he has provided usable, actionable, and results-oriented information. He has taught me that sales is a process. I have found his knowledge and methodology immensely helpful in keeping my team on track and getting the results I want. And I am beyond excited that he is divulging his personal Sales Playbook so I can take my team and my company to the next level."

KAREN CAPLAN, CEO and president, Frieda's Specialty Produce

"This is another powerful and valuable book from Jack Daly, who embodies MOTIVATION. Even those of us who think we are highly motivated cannot compete with Jack, who generously shares his experiences. I have seen the quality of his Playbook, and it is world-class. Jack knows winning sales teams better than anyone I have met, and this Playbook will tell you how to set up your own–step-by-step."

ROB FOLLOWS, founding CEO, STS Capital Partners; world leader in International M&A; Seven Summits and Everest completed, 2006

"Business is faster and more complex than ever. I love that Jack and Dan provide a real-life, Best Practices, and easy-to-use strategy that is adaptable to any business. We will use it to consistently deliver the plan throughout the entire sales team."

KEITH ALPER, CEO and founder, Nitrous Effect | An Agency Collective

"Jack Daly's *Hyper Sales Growth* and *The Sales Playbook* have literally changed my company's life . . . to the tune of 400 percent growth since implementation thirty-six months ago. Read it, and reap the rewards."

ADAM D. WITTY, founder and CEO, Advantage Media Group

"When you witness a high-energy Jack Daly presentation, you are always left wanting more. He writes his first book *Hyper Sales Growth*, and fittingly, his readers and fans *demand* a sequel–or 'Playbook' to help execute on his ideas, and this book delivers! This is a 'must-read' for all sales departments."

DAN GOULD, president/entrepreneur, Synergy; two-time Inc. 500 fastest-growing company.

"For nearing twenty years, I have been a great fan of Jack Daly and his incredible, well-proven approach to sales and sales management.

By exclusively using Jack Daly's sales and sales-management principles, OptiFuse has grown into one of the fastest-growing companies in America.

His book, *Hyper Sales Growth*, has become required reading for everyone at our company because like Jack explains so well . . . every person in the company is in sales, whether they like it or not.

After reading Jack and Dan's newest book, *The Sales Playbook for Hyper Sales Growth*, I now have a practical step-by-step approach to help my company not only understand all of the sales and sales-management theories that Jack professes but also help to put all of that theory into action. I fully expect to be ordering dozens of copies so that each member of my staff can help us to implement the 'Best Practices' set forth by Jack and Dan.

If you only read one book this year, I highly recommend that it be *The Sales Playbook for Hyper Sales Growth* . . . well, that is if you want to increase the sales performance of your company."

JIM KALB, president, OptiFuse

"*The Sales Playbook for Hyper Sales Growth* is a book for every business no matter the size. The systems and processes detailed in this book will positively impact many businesses, sales teams, and people in incredible ways. After I saw Jack speak at an event in 2007, my team immediately took action and followed the system and processes laid out in the book, which helped us hyper grow our business over a four-year period and successfully exit in 2012. I could not imagine sending a sales team out in the field without a Playbook. GAME CHANGER!"

DAVID SOBEL, partner, CEO Coaching International; former partner, Home Warranty of America

"Daly and Larson have done it again! Their rock-solid plays will get your whole sales team hitting goals just like your top performers. This time, they go way beyond sales psychology to give us invaluable insights into coaching and management. It's great to read their energetic and positive ideas."

BEN RIDLER, founder and CEO, Results.com

"I have seen Jack speak over a dozen times, I have spent hundreds of hours by his side learning at MIT, I have run for countless hours side-by-side at marathons and half Ironmans with him, he has spent nights in my home and we have had many meals together, and each and every time, there are nuggets of easy-to-implement in business tools, systems, processes, and ideas that all have an immediate positive effect—in business and in life. Much love and thanks for continuing to raise the bar. Giddy Up."

KRIS KAPLAN, K2 Coaching

"I have benefited greatly from the teachings of Jack Daly over the years, for both business and personal success. His expertise and ability to educate salespeople, sales management, and senior leaders on how to raise their sales game in any industry to new levels is both proven and powerful. This book, *The Sales Playbook for Hyper Sales Growth*, provides a best practice for sales organizations to leverage if serious about achieving Hyper Sales Growth. Jack lives life by design, and this book outlines concrete steps for creating a Sales-Playbook approach to achieve sales success by design."

DON ANTONUCCI, president, Regence BlueShield

"The book *Hyper Sales Growth* was the first beautiful materialization of Jack's advanced sales insights and energy. This new *Sales Playbook* is again the perfect blend between high-energy inspiration and simple, down-to-earth practical formats, checklists, and 'how tos.' Together they make undeniably the best sales system in the world."

KEES DE JONG, entrepreneur, speaker, investor, mentor, and columnist; cofounder, Spark Leadership Foundation

"Twenty years ago I had a front-row seat at a conference where Jack Daly was the keynote speaker. To this day, he remains the most impactful sales speaker I have seen. Period. The strategy he described in one hour became the backbone of our sales culture for our twelve companies. We've already adopted *The Sales Playbook for Hyper Sales Growth* as our next-generation 'go-to' sales strategy. And the results have already been stunning. If you want hyper sales growth, this is your Playbook!"

TROY HAZARD, entrepreneur, speaker, author, television host

"Having been in some sales capacity for the majority of my career (twenty-five-plus years), I find the common-sense approach in Jack's lessons both refreshing and real! Having a TRUE plan for success is a must in today's crazy competitive market. And having been a 'disciple' of Jack's training now for the past six years, I can say that this works! No doubt about it!

We have been working on our own handbook and know the work involved. So to have the ability to now have this amazing Playbook will only strengthen the tools we have been utilizing in our organization and will continue to GROW the amazing sales team we have!

Thanks for this AWESOME tool—I look forward to implementing it with our team!"

TODD HUCKABONE, director of sales, North America, PHILLIP JEFFRIES

"We have employed Jack's service for over ten years, for both our sales teams as well as inside personnel. Jack delivers a high-energy, rational, common-sense approach to sales that focuses on two really key areas: people relationships and regular discipline. The tools he provides have become mainstay for our organization's sales success. All new sales individuals participate in the Jack Daly course when joining our organization."

ED MCKENNA, president, McKenna Companies

"I had the pleasure to meet Jack almost fifteen years ago and learn some valuable lessons from him about developing sales in my businesses. Jack's expertise has been invaluable when my company was stuck selling or just wanted more. Having grown and sold five businesses, I now coach business leaders on how to develop strategy for their businesses. The majority of the time, sales are an issue. You may have sales, but are they the right sales that are maximizing the return for you and your customers? Jack's book, *Hyper Sales Growth,* is the book I turn to help business leaders enhance their sales. Now I am really excited because a few years ago, I had the opportunity to meet Dan Larson who gave me the key to bringing Hyper Sales Growth to life. Developing the Sales Playbook was the missing element. Dan took the decade of experience working with Jack and developed the details so business owners can get their Sales Playbook working for them quickly. If you want more of the right sales I strongly suggest reading this book and investing your time in the *Sales Playbook* the Hyper Sales Growth way."

DAVID CHAVEZ, CEO, Assured Strategies

"*The Sales Playbook for Hyper Sales Growth* is a game changer for any business and business owner. It sets the framework and plan for how to super-charge your sales team for growth! The ideas can relate to any business, and it is fun putting them into play and seeing the results unfold before your eyes!"

RIAD NIZAM, senior VP of sales, Master Electronics

"Having worked with both Jack and Dan for many years, I'm a firm believer of the concepts and skills they preach. *The Sales Playbook* enhances their teachings by providing clear and proven steps to achieve success. It is a must-read for salespeople, Sales Managers, and business owners who want to hyper grow sales.

ROGER LIN, Keysource Foods, LLC

"After so many years of convincing the entrepreneurial community that we needed a Sales Playbook, Jack and Dan finally wrote the 'how-to' guide on building a strong Sales Playbook. Before, this was only available to their top consulting clients, and now it's at your fingertips . . . now build a great sales organization and skyrocket your sales!"

DANIEL MARCOS, CEO, Growth Institute

"*The Sales Playbook* is brilliant, practical, and straightforward—a winning combination. There is no doubt that any company, large or small, can increase growth, profitability, and overall performance by reading this book and creating their own Playbook. If you are ready to transform your sales team and their performance, don't wait another moment—commit to this process, and results are sure to follow. A game changer by Jack and Dan. Way to go!"

DAVE GALBENSKI, founder, Lumen Legal;
former global chairman, Entrepreneurs' Organization (EO)

"My companies have been using Jack Daly for years, and the feedback is always through the roof for his unique way of commanding the attention of any audience. The most compliments I get from my staff are all of the real take-away items they obtain from Jack. We have all been to seminars where you are just counting the hours to leave. Not with Jack—you are counting the real solutions, and before you know it, time is up and it seems like you just got started. To this day, I quote Jack all the time to make me look way smarter than I really am!"

CHUCK BRENNAN, founder, president, and CEO, DLC Empire, LLC / Badlands Pawn

"The Sales Playbook for Hyper Sales Growth is a gem, one of a kind! Jack and Dan have shared their winning formula that will give you the 'unfair' advantage you need to crush the competition."

LARRY ZOGBY, president, RDS Same Day Delivery

"How many of us would dare to go public—not only with our personal and professional goals but also be publicly accountable for our progress toward those goals? Jack Daly does that. There is nothing he presents that he's not already applying in his own life. I've known Jack for twenty-plus years, as a client and a friend. He's a man of his word—a man who boldly gets things done. More than anyone I can name, Jack Daly will challenge, confront, and test one's most rigidly held assumptions. He will cajole, coach, and encourage with positivity and practical applications based on his astonishing record of success."

MARILYN MURPHY, CEO, The CTP Group, and "creative queen"

"The truth is, I only got to know Jack quite recently. But in that short time, I have secured massive learnings from him, and I never cease to be further informed when I listen to his wisdoms. What I love about this latest book is it doesn't just show you how—it gives you the template. *The Sales Playbook* has over thirty years of wisdom *and* his Playbook. What an investment!"

GERRY DUFFY, motivational speaker, author, and extreme sports enthusiast

"This book is perfect for a new salesperson looking to jump-start their career. It's just as valuable for the veteran as an excellent reminder of the skills needed to stay a great salesperson. Jack's sales advice has been the key to my success with launching several venture-backed companies."

JEFF ELLMAN, cofounder, Hireology & UrbanBound

"Jack and Dan have come together to share proven Best Practices on how to get the most out of a sales organization. Their philosophies are logical and easy to adapt to any organization dealing in a competitive environment and revolve around four ideas: having the right people on the team, creating the right processes, developing skills through training and practice, and implementing sales-management techniques to stay focused on the end goal."

MIKE WIEN, professor of franchising, Georgia State University; founder, The Specific Edge Institute; four-time competitor, Ironman World Championship

"I met Jack at an EO event in LA in 1996 at one of his first sales training workshops. I left with a tool kit of practical sales techniques for our business, which subsequently grew exponentially. We have been a disciple of Jack's no-nonsense, real-world teachings ever since. Jack's infectious energy and zest for life fuels an amazing lifestyle committed to family, friends, and a list of impressive goals and accomplishments. Jack is a friend and mentor and has made a fantastic impact on our international growth and success. If you are serious about exponentially growing your business, *The Sales Playbook* is a must-read."

BOB KIRSTIUK, cofounder and CEO, Advantage Parts Solutions

"Building a successful business in today's world is no easy matter. Having a Playbook and resource guide to help you grow your business with a step-by-step plan is required. This is a powerful source to help you shorten your path to success."

CINDY ERTMAN, EVP and national Sales Manager, RPM Mortgage;
CEO and founder, The Defining Difference

"Jack Daly was the keynote at our sales kickoff a handful of years ago. Our entire organization is still pumped up from that experience! Without a doubt, this book and its messages will yield the same result for anyone looking for massive growth and action. Onward and upward."

RYAN M. LANDRY, VP and general manager, New Horizons Learning Group

"I applaud Jack and Dan for this extraordinary gift to all of us in sales. I've admired Jack for a decade and have used his sales-management and coaching principles to affect my business, as well as dozens of my clients. The simplicity of knowing what to do and how to do it is made perfectly clear. Now, it's up to me. I'm in!"

DAVID ZELMAN, PhD, president and CEO, The Transitions Institute

"Jack does it again! This book captures in sharp detail the map and unprecedented changes needed to drive solid sales behaviors and values. More importantly, it offers a clear guide to sales leaders and their teams seeking to adapt and evolve to meet the demands of today's customer! It's a tool that every business needs to drive revenue to the next level!"

DARLENE KIRK, CEO, Kirk's Global Compass

THE SALES
PLAYBOOK
for *HYPER SALES* GROWTH

Work smarter. *Earn more.*

THE SALES
PLAYBOOK
for *HYPER SALES* GROWTH

JACK DALY & DAN LARSON

Advantage®

Published by Advantage, Charleston, South Carolina.
Member of Advantage Media Group.

ADVANTAGE is a registered trademark and the Advantage colophon is a trademark of Advantage Media Group, Inc.

Printed in the United States of America.

ISBN: 978-1-59932-842-3
LCCN: 2016953156

Cover design by George Stevens.

This publication is designed to provide accurate and authoritative information in regard to the subject matter covered. It is sold with the understanding that the publisher is not engaged in rendering legal, accounting, or other professional services. If legal advice or other expert assistance is required, the services of a competent professional person should be sought.

TreeNeutral
Advantage Media Group is proud to be a part of the Tree Neutral® program. Tree Neutral offsets the number of trees consumed in the production and printing of this book by taking proactive steps such as planting trees in direct proportion to the number of trees used to print books. To learn more about Tree Neutral, please visit **www.treeneutral.com.**

Advantage Media Group is a publisher of business, self-improvement, and professional development books. We help entrepreneurs, business leaders, and professionals share their Stories, Passion, and Knowledge to help others Learn & Grow. Do you have a manuscript or book idea that you would like us to consider for publishing? Please visit **advantagefamily.com** or call **1.866.775.1696.**

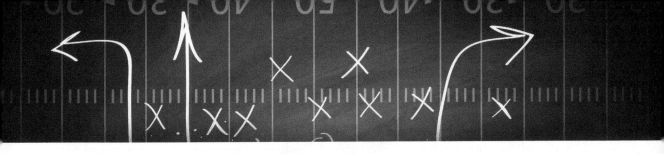

DEDICATION

FROM JACK:

I never contemplated writing this book. After writing *Hyper Sales Growth,* I figured I was done. Down the road I had, and continue to have, aspirations of writing a personal memoir, a looking-back journey on my triathlon/marathon/top-golf-course journey, and a series of books for kids to aspire to become entrepreneurs. But as far as books on sales and sales management, I figured I was done.

This book is inspired by, and thereby dedicated to, all the many readers of *Hyper Sales Growth* who contacted me with such positivity and enthusiasm and said, "Hey Jack, you've certainly convinced me that I should have a Sales Playbook. Well, I'm ready—I just don't know how and where to begin!" I reached out to my partner, Dan Larson, and asked if he would help me in this effort, as he has done so much heavy lifting in implementing my systems and processes with countless clients, and he never hesitated. (I suspect he didn't realize how much was going to be asked of him!) So, thanks to you, Dan, and most especially, thanks to all out there who have not only read or listened to my ideas on how to build a fast-growing, profitable business, but more importantly, have taken ACTION!

FROM DAN:

I learned a simple definition of leverage in business from Jack long ago: work to get more out of everything you're doing, often by doing less. Today we describe this as "work smarter, earn more."

Sales is a performance game with a very clear scorecard. Core for me in writing this book is a huge level of respect for what it takes to win the sales game—that is, all the players at every level doing the hard work, sweat, long hours, pushing through a lot of rejection to get a "yes," and figuring out how to win more. Winning the game requires owners and Sales Managers working hard to put a sales team together and trying to stay focused and produce the results needed. While I've learned what it takes to succeed, I now have a burning desire to help others leverage what we know and have proven to work so well.

I've been coaching company leaders and sales teams for well over a decade to implement Jack's Hyper Sales Growth systems and processes in just about every situation, size, and type of company. I'm convinced the need to know how to build a Playbook is enormous and ongoing.

Having a Playbook isn't the total answer, but it is the critical work tool that equips companies and teams to leverage their efforts to earn more and have more fun by winning bigger. So this book is dedicated to all my fellow sales professionals who are looking for a better way to win bigger.

Finally, I could write a book on what an incredible trainer, mentor, and "fire starter" Jack Daly has been for me. Thirteen years ago I had no idea exactly what I was getting into with Jack, but it has been an absolutely jam-packed thrill ride of pushing, learning, doing, proving, and improving—as well as laughs and fun—every step of the way.

Jack does so many remarkable things in his remarkably full life. So many times, while talking with him about his latest adventures, I shake my head, trying to understand how it's all possible. I don't know anyone who pours so much of himself into everything he does, in a nonstop demanding schedule, and yet somehow gets it all done exceptionally well. Jack, I still find you truly amazing. I'm grateful to be a partner with you in writing this book.

Thank you to Jack for being such an inspiration, and thank you to the readers who are willing to learn and take action on these ideas.

TABLE OF CONTENTS

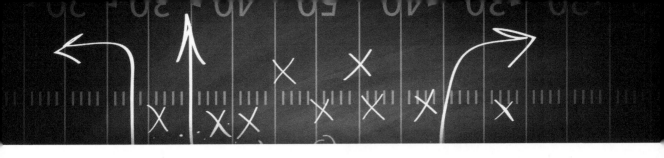

PREFACE

There isn't a coach in any sport on any level who would consider putting players on the field, on the ice, or on the court without proper preparation, without practice. Why doesn't the same go for sales teams?

Companies often ask me (Jack Daly) to come in and teach the Hyper Sales Growth concepts to their sales teams, to which I say, "Terrific—as a start, could you do me a favor and send me your most recent Sales Playbook with all of your current systems and processes so that I know how your people are doing it now?"

About 98 percent of the time, the silence on the other end of the line is deafening. What that tells me is that the vast majority of companies are sending their salespeople out onto the field without leveraging the systems and processes that have proven to work best for their company, that enable them to win more than they lose.

I have to tell you, there isn't a coach in the world who would send his players out onto the field with nothing more than a kiss for good luck and a general "Go for it!"

That would be absurd, right? How would the players respond to that approach? They'd want to know when they were going to practice and what plays they needed to run, and here's the coach saying, "Nah, we've got ABC team coming in tomorrow night. Let's just take the field then and see if we can win."

Most people practically belly laugh at the absurdity of that analogy, and yet that's exactly what we're doing with our businesses. That's why, when Sales Managers hear wise sayings such as "Inspect what you expect" from thought leaders and finally start tracking their salespeople, only to find that so many of them aren't doing that well, they have to realize that it's not the salespeople's fault. It's the Sales Managers'. What are they thinking when they put a salesperson in the field without systems, processes, or even practice?

That's the value of a Playbook, of having a regularly updated sales guide that contains all the systems and processes that your company knows will result in the highest payoffs.

In my 2014 book *Hyper Sales Growth*, I gave people, in a narrative form, the basics of how to build a winning culture, what a Sales Manager should be doing, and how to determine what the High Payoff Activities are for your company's Sales Managers and salespeople.

What our readers and those who hear our presentations have come back to us and said is, "Man, that was very helpful, but how do I build a Playbook?"

We've answered that question with this book. Do you want to see the forms, the systems, and the processes, as well as the order that you should be implementing them in your company? Then this is the book you need to build your company's definitive Sales Playbook for Hyper Sales Growth.

A series of tips like this throughout the book will help you keep your eye on the ball:

inSITE-app to get PLAYBOOK RESOURCES:
A unique feature of this book is that downloadable sales tools, templates, and videos are available to assist and accelerate your learning and building of your Playbook. All of these features are available by downloading the free inSITE-app in the Apple or Google Play Stores!
Please register your FREE account at http://leveragesalescoach.com/resources. Simply click "Register for Playbook Resources" and create a FREE account to access the inSITE-app to get PLAYBOOK RESOURCES on your mobile device or computer. Throughout the book the laptop icon will refer you to a downloadable tool, template, or video available in the inSITE-app. TAKE ACTION and USE the resources in this book!

SCORING PLAY:

Every company should build its own Playbook based on its industry, its company culture, and its specific knowledge of what works. Additionally, the process of building your own Playbook *with and through your team's inputs* creates buy-in and promotes learning. This book will help greatly in that process.

ON PROCESS:

In my three decades of coaching, I've learned that the process is much more important than the result.

NICK SABAN, head football coach, University of Alabama

ACKNOWLEDGMENTS

I can't imagine life without a mentor. Thanks Jim Pratt, you taught me so much about business, and even better, about life.

Speaking of mentors, a big shout out to the Top 10 Percenters. You guys show the way for all of us to learn the top plays for inclusion in our Sales Playbooks.

To my many clients who have entrusted their business to me in charting a course for successful growth in revenues and profits. I know I've contributed, but your success has been without parallel. Along the way I've learned much and reflect such in this Sales Playbook.

To my publisher, Adam Witty, and his talented Advantage Team. Three books in three years, and you've made it seem easy. You've created a monster; more to come!

Dan, *Hyper Sales Growth* was it for me. Without all your critical contributions as coauthor, this book wouldn't exist. Thanks for taking the brunt of the heavy lifting—true sales muscle is in evidence throughout the book.

While I take pride in "no employees," I sure have one helluva support team! There is no possible way I could travel so much, speak so much, and play so much without you all making it happen. I get the adulation and take the stage bows. You all make it happen behind the scenes. Not a day goes by without feelings of gratitude to each of you.

And the best for last—to my wife of forty-six-plus years, Bonnie. Those who know her well, and those who don't, all call her "Saint Bonnie." I get it! If it were just writing a book, that would be "one thing." With me, it's never "one thing." Yet, ever since I met her, she's been my number-one supporter. Thanks for coauthoring our book of life: I said "Will you…"; you said "I do."

–JACK DALY

"Don't wish it was easier, wish you were better." Jack Daly said this to me many years ago, quoting Jim Rohn. It has never left me. It is "haunting" at times, but inspiring all the same. Thanks, Jack, for being a mentor, a partner, a goal achiever, a butt kicker, and a coauthor with me, pushing me to dig deeper and deliver more in every way I can.

Thank you to the Learning Innovators: I have always been a hungry learner. Since my earliest days thirty years ago working with business owners, my passion has been to help people win bigger by finding a better way. So a huge thank-you to every business leader out there that I've worked with—true professionals who are great at what they do, yet open and coachable enough to explore better ideas and then put them into action. Pursuing the better way with you has stretched and grown me, making me better in the process.

To my team of coaches at Leverage Sales Coaching: Patrick Ryan, Anthony DiMarco, Patrick Martinez, Michael March, and Dan Caulfield. Huge appreciation to you for being in the game with me—solving challenges with clients and collaborating to sort out the best Action Plan to succeed. You are a big reason I'm doing this; in helping our clients get the best Playbook practices to win, we have plenty to do, and this book is intended to help our clients and us as coaches implement faster ideas that work.

To family, friends, and partners: My close inner circle has put up with me being absorbed in building this book for so long. A big-time thank-you to my wonderful kids, Sydney and Jaxon, for your love, patience, and understanding. And to my "compadres at the gym," Dan Smith, Lisa Bender, and Laurie Rood, for your ongoing interest and encouragement. And a special thank-you to Jennifer Geiger and Gabriel Clift with Jack Daly, and Darlene Kirk at Kirk's Global Compass, for your insights, encouragement, and support, which have been so valuable to me.

–DAN LARSON

THE TEASE

As a salesperson, how much time do you spend learning proven sales techniques from your company's Top Producers? How much time do you spend practicing those techniques in-house, refining them with other team members before taking your final, polished approach on the road? And how much time each day or week does your Sales Manager spend helping you develop those high-performing techniques and processes?

Same question for you, Sales Managers: How much of your day or week is dedicated to growing your sales team? How much time do you spend teaching or arranging for the mentoring or practicing of proven sales techniques? Are you teaching your salespeople how to fish, or are you just telling them how many fish they need to bring in to meet quota?

In *The Sales Playbook for Hyper Sales Growth*, we not only delve into the necessity of developing these processes within a company but also provide valuable techniques, tools, and procedures that sales teams can begin implementing immediately.

The Sales Playbook for Hyper Sales Growth is the highly anticipated follow-up to Jack Daly's 2014 hit *Hyper Sales Growth*, offering the structure, practice, and actionable tools necessary for a company to build its own customized Sales Playbook.

Divided into three comprehensive sections that address salespeople, the Sales Manager, and, lastly, the actions needed to create and put your Playbook into action, *The Sales Playbook for Hyper Sales Growth* deep-dives into the following essential areas:

People
- The three high-payoff things done by your Top Producers

- The A-B-C-D ranking system

- The importance of mindset, attitude, behaviors, and activities to achieve results

Processes

- Goal Achievement Plan

- Sales Process clarification

- CRM reporting

- Time and focus management

- Proactive Pipeline Management

- Touch System

Practices

- Personality Styles

- Best Questions and Active Listening

- Objection Responses

- Success Stories

- Sales-Ready Messages

- Model the Masters: the value of mentoring programs

- Sales meetings

- Role Practice

Sales Management

- The Sales Manager's role and purpose

- Key roles of a highly effective Sales Manager

- Sales growth plan: what, when, how

- Sales Manager's Checklist: keys to success

- Sales Manager's calendar of Key Activities

Action Plan/*Scoring Plays*

- The best get coached.

- What are your Scoring Plays?

There are twelve key elements for any Sales Manager that should be addressed regularly to train, grow, and develop a high-performance sales team. These elements fall into Three Vital Areas:

1. PEOPLE: Team Development

- Ranking the salespeople: minimum standards of performance

- Recruiting and upgrading the sales team

2. PROCESSES: Management Processes

- Goal Achievement Plan (GAP) and Key Activities Inspection Process

- Sales Process Steps, Key Activities, and Best Practices: inspect and rank

- Proactive Pipeline Management: inspect the baskets

- Prospecting Touch System inspection

3. PRACTICES: Training and Development

- Sales Success Guide building and training

- Effective sales meetings that train and develop

- Sales Process Steps, Key Activities, and Best Practices: train and practice

- Role Practice process

- One-on-one sessions

- Field calls that train and develop

How much time do you commit to each area? How much time *should* you commit? In Chapter 8, we give a clear breakdown on where the best Sales Managers should be focusing their time and for how long, as well as Key Activities needed to grow their team in Quality and Quantity.

With your company's customized Sales Playbook, the message should be clear and resounding: This is our guide to solid wins. We're going to use it to practice and prepare, and when we all work together, we're going to win a lot more than we're going to lose.

This is no time for individual sales reps claiming they "have their own style." This is about leveraging Best Practices. When the whole team works together, that's when the truly epic wins are achieved.

ON PREPARATION:

I've learned that possibly the greatest detractor from high performance is fear: fear that you are not prepared, fear that you are in over your head, fear that you are not worthy, and ultimately, fear of failure. If you can eliminate that fear–not through arrogance or just wishing difficulties away, but through hard work and preparation–you will put yourself in an incredibly powerful position to take on the challenges you face.

PETE CARROLL, Head Football Coach, Seattle Seahawks

JACK DALY

Jack Daly is an international expert in sales and sales management, bringing with him **thirty-plus years of field-proven experience that started with CPA firm Arthur Andersen and has since led to CEO positions with several national companies.**

An internationally recognized speaker, Jack delivers explosive keynote and general- session presentations, interactive workshops, in-depth seminars, and lively training sessions that inspire audiences to take action in the areas of sales, sales management, corporate culture, customer loyalty, and personal motivation.

Additionally, his street-tested techniques and proven methodologies are designed to draw higher results from your Sales Manager and sales team's efforts. **Thousands of companies and professionals have benefited personally, financially, and professionally using the concepts that Jack teaches.**

Consistent with *The Sales Playbook for Hyper Sales Growth*, Jack has followed a similar process with regard to his personal life. His "Life-by-Design" approach (see www.jackdaly. net) developed early on in his life means more than a life well-planned—it's about a life well-lived. With meticulous care, Jack planned, tracked, measured, and built an accountability process covering health, family, travel, and "bucket-list" aspirations to optimize performance results. Married almost fifty years to his high school sweetheart, Jack has completed fifteen Ironmans, including the World Championship and Team USA, and eighty-plus marathons, and is well on his way to having run one marathon in every state and continent. He's played ninety of the top hundred golf courses in the United States, taken on the world's largest bungee jump, and continues to add new challenges to his list. Jack lives an active and stimulating life, much of it taking place as a result of a process similar to *The Sales Playbook for Hyper Sales Growth*, leveraging a concept of Modeling the Masters and systems of goals/measurement/accountability that drive above-average results.

DAN LARSON

As president, CEO, and head sales coach for Leverage Sales Coaching, Dan Larson has led a talented team of coaches and support staff in offering high-quality sales and sales development services that coach and train owners, executives, and all levels of Managers and salespeople on how to increase their individual performances and the performances of their team and company.

With thought leadership and directional advice from industry leaders such as Jack Daly and various CEO coach organizations and CEO enclaves, Leverage Sales Coaching maintains a close network of trusted referral specialists working around the United States, Canada, Australia, and the United Kingdom, all with a uniform purpose in mind for their clients: **Grow your Managers. Grow your sales team. Multiply results.**

Dan has worked closely with Jack Daly since 2003 as a sales coach and in developing training programs. He knows the Jack Daly sales systems thoroughly in the areas of sales, sales management, and leadership/culture. He is Jack's partner in developing his extensive online sales training programs and tools. Dan also cocreated a comprehensive two-day intense training program to transform Sales Managers from being "sales minded" to becoming Sales Development Leaders.

Dan designed the Leverage Sales Coaching Master Track to provide clients with a sales-leadership and management system based on Jack Daly's *Hyper Sales Growth* principles. The LSC Master Track method includes street-tested sales systems, processes, tools, templates, and models needed to train and motivate a sales team to achieve greater results.

Dan leads from twelve-plus years of coaching experience and twenty-eight-plus years of business and sales achievement. He brings a career of a success mindset in sales, sales management, corporate executive, and entrepreneurial experience together to drive for increasing results.

JACK AND DAN'S PARTNERSHIP

Jack Daly and Dan Larson have known each other for more than a decade. While Jack travels about two hundred thousand or more air miles every year speaking and spreading the message of culture, sales management, and sales, Dan works more behind the scenes. Jack delivers the broad concept while Dan offers up the details, working out valuable concepts such as what activities a Sales Manager or salesperson should be involved in.

According to Jack, "At the end of the day, there are companies that can choose—and people who can choose—to go about running their business and building their business by taking the information that I share on the stage and implementing it into the business on their own.

"Then there are those people who raise their hands and say, 'I'd like somebody to help me and hold my hand a little bit closer. I'd like somebody to give me guidance.' That's where Dan comes into play."

We call it Leverage Sales Coaching. Leverage Sales Coaching is a business that is comprised of coaches led by Dan who intimately know Jack's material and work with Jack's clients to implement the proven Jack Daly systems and processes on culture, sales management, and sales.

The coaches at Leverage Sales Coaching are very skilled at using the experience they've had with a variety of businesses and clients to facilitate and expedite the implementation of a customized Sales Playbook based on the proven systems and processes of Hyper Sales Growth. **For more information, visit leveragesalescoach.com, or call (800) 565-6516.**

INTRODUCTION

There is a common misconception that salespeople are born, not made.

The fact is that even if you're born with all the innate talents of a rock-star salesperson, none of it means a thing if you can't apply those talents effectively, especially within a team construct.

Imagine a high school All-American going to a premier college on a full football scholarship. On the first day of practice, the coach hands him the Playbook that over the years has led the team to become one of the dominant college squads in the nation. What if that new team member looks the coach in the eye and says, "I don't need this. I have my own style." How will that fly with the coach and the rest of the team?

It won't. That kid can have all the talent in the world, but if he can't apply those talents within a team construct, he's not worth one shiny nickel, let alone a full scholarship.

A team relies on its proven, time-tested written systems to produce success. Over the years, the team embraces these systems because they work, and the best players understand that it is no affront to their talent to abide by the team's Playbook.

A Sales Manager needs to know every in and out of his or her Playbook and how to keep the team on track by following proven guidelines for success. It takes consistent practice and preparation, but in the end, sticking to a solid, time-tested game plan means winning a lot more than you lose.

The Sales Playbook for Hyper Sales Growth breaks these essential elements of a successful team into three parts:

Part I: Sales Team Playbook identifies the Key Activities that the Top Producers, the best-performing salespeople, must perform daily to separate themselves from the rest, winning new customers, growing the ones they have, and differentiating themselves from the competition.

Part II: Sales Manager Playbook describes the Six Keys to Hyper Sales Growth and how to create your own Sales Manager Playbook, as well as time-tested methods for recruiting top performers, coaching, training, and building a high-performance sales team. Effective sales management is vital to both growing sales and growing your sales team in Quantity and Quality.

Part III: Action Plan is just that: a plan for getting started on creating and putting your Playbook into action, including free tools, resources, and inspiration to get moving.

This book is for those who are serious about making changes within their company to grow results. The concepts we'll cover apply to everyone from top-level executives and entrepreneurs to Sales Managers and salespeople, and there are action items for each that can be taken or implemented immediately. For those readers inclined to say, "Show it to me in one chart," here's a preview of the concepts:

- **Foundation of Hyper Sales Growth**

- **Install sales systems, processes, tools, and Best Practices:**

  □ Then, practice them regularly.

  □ *If you're not practicing in-house, you're practicing on your customers.*

  □ **Work smarter. Earn more.**

- **Build a stronger Sales Game Plan to develop the sales team to become your competitive advantage.**

LINKS in the SALES CHAIN

Where does *YOUR* sales chain break?

Find the weak links & fix them.

Work smarter. Earn more.

1. **Prospecting**

2. **Qualifying**

3. **Appointment Setting**

4. **Presenting**

5. **Objections Management**

6. **Closing**

7. **Follow-Up / Through**

THE PURPOSE OF A PLAYBOOK

The purpose of a Playbook is not to build and own a Playbook; the purpose is to get the manager and team to consistently *practice* and *act* on High Payoff Activities (HPAs) and Best Sales Practices to lift results. A Playbook is essential to equipping the manager and the team, guiding them through the Six Keys that improve performance, drive sales, and push a company into hyper growth.

The Playbook is a collection of Best Practices in the areas of People, Processes, and Practices that can be learned and repeated.

A Sales Manager's job is to direct the salespeople's mindsets, attitudes, and behaviors so that their focus is on the HPAs that drive results. The direction is driven through a sales-leadership approach focused on training, growing, and developing a team of Top Producers. The Sales Manager sets and raises the bar and works to lead his or her team to *want* to take on those all-important HPAs. The salesperson accepts some guidance and coaching to improve performance.

ON TEAM BUILDING:

You don't get the team you want—you get the team you build.

URBAN MEYER, head football coach, Ohio State

READY FOR GAME DAY

Some people will read this guide and feel reassured that they know their business well and that they have the in-house talent to implement the systems and processes that we are sharing here. They may feel they will have everything they need to build their Playbook and increase their opportunities for success. If that's the case, big applause here. We are delighted!

However, many others will read this book and say, "This makes all the sense in the world, but we have too much to do and too little time. Sure, we see the value of this, but we do not have the time or expertise to set it up. We would love to find a way for someone to help us implement it."

They are looking, in effect, for a customized approach.

If you don't have the time or available talent to set up your team Playbook or are looking for ways to speed up or augment your efforts, we also provide several options for coaching, training, and Playbook building. For more details, contact us at (800) 565-6516, e-mail to info@leveragesalescoach.com, or visit leveragesalescoach.com and click Free Coaching Session.

If you're a salesperson or Sales Manager looking to hyper grow your sales and are willing to accept new ideas and break out of the status quo to do it, then this is your book.

So let's get started.

PART I

THE SALES PLAYBOOK

The very top salespeople are maniacally focused on what we call HPAs, or High Payoff Activities. As a salesperson, once you've decided what those High Payoff Activities are, you shouldn't go home on any given night until you get your HPAs done.

The problem, however, is that companies are constantly asking their salespeople to do things that aren't HPAs.

We've all heard it said that there's no such thing as a problem, just an opportunity. The problem—or rather, opportunity—here is that excellent salespeople are tying up their time on things that aren't generating business. **A sales force of ten people may in fact only amount to a sales force of five because more than 50 percent of each salesperson's time is being spent on non-HPAs.**

Actively look for ways to reduce the salesperson's nonselling time to free up their HPA selling time. The more a salesperson can stay focused on HPAs, the more money he or she will make, and the more business the company will generate.

DRIVING HIGH PAYOFF ACTIVITIES

Here Jack Daly shares a weakness: I don't do well with technology. I love being out on the road, I love interacting with people, and I love figuring out their business and helping them determine what their needs are. But if you put me in front of a keyboard and tell me to update my Customer Relationship Management (CRM) system's contact database, I'm going to be fearful that I'll make a mistake on the keyboard, and I'm going to be slow as hell. I'm also going to hate whoever made me do that data-entry work. It's just insane! While I'm sitting there, slowly pecking away at the keyboard, I could be out meeting another prospect, doing what I love, and bringing business in. (Some version of this exists with every salesperson working on non-HPAs.)

Updating databases is not an HPA for me. Now, don't get me wrong. I am a huge advocate for leveraging a contact-management system. Later in this book we will detail how to do just that. However, data entry is not in my skill set and not a skill I aspire to at this stage of life.

What are the things you do well that generate business? Now, figure out everything else that people are telling you to do, or that you're voluntarily doing, that's not an HPA for you and list it. Then figure out how to get items on that list off your plate and onto someone else's.

High Payoff Activities drive high performance and vice versa. I could hire a sixteen-year-old who has tremendous database skills, and I could pay that kid $8 or $10 an hour to enter data while I'm out in the field, doing what I'm good at, and generating more dollars per hour than $8–$10 in additional personal income. This is a "win-win-win." The kid is happy, the company is happy, and I, the salesperson, am happy, all by focusing on the HPAs.

Figure out what your HPAs are, and then do them. Whether the company pays for an assistant, or maybe two or three salespeople share an assistant, get as much off your desk as you possibly can and focus on what you're good at.

PLAYBOOK RESOURCES:
SEE SALES PLAYBOOK VIDEO, The Power of Leverage, High Payoff Activities
inSITE-app & http://leveragesalescoach.com/resources

The Profession of Sales is for Sales Professionals

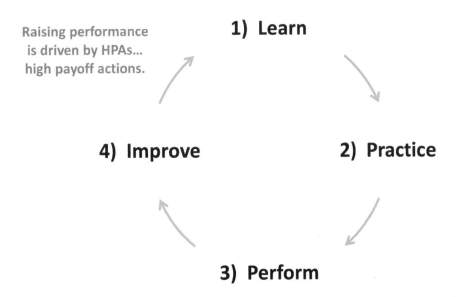

Raising performance is driven by HPAs... high payoff actions.

1) Learn

2) Practice

3) Perform

4) Improve

SCORING PLAY:

Ask yourself two key questions to help you focus on your HPAs and how to improve them:

1) What end results are you measured on?

2) What HPAs really matter to drive your performance that leads to your results?

Use the provided **Sales HPAs Checklist** tool to sort what you do well and what you could improve on.

- How many of the activities in the "I Need to Improve" list could be improved by changing your approach or by getting training to improve those activities?

  □ Can you strengthen those weaknesses so that they result in more sales?

- For your "Performing Well" list, consider what you're currently doing and how you can strengthen those activities to improve results. Instead of "making calls," for example, you could say, "making calls within one hour of first contact."

My Sales HPAs Checklist

Key Area	My Sales HPAs	An important HPA	I'm Performing well	I'm OK at this	I need to Learn or Improve
Sales Plan	Territory Mgmt/Planning	☐	☐	☐	☐
	Prep / Planning / Strategy	☐	☐	☐	☐
	Profit Analysis	☐	☐	☐	☐
	Organization-Action Plans-Prioritizing	☐	☐	☐	☐
	Key Account Planning & Growth	☐	☐	☐	☐
	Goal Pursuit / Achievement	☐	☐	☐	☐
	Manager Communication	☐	☐	☐	☐
	Win / Loss Review	☐	☐	☐	☐
Preparation	Best Questions Practicing	☐	☐	☐	☐
	Innovating Ideas that Sell	☐	☐	☐	☐
Prospecting	Target List Planning	☐	☐	☐	☐
	Ask Questions & Effective Listening	☐	☐	☐	☐
	Prospecting / Door-Opening	☐	☐	☐	☐
	Networking – Ext. & Internal	☐	☐	☐	☐
	Calling Cold & Warm	☐	☐	☐	☐
	Developing COI Channel Partners	☐	☐	☐	☐
	Networking Events & Social Media	☐	☐	☐	☐
	Conferences / Trade Shows	☐	☐	☐	☐
Qualifying	Qualifying to Fit Criteria / Identify HVNs	☐	☐	☐	☐
Presenting	Presenting Solutions to HVNs	☐	☐	☐	☐
	Objection Mgmt/Tough Questions	☐	☐	☐	☐
	Demos / Sampling	☐	☐	☐	☐
	Cross-Selling/Upselling	☐	☐	☐	☐
	Selling to Consensus Buy-in	☐	☐	☐	☐
	Selling Value/Pricing Strategy	☐	☐	☐	☐
	Problem Solving/Creativity	☐	☐	☐	☐
	Managing Customer Expectations	☐	☐	☐	☐
Closing	Closing / Ask for the Business	☐	☐	☐	☐
	Price Negotiations	☐	☐	☐	☐
Pipeline Mgmt	Pipeline Mgmt. / CRM Reporting	☐	☐	☐	☐
	Touch System to Differentiate	☐	☐	☐	☐
Follow-up	Follow-up / Follow-thru	☐	☐	☐	☐
Messaging	Create Perception of Value / Differentiate	☐	☐	☐	☐
Training	Continuous Learning / Practicing	☐	☐	☐	☐
	Mentoring	☐	☐	☐	☐
	Model the Masters	☐	☐	☐	☐
	Role Practicing	☐	☐	☐	☐
	Ride-Alongs with Manager	☐	☐	☐	☐
Time Mgmt	Time & Prioritization Focus	☐	☐	☐	☐

The Profession of Sales is for Sales Professionals

Raising performance is driven by HPAs... high payoff actions.

1) Learn
2) Practice
3) Perform
4) Improve

PLAYBOOK RESOURCES:

SEE SALES PLAYBOOK, Sales HPAs Checklist

inSITE-app & http://leveragesalescoach.com/resources

You will find video references interspersed throughout the book to enhance the content that you are reading.

SCORING PLAY:
Choose your three weakest areas and three strongest areas, and set a goal for improving both by a set percentage by the end of the quarter. Keep those goals visible at all times as encouragement to blast your old sales records out of the water! Identify your non-HPAs and figure out how to shift them elsewhere.

BUILDING A STRONG SALES GAME PLAN

This is where we begin showing you what to put into your Sales Playbook. It's not too soon for you to begin physically creating your own Playbook or rewriting one you already have using the forms, processes, and free tools we are providing to help you achieve your goals. As we said in the Introduction, we are available to customize implementation for your company if you need extra help.

Your Sales Playbook will cover the Three Vital Areas—People, Processes, and Practices—which lead you to the Sales Game Plan and Scoring Plays that will bring results for your company in your industry.

In the next four chapters, we discuss Best Sales Practices and how to work smarter. You will read about how Top Producers work and the importance of mindset, attitude, behaviors, and activities in achieving high-payoff results. We go over the Sales Process, Personality Styles training and identification (to be more effective with more people), CRM usage for Proactive Pipeline Management, and driving a consistent Touch System.

Successfully applying the information will require self-assessment—the willingness to measure and rank yourself in order to improve. We will discuss the "magic" of a Goal Achievement Plan backed with accountability. But in the end, your successful results will depend on you managing your time to focus on your HPAs.

SMART SELLING FOR HYPER SALES GROWTH

We ask salespeople whether they work hard, and inevitably they tell us, "Of course I work hard." More importantly, are they willing to work *smarter* to get paid more for the hard work they are already doing? It's a pivotal question, and who would answer no?

The sales professional will always answer with an enthusiastic yes. And that's where we come in. We help companies model those top performers, observing their patterns of success and implementing those patterns more systematically. We develop the means for working smarter. We focus on the people, on the processes and tools, and on the practices that are sure to bring the best results.

Because the reality of sales is that **people do not want to be sold**. We've never met anyone who enjoys having someone try to sell them something. Instead, when it comes to selling strategies, the paradox is that to sell smarter, salespeople need to **quit selling**. It doesn't work.

Selling a product, idea, or service in today's economy takes more effort than it did even five years ago. Technology has allowed businesses to connect all over the world, which means that most consumers, customers, or clients have many options available. To win new customers and grow current ones, **a salesperson must work to build trusting relationships.** Learn the importance of leveraging your business's unique competitive advantages to create specific processes and tools for your sales team to ensure the growth of your company.

Salespeople need to hear from their manager that they should care more about the customer than about the sale because the point is that **better salespeople call on fewer people and write more business.** The key is to call on the right people.

It has become clear in today's business climate that **knowing "what" to do is not enough;** smart selling requires the **"why"** and the **"how."** The key to growing your business pivots on a Sales Manager and team executing effective systems and processes to both win new customers and retain and develop existing business. This means identifying the things that need to be done—the "what" and the "why"—and becoming properly motivated to actively engage in the "how" of putting the Best Sales Practices and processes in place.

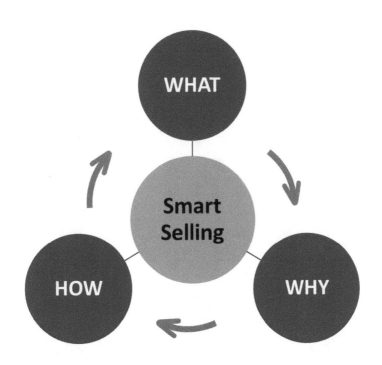

CHAPTER 1

PEOPLE:
ATTRIBUTES OF THE TOP PRODUCERS

ON PHILOSOPHY FOR SUCCESS:

The characteristics that made up our 2003 national championship team are the same attributes that form my philosophy for success. Terms like conviction, dominate, adversity, perseverance, commitment, attitude, teamwork, road map, pride, relentless, and intensity. Now, how good do you want to be?

NICK SABAN

 CHAPTER GAME PLAN

This chapter is about you, the salesperson. It stresses the value of working hard while working smarter to earn more and the importance of collaborating with your team and knowing how to contribute in order to reap the biggest rewards. It also discusses motivation and the boost you get by changing your mindset from *I have to* to *I **want** to*.

Make no mistake about this: becoming a Top Producer and achieving Hyper Sales Growth is hard. You will be signing up for more rejection because you will be told "no" more than anything else. You may feel you are putting your income at risk based on your performance. It may often seem like your job is trying to please all parties, all the time. And it certainly will feel like there are just *not* enough hours in the day.

Sales is a great career that makes a difference for our prospects and customers–our public. We bring them opportunities and creative solutions to their challenges. And a sales career gives you the ability to generate above-average compensation! But it's also a career that requires *passion* and *grit*. If you take on a position in sales and view it as "just a job," your public will sense that and consequently avoid you. This is even true for those working 100 percent of the time over the phone; the prospect can sense your enthusiasm or lack of it.

The best Sales Playbook in the world will not magically transform a salesperson who doesn't have the passion to be a Top Producer. This includes a strong *belief* in the industry, company, and products you represent. Without this belief, all the systems and processes in the world won't help.

Successful sales professionals sell from a position of strength, not weakness. You cannot be successful in representing your product or service without this passion, grit, and belief. Because of this, it all starts with PEOPLE.

STOP SELLING—START LISTENING

The reality is that people do not want to be sold to, and any salesperson who is still trying that old tactic needs to stop. Instead of focusing on your company and your own "why," you should be focusing on the customer.

Salespeople need to shut up and listen to the customer—to ask good questions but talk less. Here's the difference between the *company-focused* "pitch-fest" approach and the *customer-focused* sales approach.

People buy for *their* reasons based on what's relevant, meaningful, and important to *them*. They buy what aligns with them and helps them achieve their personal and business goals. Therefore, to sell effectively, you need to answer your potential clients' "whys" and make it easier for them to say yes.

SALES TEAM SCRIMMAGE
TIE TO YOUR CUSTOMERS' WHYS

Answer the following questions from the perspective of a potential client. This is what your prospects are asking themselves:

- *Why your company?*

- *Why you, personally?*

- *Why should I buy?*

- *Why is this a benefit to me?*

- *Why does it make my life, my business, better?*

- *Why is this a problem solver?*

How do you answer their whys? The answers are your customers' End Zone Benefits. When your answers speak to *their* reasons in a direct, powerful, compelling, relatable, and connective way, it resonates with them.

Top Producers have learned to focus on the customer's needs. It's all about them.

Regardless of the industry, all Top Producers understand **what** they need to do and **why** they need to do it, and they do **three high-payoff things**:

1. They understand the **amount of activity** needed to do their jobs well.

2. They are **effective** at carrying out those activities.

3. They are **consistent with their systems and processes** so that their HPAs are done in a reliable way.

THREE high payoff things done by Top Producers

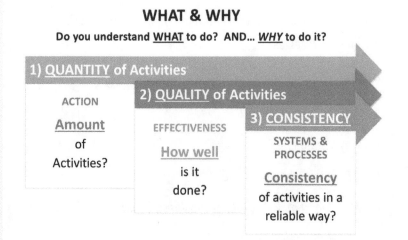

Top Producers make more money, because they find a way to get it done. They achieve their goals when others don't. **WHY? Because they do best sales practices *consistently*.** They are open and willing to learn what works. They take action. And they have the discipline to do it consistently by committing to follow systems & processes that increase their success.

WHAT & WHY

Do you understand **WHAT** to do? AND... *WHY* to do it?

1) QUANTITY of Activities

ACTION

Amount of Activities?

2) QUALITY of Activities

EFFECTIVENESS

How well is it done?

3) CONSISTENCY

SYSTEMS & PROCESSES

Consistency of activities in a reliable way?

You can't approach the sales business with anything less than a professional mindset to become a Top Producer. A good salesperson knows that he or she needs to prepare, plan, and practice. The Top Producers don't "wing it" when it comes to potential clients: they've prepared, they have their plan, they've practiced it with fellow associates, and **they're ready to sell professionally.**

The sales world is a competitive place, and as with every other occupation, **continuous learning is what drives the income of Top Producers.** Consider any profession: doctors, lawyers, CPAs, and others. In every one, *the top earners are learners.* They use the systems, tools, processes, and Best Practices in place to learn and grow.

SMART-SELLING PEOPLE EARN MORE

For Top Producers in the sales profession, learning more to earn more is a continuous process. From our coaching experiences close to the playing field, we know that the most productive mindset to build exceptional results has two requirements:

1. **Are you Coachable?** Are you teachable, open, and willing to learn and accept new ideas?

2. **Are you willing to Take Action on ideas**? Will you implement and immediately put new ideas into action?

The two requirements together make up an Achiever mindset. But if one or both are not in place, people will struggle or fail to improve their results. The tenet "Work smarter. Earn more," requires paying attention to what's working and what's not working so that you can pinpoint exactly where and how to improve. It's not just about working hard.

> **Are you Coachable?**
>
> *"Those who can't change their minds can't change anything."*
>
> George Bernard Shaw

SCORING PLAY:

Offer to take one of the top salespeople at your company to lunch and tell that person what you've been trying, and then ask his or her opinion. By putting yourself in the position of a student, you not only flatter these top performers, but they're also more willing to share with you some of the tips and tricks of the trade that they've learned over the years. The "Model the Masters" section of Chapter 3 has more related ideas.

A WORD FROM DAN . . .
THE BREAKFAST CLUB

It was a breakfast club, of sorts, that made a major difference as we worked with a data-management company whose leads had plummeted, revealing severe deficiencies in its sales structure and capability to generate new business.

We identified some talented salespeople who were not the top performers but who were leaning in, wanting to learn how to do a better job. They began gathering informally, sitting down over coffee for an hour before work each day for a meeting on Best Practices. They talked about what we had been teaching them and the specific steps toward success. They kicked around ideas.

The breakfast club began with just a few motivated people, and they found that they were having fun as well as markedly improving their performance. Soon, others on the team noticed the camaraderie and the improvement in sales, and they joined in. Even the top performers wondered if they might be missing something as they saw others attaining results much like their own. This momentum arose from the front line. Nobody told them they had to do this. Yes, we planted the seed by suggesting that such gatherings would be beneficial, but that seed quickly sprouted and grew strong.

That's how you get things going. Those are the keys to the car. The kind of people who started that breakfast club—the kind who yearn to be better but who are not quite there yet—are the catalysts for change. Their attitude and their desire will pull everyone higher. That is the mindset that we need to encourage: *What else can I do? What more can I learn? How might I improve?* Even with just a few such people, you have enough to get started. Success breeds success. It releases energy. It is the ultimate encourager.

DAN LARSON

COLLABORATORS AND CONTRIBUTORS

Working smarter requires knowing how to work well with your team, using their talents and knowledge to your mutual advantage.

You need to ask yourself several questions to know exactly how to work smarter:

- Are you ready to collaborate?

- Are you ready to contribute, rather than sitting there waiting for the Sales Manager to just chew through the stuff?

- Do you want to advance ideas and ask questions?

- Would it be helpful if you and others on the team could talk about the top five objections you hear from prospects and how they might best be handled?

- Would you be eager to share what you have learned that works well, particularly if your teammates shared, too?

As a salesperson, you could be the one to start the trend. You do not need to wait for the Sales Manager to initiate collaboration. Go into sales team meetings expecting to contribute and collaborate. Meetings should not be a boring waste of time; they should be a resource for learning and improving your sales skills.

The meetings are an opportunity for salespeople to learn to lead by example and to shape and write your company's Sales Playbook for Hyper Sales Growth. Share your successes, and talk about how they might be replicated. Share your horror stories, and ask for help on how to handle the customer from hell. Solicit ideas. You might find that the junior salesperson who just joined the team has some brilliant insights. If you can help the sales meeting evolve into a brainstorming session, you and the company will be better off.

"MAKE ME" OR "MAKE ME WANT TO"

There are two types of motivation in the world: *making* **someone do something** and **making them** *want to* **do something**. Sometimes we're made to do things, but what's more useful is when we learn how to make ourselves *want* to do something. When you do something that you want to achieve, when you accomplish a personal goal, then you feel motivated.

Earlier we compared the Sales Manager's best approach as teaching someone to fish rather than telling them how many fish they have to catch. Along the same lines, the salesperson who sets out with his or her own goals in mind is most likely to muster the skill and determination to meet those goals and bring home a great catch.

Why do you put your feet on the floor in the morning and get moving? Your "why," if it is a burning desire, is what can make you a Top Producer who outperforms the rest of the team.

A few years back, one sales rep shared his "why" with us:

> You want to know the real reason? My parents basically abandoned me as a kid. They were into drugs and all kinds of stuff. And my Grandma stepped in and raised me. She basically saved my life. And now that she is older, I want to make Grandma's life better. So that's why I get up in the morning, and that's why I charge hard.

You might think that everyone knows their motivation, but it is not something people often talk about. They may not have really identified it or clarified it. They should. That's what is going to give them the Achiever mindset, an attitude that combines the desire for success with the open mind to listen and learn to compete and win.

PERFORMANCE RATINGS

At this point, it's helpful to define the levels of performance that motivation—a term encompassing the grit, the drive, the will to achieve a goal, and the desire to take on challenges and overcome setbacks—plays in determining. We use a simple A-B-C-D scale.

Rank the Sales Team

A – Achievers

B – Be Better

C – Content

D – Don't Move much!

Where does the Sales Manager invest their time?

"A" Player: These are the achievers. One way or another, they find a way to get it done. They achieve their budget and then some. No matter what they are dealing with, they find a way to win. They do what it takes, and they often make it look so easy.

"B" Player: "B" players are those who are hoping to "be better." They are not "A" players yet. They might even be relatively new on the job, but they are striving. They're looking for what they can learn, and they're energetic about applying it. Their whole mindset is one of improving.

And here, before we get to "C," is a big, fat red line. This line represents the division between the top "A" and "B" players and the bottom "C" and "D" players when it comes to motivation, drive, willingness, ability, and preparation.

"C" Player: The "Cs" are the complacent ones. They're satisfied and do not generally want to work harder. They're really not willing to invest more or to put more drive or energy into it, and most of the time they really do not want to be an "A" player. They would like to make more money but do not want to do what it takes to get there. They're just not motivated enough.

"D" Player: You might think of this letter as standing for "Don't." "D" players don't sell much, don't move much. They remind us of dogs on a porch; they keep their heads down, and they'll stay on the porch as long as they keep getting fed. We have encountered many companies with a large number of people who are really nice and have been there a long time but do not sell much. Since they're nice, though, and because of their seniority, the company makes room for them on the porch. You need to deal with the underperformers and help them move on to another opportunity.

When we talk with companies looking to hire us to coach their sales teams, we understand that we are measured on helping them produce three things:

1. **Change:** Something needs to change to significantly improve their outcomes.

2. **Action:** The change must be driven by sufficient action.

3. **Results:** A dramatic improvement in results will happen.

We ask them about the two requirements for Top Producers discussed earlier: Is your sales team Coachable? Are they willing to Take Action on ideas?

If their people are not open-minded or are so stubborn they believe they have nothing to learn, no real change will happen. And if they can't take those ideas and get busy applying them, trying them, and working at them, then even the best ideas will fail.

We find that the "A" and the "B" players commonly have no problem with those two simple requirements. We find that the "C" players may or may not be open-minded, but they are unwilling or fail to take sufficient action. They're just not motivated enough.

What is needed from the team is an overall Achiever mindset so that real progress can be made. Anything less is a detriment to the entire team.

SELF-ASSESSMENT: WHAT STYLE OF TEAM PLAYER ARE YOU?

Decades of research has established that people can be grouped into distinct Personality Styles.[1] For salespeople, this is more than an academic exercise or parlor game. It is a key to knowing how to interact most effectively with prospects and customers. To implement your Sales Playbook, you must understand this breakdown of four Personality Styles that each of us principally falls into:

1. Analytical

2. Driver

3. Amiable

4. Expressive

Personality Styles

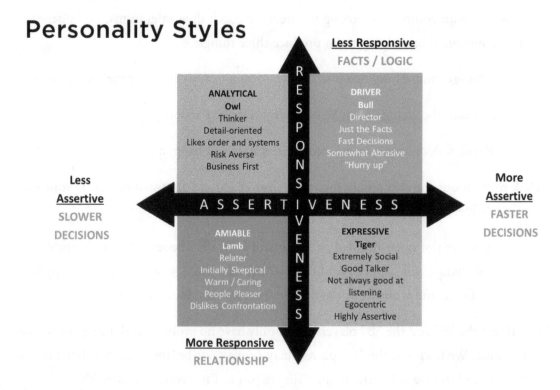

---

1   Wilson Learning Library, *The Social Styles Handbook: Adapt Your Style to Win Trust* (Nova Vista Publishing, 2011).

We each have elements of the four Personality Styles within us, but one generally dominates. The less-assertive type people, who are slower to come to decisions, are the Amiables and the Analyticals. The more assertive types and the quicker decision makers are the Expressives and the Drivers. The Amiables and the Expressives tend to emphasize relationships, people, and feelings. The Analyticals and the Drivers tend to emphasize facts and logic.

You can identify the dominant personality style of yourself and others by asking just two questions:

1. Are you more assertive, or less so?

2. Do you tend to make decisions using facts and logic, or based on emotion—your feelings about people and relationships?

If those two questions can't help you identify your personality style, ask a few friends how they see you, and then compare their answers to the graph.

Although it's not always true, salespeople tend to be Expressives. They find it easy to talk and make social connections. They are naturals at painting pictures verbally. They may need to work harder at understanding the Analytical mindset, which wants to gather the facts and then deliberate. At times it can feel as if Expressives and Analyticals are not even speaking the same language.

What is the lesson for the salesperson? First, know who you are and where you stand. If you are an extreme Expressive or an extreme Driver, understand that the people you have trouble connecting with are the ones who are the opposites of you, so you'll have to work harder to make a good connection.

If you know whom you are dealing with, you can adjust your style accordingly.

If you'd like a detailed personality assessment, we offer a *free* sample talent assessment. We offer seven different categories of DiSC® talent-assessment reports, useful in talent needs for different roles in sales, management, or executive, job-fit reports, or basic talent reports. For your free code, call us at (800) 565–6516, e-mail to info@leveragesalescoach.com, or visit leveragesalescoach.com and click Free Coaching Session.

Another great resource, which we originally mentioned in *Hyper Sales Growth*, is *The Platinum Rule for Sales Mastery* by Tony Alessandra. This book speaks the language of your targets and teaches you how to give them what they want and need in order to feel comfortable buying from you. But to do that, you need to understand their personality.[2] When you get good at this, and are willing to adjust accordingly, you will reap big dividends.

See a free video link at www.HSGvideosPlatinumRule.

PLAYBOOK RESOURCES:

SEE PEOPLE VIDEO, Jack on Sales, 70% of Salespeople are Expressives, 4 Personality Styles, Tony Alessandra Descriptions

inSITE-app & http://leveragesalescoach.com/resources

SALES TEAM SCRIMMAGE
IN THE BUYERS' SHOES

Imagine yourself as a buyer considering a substantial purchase. You are getting calls from umpteen salespeople from different companies, hither and yon. They all are selling pretty much the same thing, it seems, and they all sound the same: "Our people make the difference. We have been around since 1492. We service what we sell. We are the best of the best!" Platitude after platitude, blah, blah, blah.

Let's face it: if you think "We service what we sell" is what makes you special and different, try to imagine any buyer who wouldn't expect that as a matter of course. You need to describe what differentiates your company in a way that stands out from the crowd. What is your Value Proposition? Think about it. If all you can come up with is "our people, our service, our quality," you are not trying hard enough. You need to describe something unique.

You cannot afford to be boring.

During a sales team meeting, set up the following exercise: Have a salesperson describe what differentiates your company from the rest of the pack. Every time that salesperson uses a boring, run-of-the-mill platitude, have the rest of the sales team shout "Beep!" or use an actual buzzer. Either way, the salesperson is forced to listen to himself or herself. At the end of it, each salesperson gets a tally

2   Tony Alessandra, Scott Michael Zimmerman, and Joseph La Lopa, *The Platinum Rule for Sales Mastery* (Platinum Rule Press, 2007).

of how many buzzer stops he or she got. At the next meeting, or during some practice time with an associate, do some brainstorming on unique Value Proposition angles, then run through the practice again and shoot for a buzzer-less presentation. 🏈

DEVELOPING YOUR UNIQUE VALUE PROPOSITION

These are some tactics that will help you develop a strong Value Proposition:

Reassure your prospects that you will be highly responsive, and follow up with that promise. If you do not have an immediate answer, tell them that you will get back to them quickly, and be specific about when you will follow up. Let them know you will get on it, stay on it, and make sure it happens. Tell them about your experience in the industry, your accomplishments, and the insights that you have contributed. How do you, personally, stand out as unique, different, and special?

Paint a picture for your potential clients that clearly and compellingly answers the questions "Why you? Why your company?" Help them clearly see the benefits and advantages and how you can make life better for them. Show them how you can help them streamline and boost their efficiency—even if your price is a little higher than the competition's, you will more than make up for that in value. In other words, talk about more than the features of your product or service. Zero in on how you can improve the buyer's situation. The prospect is wondering, "So just what can you do for me?"

About 85 percent of phone calls wind up as voice mail, so leave a message that means something.[3] Many salespeople just leave a voice mail that touches base, and you can be sure that the prospect has had several calls like that already on any given day. Instead of "Hi, just checking in with you, wondering if you are ready to buy," try something like this: "If elevating your sales team through coaching and training is still important to you, could you give me a call back before 10:15 a.m. tomorrow? Here's my number."

Without overpromising, do your best to **project the results that your prospect could expect**. After you identify the buyer's needs and problems, help them to see your product or your service in action. Tell them the percentage of gain you expect them to realize in a

---

3   Howard Brown "9 Voicemail Tips to Dramatically Improve Return Calls," RingLead, August 12, 2014, https://www.ringlead.com/blog/voicemail-tips/.

particular area after they make this purchase from you. If you are able to produce some accurate figures, that too can be a powerful part of the Sales-Ready Message that you deliver. For more on Sales-Ready Messaging, see Chapter 3.

In her book *Creating Competitive Advantage,* Jaynie Smith shares powerful points on how to differentiate yourself from the competition. For example, consider Jack's differentiators of "Why Jack Daly?" on his business card—the more specific and unique you can be, the more you stand out to your potential client, the better. Everyone has something that makes them unique. Discover yours and shout it out!

WHY *jack* **DALY** ?

JACK SPEAKS FROM EXPERIENCE

1. History of proven growth of clients' businesses from individual success stories to international-size firms.
2. Proven CEO/Entrepreneur, having built 6 companies into national firms.
3. Co-owner/senior exec. of INC #10 and Entrepreneur of the Year award winner.
4. Vistage UK Overseas Speaker of the Year.
5. TEC Australia Speaker of the Year.

6. Spoken to audiences in several countries on 6 continents.
7. BS Accounting, MBA, Captain in US Army, accomplished author of books, audio and DVD programs, online webcasts and more.
8. Led sales forces numbering in the thousands.
9. Competed in Ironman World Champion-ship. Is an Ironman on 5 continents.
10. Amazon Bestselling author of *Hyper Sales Growth* & *Paper Napkin Wisdom*.

RESULTS- that's what all of the above is about. Jack Daly delivers results.

How do you stand out? What makes your product or service truly unique? What statistics can you share that will surprise and encourage your potential clients? How responsive, how innovative, how trustworthy has your business proven to be? Sell them with your unique Value Proposition, but also sell them on *you*, and the sale is more likely to follow.

THE FIVE FOUNDATIONAL LAWS OF SELF-RENEWAL

This chapter began with discussion of the importance of *passion* and *grit*. We've talked about the importance and value of passion in selling, so let's close with the best way to get that grit.

It's called **The Five Foundational Laws of Self-Renewal,** and abiding by each law can not only give you the passion and grit you need to be a better salesperson but likely also help you be a better person all around.

1. **The Law of Self-Discipline:** Doing what you say you are going to do, when you say you are going to do it, whether you want to or not.

2. **The Law of Responsibility:** Recognizing YOU are responsible for the outcomes you experience. When looking for why you're not producing, look in the mirror.

3. **The Law of Attraction:** If you really believe you can be, have, or do, you will create the circumstances and find the people to allow you to be, have, or do.

4. **The Law of Expectations:** Your life is a direct result of your expectations for it. You are what you think you are—raise the bar!

5. **The Law of Belief:** The guiding factor, principle, passion, or faith that provides direction in life. Essentially, your stake in the ground.

ON BEING RELENTLESS:
You see, it's not just about having the best players–it's about being relentless in the pursuit of your goal and resilient in the face of bad luck and adversity.
NICK SABAN

PLAYBOOK RESOURCES:
SEE PEOPLE VIDEO, Your Mindset, 5 Laws of Self-Renewal
inSITE-app & http://leveragesalescoach.com/resources

Passion sells! We have covered the mindset and motivation of those who are willing to work hard and, more importantly, work smarter to be Top Producers. Now let's dig into the Sales Processes!

CHAPTER 2

PROCESSES:
ACHIEVING GOALS STEP BY STEP

 **CHAPTER GAME PLAN**

We show you the Four Steps to creating your ideal Goal Achievement Plan, which starts with you identifying your end goal. Once you have your goal defined, you can work out how you plan to achieve it using a Goal Achievement Plan. This chapter shows you how to create your Goal Achievement Plan and how to implement it, from putting it in writing in your Sales Playbook to refining your system of measurement and implementing that all-important Touch System. Finally, by having a solid system of accountability in place, you can ensure that you're hitting every one of the steps you need to leverage your efforts for Hyper Sales Growth.

We've found that setting goals at the three levels of Minimum, Realistic, and Stretch is more useful to engage salespeople with greater belief and buy-in.

- **Minimum:** minimum results I commit to producing this period no matter what the conditions

- **Realistic:** what I realistically expect to produce this period based on known data and sales forecasts, the previous sales history, and my commitment to stay focused and work hard to perform consistently well

- **Stretch:** what I expect to produce this period if conditions are better than expected and I commit to stay focused, work smarter, and perform consistently at my best

You've got the mindset of a Top Producer and the *passion* and *grit* to achieve any goal you set your mind to. So, how are you going to make those goals a reality?

You'll do it with a little bit of backward thinking. By that, we mean that your first step is defining the goal and then working backward to achieve it by putting our step-by-step guide into your Sales Playbook.

STEP 1: MIND THE GAP

Goal Achievement Plan	
1. Focused Goals	Backward Thinking
2. Written Action Plan	Key Activities
3. System of Measurement	Tracking Performance
4. System of Accountability	Progress Reports

If you are serious about accomplishing your goal, then you will devise a plan to achieve it. You can think of this Goal Achievement Plan by its acronym, GAP.

Establishing your GAP requires some backward thinking: you focus on your goal first and understand why you want it and then calculate how and when you will get there. You establish your annual goal, for example, and then figure out how you will make it happen monthly and weekly.

PLAYBOOK RESOURCES:

SEE PROCESS VIDEO, Sales Systems, Backward Thinking

inSITE-app & http://leveragesalescoach.com/resources

 **Goal Achievement Plan Summary**

Goal Achievement Plan Overview

The Goal Achievement Plan (GAP) is an underlying foundation to the very purpose of a successful sales organization. If you are serious about achieving your goals, then you should want to create a serious plan to make it happen. We know that "Winners keep score!"

The crux of a Goal Achievement Plan is to consistently perform the high payoff activities on the high payoff target accounts to drive bigger results. Below are the key elements needed to create a GAP that works.

Goal Achievement Plan	
1. Focused Goals	Backward Thinking
2. Written Action Plan	Key Activities
3. System of Measurement	Tracking Performance
4. System of Accountability	Progress Reports

Goal Achievement Plan

- **1) Goals in Writing   Backward Thinking**
    - Break down your goals "back to front" (Annually → Quarterly → Monthly → Weekly → Daily)
    - Using your specific Key Measurements. Some examples below
        - # Existing_____Sold (accounts, units, etc)
        - # New_____Sold (accounts, units, etc)
        - Revenue $ per_____(period)
        - Average $ per_____(sale $, margin, etc for your key measurements)
- **2) Written Plan   Key Activities**
    - What Key ACTIVITIES *really matter* to drive results?
        - # Prospecting calls to target accounts → # Qualified leads
        - # Appointments set → # Presentations to key decision makers
        - # Deals won → # Relationships advancing
        - # Referral partners developing
        - Marketing visibility: # Networking events; # Trade Shows, etc.
        - Other? _____
- **3) System of Measurement   Tracking Performance**
    - How you are pacing toward your goal?
    - Use your CRM, pipeline reporting, pacing report or other system to track your progress & pacing toward your goal
- **4) System of Accountability   Progress Reports**
    - What adjustments do you need to make?
    - Look for ways to adjust activities, targets or effectiveness to be sure to stay on track

Goal Achievement Plan driven by Backward Thinking

Below are several keys to implement an effective Goal Achievement Plan using Jack Daly's "backward thinking." The end result is to develop an effective action plan to know what you need to achieve your goals.

Principles/Concept:

- **The "funnel" concept** of "begin with your end $$ needed" (e.g. $1,000,000 revenue)

- **Sales Process Steps & Key Activities**: Then backward think/reverse engineer the activity plan. Break down the amount of Key Measurements and Key Activities required at each step.

- **Three related factors affect the amount of activity you need to achieve goal:**

  - 1) **High Payoff Targets** = The right best-fit targets must be the focus

  - 2) **Key Activities** = Amount of Activity required to be sure to   hit your goal?

  - 3) **Conversion Rate** at each step is determined by how effective you are at each step?

  - Achieving your goal requires having enough leads & best-fit target opportunities in the front end of the funnel that are sufficient to reach your goal.

  - Your Conversion Rate at each step helps determine if you have sufficient target opportunities in the front end or if you need to get more.

Top 10 Best-Fit Account Rating Steps

The steps below will help you identify your **Best-Fit Target Accounts** for your highest payoff activities.

 **Goal Achievement Plan Summary**

Identify your Top 10 high payoff accounts for Existing and New Accounts:

1. Begin with your broad list of all Existing accounts and New target accounts.
2. Use the ratings steps below to identify your Top Account targets. It's recommended doing this in an Excel spreadsheet so that it can be easily sortable.
3. Identify the Best-Fit Targets using the criteria below or choose your own. Determine the most productive Top 10 Accounts to pursue and grow.

Best-Fit Account Ratings Tool used to focus your high pay-off activities on the best key account targets

Purpose: Be more objective about identifying the best target accounts to grow your business. Create a system and process that helps you target better to work smarter.

Rate your list of Prospects and Customers according to the following:

VOLUME OF BUSINESS account is doing <u>in the marketplace</u> (not with you)

- **A**   X-Large $____/ yr or more   (<u>set your own rating thresholds</u>)
- **B**   Large $____/ yr
- **C**   Med $____/ yr
- **D**   Small $____/ yr

YOUR **SHARE** OF CUSTOMER

- **1**   Does most/all buying thru your company
- **2**   Does some buying thru your company
- **3**   Does no/little buying thru your company
- **4**   Good potential as a Referral source

Best-Fit Account Rating for Top 10 Targets:

- **A2 & A3:** Focus greatest mktg/sales effort
- **B2 & B3:** Focus strong mktg/sales effort
- **C2 & C3:** Focus medium mktg/sales effort
- **A1, B1 & C1:** Maintain good relations & ensure good contacts and service

Top 10 Accounts Activities Goal:

1. Use Best-Fit Account Rating to identify the best targets for focused sales & touch program effort.
2. Sellers schedule follow-up communication plan based on progress and Best-Fit Account Rating.

Top 10 List Forms

 **Goal Achievement Plan Summary**

PROSPECTS Best-Fit Target List:

Focus precedes success. What accounts deserve your biggest focus in order to greatly increase your income?

PROSPECTS: Top 10 Best-Fit Target List					
List your best prospect targets according to your ratings & sales potential. What will each account be worth when successful?					
Target #	Company	Best-Fit Acct Rating	Account's Total Purchase Vol./Yr.	Your Current Purchase Vol./Yr.	Your Target Purchase Vol./Yr-1
1			$	$	$
2			$	$	$
3			$	$	$
4			$	$	$
5			$	$	$
6			$	$	$
7			$	$	$
8			$	$	$
9			$	$	$
10			$	$	$

LEVERAGE SALES COACHING **Goal Achievement Plan Summary**

CUSTOMERS Best-Fit Target List:

Focus precedes success. What accounts deserve your biggest focus in order to greatly increase your income?

CUSTOMERS: Top 10 Best-Fit Target List					
List your best customer targets according to your ratings & sales potential. What will each account be worth when successful?					
Target #	Company	Best-Fit Acct Rating	Account's Total Purchase Vol./Yr.	Your Current Purchase Vol./Yr.	Your Target Purchase Vol./Yr-1
1			$	$	$
2			$	$	$
3			$	$	$
4			$	$	$
5			$	$	$
6			$	$	$
7			$	$	$
8			$	$	$
9			$	$	$
10			$	$	$

 **Goal Achievement Plan Summary**

CLIENTS Best-Fit Target List:

Focus precedes success. What accounts deserve your biggest focus in order to greatly increase your income?

CLIENTS: Top 10 Best-Fit Target List					
List your best client targets according to your ratings & sales potential. What will each account be worth when successful?					
Target #	Company	Best-Fit Acct Rating	Account's Total Purchase Vol./Yr.	Your Current Purchase Vol./Yr.	Your Target Purchase Vol./Yr-1
1			$	$	$
2			$	$	$
3			$	$	$
4			$	$	$
5			$	$	$
6			$	$	$
7			$	$	$
8			$	$	$
9			$	$	$
10			$	$	$

Once you have established your clearly focused goal, you need a written Action Plan that delineates how you will achieve it. You need a system of measurement and a system of accountability so that you will stay on course.

 **PLAYBOOK RESOURCES:**

SEE PROCESS, Goal Achievement Plan

inSITE-app & http://leveragesalescoach.com/resources

THE SALES PIPELINE

The pipeline concept has been embraced much the same across all industries as the process associated with reaching sales goals. You start with opportunities and progress through stages to end with closed sales. At each stage, the conversion rate percentage grows, and the amount of activity required by the salesperson diminishes.

The Funnel – Goal Achievement Plan – ANNUAL

Conversion Rate (approx.)	Best-Fit OPPORTUNITIES		
20%	1. Prospecting / Target / Intell	5,000 Calls	Backward Thinking
50%	2. Qualifying / Needs / Best-Fit	$10M (500 Fits)	
40%	3. Appmt Set / Dec-Mkr	$4M (200 Needs)	
80%	4. Present / HV Needs	$3.2M (160 Solutions)	
63%	5. Obj Mgmt	$2M (100 Proposals)	
56%	6. Close/AFB	$1.1M (56 Agreed)	
90%	7. Follow-Up	$1M (50x - $20K Confirmed)	Goals Back-to-Front

$1,000,000

Begin with end $$ needed

The Funnel – Goal Achievement Plan – ACTIVITIES

Activity Level required for goal

Conversion Rate (approx.)	Best-Fit OPPORTUNITIES	
20%	1. Prospecting / Target / Intell	100 Calls per wk
50%	2. Qualifying / Needs / Best-Fit	20 Leads / week
40%	3. Appmt Set / Dec-Mkr	10 Qualified / week
80%	4. Present / HV Needs	4 Appmts / week
63%	5. Obj Mgmt	3.2 Presents / week
56%	6. Close/AFB	2.0 Ready to Buy / week
90%	7. Follow-Up	1 Close/Agreed / week
		1 Confirmed Sale / week

Level of Effectiveness

$1,000,000

Key Measurements & Minimum Standards

A typical sales pipeline, for example, may go through the following progression:

1. Prospecting

2. Qualifying/Identifying needs

3. Setting an appointment with a decision maker

4. Giving a presentation/Assessing high-value needs

5. Managing objections

6. Closing/AFB (ask for business)

7. Following up

In sales coaching, we use many templates and tools, but the Goal Achievement Plan is the linchpin that drives the rest of them.

STEP 2: CREATE YOUR WRITTEN PLAN

Understanding the "what" and "why" of your GAP is critical. As a salesperson, you need to know exactly what you should be doing and why it makes sense. You also need to know "how much": How much activity is required to reach that goal, and how effective are those actions?

A well-written plan for achieving your focused goal, your GAP, should include the following Four Key Elements:

1) THE PLAY BY PLAY: Exactly what action in what sequence needs to be taken to achieve your goal? Prospecting, qualifying, setting appointments with decision makers, presenting, and even following up after the sale are all actions that should be clearly defined as part of the Sales Process.

Sales Process-Scorecard Example

Below are examples of HPAs (High Payoff Activities) that really matter to drive results in each step of a sales process. Note the following attributes of the HPA descriptions:

- **Succinct, Clear, Useable:** "Bite-size" description that's still clear enough to know exactly what to do
- **Specific:** Specific actions to be taken and key questions or reminders of best sales practices
- **Quantifiable:** Wherever possible, add an amount of activity to establish Min Stds for sellers

SALES STEPS & HPAs	Tools & Training
Step 1: Prospecting << KPI: # CONTACTS >>	
Target Prospect List Prep & Planning: Prep weekly Top 10 List for prospects, customers, clients from Target List based on Pre-Qualifying Checklist	• Master Target List • Top 10 List • Pre-Qualifying Checklist
Networking/Trade Shows: Goal = 8 or more pre-qualified leads; Give cards to sales asst.; Complete a trade show recap; 24-hr follow-up touch on leads	• Networking Best Practices
Social networking: Post blog update & insights post at least 1x per week	• Social media marketing
Calling-Warm/Cold: Min 5 hours blocked/week for directors and above, inside sales calling your top 20 list	• Calling Best Practices • Top 10 List TODAY • Pre-Qualifying Checklist • 10 Tips Better Voicemails
Leads Tracking & Follow-Up: 24 hr or less follow-up, track in CRM	• CRM
Step 2: Qualifying Phone Call/Meeting << KPI: # QUALIFIED >>	
Advance prep work on target: Identify Decision-makers & key influencers	
Qualifying Checklist: Questions List to determine deeper Qualifying criteria; Current buying program; Questions list; Consultative selling training	• Qualifying Checklist • Questions list • Consultative selling training
Step 3: Appmt Setting << KPI: # APPMTS that STICK >>	
Appointment setting: "Calendar handy?"; Suggest specific time/date; Ensure right people will be there; Outline agenda for meeting-1; Meet/exceed Appmt activity Success Goals each month	• Appmt Setting Best Practices • Success Goals
Opportunity Brief: Create and review Opportunity Brief with Mgr	• Opportunity Brief
Meeting Reminder/Confirm: Send reminder & confirm 24 hrs in advance	
Step 4: Needs Analysis: Mutual-Fit	
Role Practice Tough Questions: Anticipate prospect's tough questions. Who will answer (if team selling)?	• Role practice training
Needs Analysis meeting: Get prospect talking; Understand their needs & priorities; Probing questions to learn business objectives & core issues; Identify HVNs; Reason to proceed/Solution awareness/End results/Value we deliver	• Qualifying Checklist • Questions list • Consultative selling training

Step 5: Presentation << KPI: # PRESENTATIONS >>	
Presentation Prep meeting: Focus on HVNs (High value needs) = Know their 'end zone' (what matters most to client)	
Create Presentation: Focus on THEIR needs and smart solutions, discuss measurable value, relevant success examples	• Presentation templates
Role Practice: Practice Q&A and buyer's tough questions	• Role practice cheat sheet
Solution Presentation: Customer-focused presentation, interactive questions, Focus on THEIR reasons/HVNs	• Presentation notes cheat sheet
Follow-up: Recap next steps who-what-when for all, Send calendar to all	• Calendar invitation
Step 6: Closing / Won or Lost << KPI: # WINS >>	
Negotiate with Buyer/Mgr: Negotiate terms, discuss & confirm	
Closing: Recap solution plan that meets their needs, terms, and timeline	
Agreement Signature: Get signature or follow up to secure signature	
Submit signed order & process it: Alert Mgr, fulfillment or operational team	
Win/Loss ratio: 50% or higher?	
Success Review: What worked? What didn't? What can we learn? What needs to be improved?	• Success Review tool
Step 7: Follow-Up / Follow-Through	
Follow-up/Follow Through: Recap actions; Who is doing what by when? Calendar follow-up actions and follow-through	
KEY ACTIVITIES	
Total Score	

2) HPAs: What are the High Payoff Activities driving the action? For example, what are the HPAs that will drive the best prospecting, the best qualifying, and the best presentations? What doesn't just produce results but produces the best results?

Here are some examples: face-to-face visits, phone calls, networking events, trade shows, follow-up and follow-through, time and prioritization focus.

3) BEST PRACTICES: What Best Practices will lead to the best results at each stage of the pipeline? For example, we know that conversion rates will rise when you do a better job of qualifying prospects at the front end and that you close deals at a much higher rate when you present to the right people in the right way.

4) KPIs: Key Performance Indicators are just that—a measurement of how well you're doing. KPIs are measured in two ways: **lagging indicators**, which show the results of sales the previous month, quarter, or year; and **leading indicators**, which show whether you are getting enough leads and opportunities at the front end in real time so that you can stay on track to achieve your goals. In essence, **your KPIs give you a real-time sense of the health of your pipeline**. Here are some examples: number of new contacts made, number prequalified, number presentations, number closed, total dollars closed for period.

PLAYBOOK RESOURCES:
SEE PROCESS, Sales Process Scorecard
inSITE-app & http://leveragesalescoach.com/resources

STEP 3: SYSTEMS OF MEASUREMENT: CRM AND PIPELINE MANAGEMENT

There are two fundamental tools for sales that are essentially joined at the hip: the Customer Relationship Management (CRM) system and the Pipeline Management system.

Customer Relationship Management

Customer Relationship Management organizes all contacts and manages where prospects, customers, and clients are in the deal-making process. Whereas Pipeline Management keeps track of what specifically is advancing or stalling in the pipeline, CRM delivers a general report of where things stand and what opportunities are currently available.

In essence, the CRM is a dashboard, offering a high-level view of how well things are functioning in the Sales Process. It shows what's recently closed in a particular period and projects what future sales will likely be depending on where things are in the pipeline and their respective values.

For example, if a salesperson's goal is to get $100,000 this month in sales, but he only has the potential for $30,000 in the pipeline, he will know that even if everything in the pipeline closes, which is unlikely, he has no shot of making his goal. However, if he has $250,000 in the pipeline, even if it does not all close, he can predict a good chance of hitting his $100,000 number.

Proactive Pipeline Management

Managing your sales pipeline is critically important as it works in tandem with your CRM, letting you know where people are in the process, what needs should be addressed, where you can push, and where you need to focus your time.

Every sales pipeline has four categories, or baskets, of people:

1. Prospects

2. Customers

3. Clients

4. Centers of Influence

Prospects are people who have been qualified as leads, or at least have been identified as good targets. However, they have not yet done business with you. **Customers** are people who have done some business with you but only occasionally. They may not be regulars. A **Client** is someone who is spending significant money with you regularly. A **Center of Influence (COI)** may never buy or use your product/service but could send you a lifetime of business.

Pipeline Management is the manner in which you deal with those people as you get them to move along toward the goal. Your objective is to get them to buy more regularly, to become clients.

Sales Key Activities Dashboard

	Regional Sales Manager		Rudy								
	Week Start Date		02/15/16								

	Name	KEY ACTIVITIES - LEADING KPIs					KEY RESULTS - LAGGING KPIs				
		# Contacts (min 50)	# Qualifd (min 25)	# Appmts (min 10)	# Presents (min 6)	# Wins (min 3)	# Units Sold			Total # Units Sold	Amount Sold
							A	B	C		
1	Chris	55	30	13	8	5	22	36	25	83	$33,200
2	Matt	52	27	12	8	5	20	32	30	82	$32,800
3	Kent	44	24	10	7	5	18	29	28	75	$30,000
4	Paul	42	23	10	6	3	20	26	21	67	$26,800
5	Michelle	40	20	9	5	3	18	29	19	66	$26,400
6	Ed	38	18	8	5	3	15	22	18	55	$22,000
7	Frank	35	17	9	5	2	14	24	25	63	$25,200
8	Ray	33	15	7	3	2	12	19	20	51	$20,400
9	Robin	31	14	6	3	1	15	18	16	49	$19,600
10	Robert	28	18	7	4	2	14	22	17	53	$21,200
Team Totals		398	206	91	54	31	168	257	219	644	$257,600
		80%	82%	91%	90%	103%	84%	129%	110%	107%	$400

LEVERAGE SALES COACHING

PLAYBOOK RESOURCES:

SEE PROCESS, Sales Key Activities Dashboard

inSITE-app & http://leveragesalescoach.com/resources

SALES TEAM SCRIMMAGE
NARROWING YOUR FOCUS

In your specific industry, you're aware of what your competitors are offering. So, how does your service or product stand out? How does it speak specifically to a particular niche in the broader pool of prospects? Who needs your product or services the most?

Working together as a team, brainstorm on those particular qualities that make your company, your service, or your product stand out. These can be actual functions of the product or emotions that the product or service evokes. Think outside the box and describe your uniqueness in as many ways as you can.

Once you have your unique characteristics listed, work on narrowing the niche of potential clients that would benefit most from these aspects of your product or service.

TIP: Consider the profile of the best customers that you or your company already have. What are their traits and characteristics? The target might not perfectly match the ideal, but it will help you narrow your search.

Remember, success leaves clues:

- What led to the success that you and your company have had with your best customers?

- What does a good fit look like, as opposed to an ideal fit?

- If an A customer is perfect, what are the characteristics of a B customer?

- How about a C?

Once you're clear on precisely what you are looking for, you will find it far easier to narrow your focus, rather than using up your energy trying to chase everybody. Remember the top performers tend to call on fewer people but write more business. The key is they invest their time with the right people.

INSPECTING THE BASKETS: THE PIPELINE TOP TEN

Inspect the Baskets

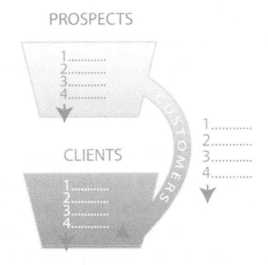

- Top 10 Prospects – Customers – Clients?

- What ways have you touched them?

- What frequency?

- What can you do to advance them?

When it comes to Pipeline Management, the essential question you need to answer is: **What can I do to advance my top ten prospects, customers, clients, and COIs?**

Once you've identified the most likely opportunities in each basket of your pipeline—prospects, customers, clients, and COIs—you will need to keep track of what stage each lead is in, the opportunities you can pursue in each stage, and the next steps that you will take.

This management is not just keeping track. **Proactive Pipeline Management** means that at each stage, you always ask yourself, *Now what? What's standing in the way? What can I do next to get them closer to the deal?*

Even when you get to the finish line and close, you still need to follow up and follow through. If you drop the ball at this point, you could have a brand-new customer who is unhappy. You need to keep up the momentum and keep the customer pleased with you.

PLAYBOOK RESOURCES:
SEE PROCESS VIDEO, Sales Systems, Proactive Sales Pipeline Management
inSITE-app & http://leveragesalescoach.com/resources

ESTABLISHING A TOUCH SYSTEM

When it comes to your top ten in each basket of the pipeline, are you keeping track of how often and when they've been "touched"? That is, when was the last time you had a face-to-face conversation with them, or got in touch by phone call, snail mail, e-mail, social media, or text?

WHAT'S YOUR FREQUENCY?

Experience has shown that it takes nine touches just to build basic recognition that you exist, and those nine touches will not get someone ready to buy. In fact, the number of touches needed has been increasing as businesspeople tend to hide behind voice mail and e-mail and whatever else they use as a gatekeeper. If they want to hide, it is not hard.

With so many touches required just to break through, you can see that a systematic approach is essential so that you do not have to start from scratch every time.

The nature of the touches can vary widely. You might communicate about general business information. You might talk about news and insights that are relevant to their industry. You might let them know what sets you or your company apart. Sometimes, the touch can be just to share something fun or something personal.

A good Touch System does more than just keep track of how often and when you've touched base with a potential client. It also measures the quality of those touches, which is what wins a new client. Frequent, ineffective contacts can become annoying and turn off a potential customer. Quality touches are those that generate trust. They help your contact get to know you, and the more they get to know and like you, the more they trust you—and ultimately a sale is a transfer of trust.

Proactive Pipeline Mgmt. – Touch System
Inspect the Baskets

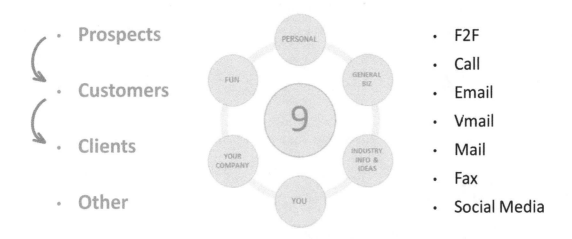

- Prospects
- Customers
- Clients
- Other

PERSONAL
GENERAL BIZ
FUN
9
INDUSTRY INFO & IDEAS
YOUR COMPANY
YOU

- F2F
- Call
- Email
- Vmail
- Mail
- Fax
- Social Media

PLAYBOOK RESOURCES:
SEE PROCESS VIDEO, Sales Systems, How to Build Your Touch System, Tools to Touch inSITE-app & http://leveragesalescoach.com/resources

A WORD FROM DAN . . .
THE POWER OF CONNECTION

Years ago, I worked with a salesman who was trying to figure out why a potential buyer kept giving him the cold shoulder. The good news was that the buyer at least was taking his calls. The bad news was that things were going nowhere.

The salesman learned, through social media and other contacts, that this particular person was a big fan of the Iowa State Hawkeyes. His office was plastered with tokens of his allegiance to the team.

"Why don't you hop on the Hawkeyes' website," I suggested to him, "and buy a keychain, buy a key fob, whatever, and just pop it in the mail to him? Nothing related to business, but just say, 'Hey, next time you go tailgating at a Hawkeyes game, here's something new to show off.'"

He took my advice, and later he told me that it had changed the man's demeanor when he would take his calls. The conversations were warmer and friendlier. They ended up doing business, and he thinks the Hawkeyes connection was a significant breakthrough.

It takes the human touch. You need to reach out to people regularly, in a variety of creative and memorable ways. When you are able to connect, you have progressed appreciably toward the sale. This is not to say a key fob in the mail is what it takes. What it takes is learning enough about a fellow human being to make a meaningful connection.

DAN LARSON

As you consider your current Touch System, ask yourself:

- How often do prospects return my phone or e-mail messages? How eager are they to have a conversation with me?

- How often do prospects disappear into a black hole, even when they seemed really interested?

- How often do prospects I forecasted to close instead sign with a competitor or, worse, stay with the status quo?

SCORING PLAY:

What are the HPAs that have helped you advance people in your pipeline in the past? What are some HPAs that have worked for other sales team members at different points in the process? Collect your own and work with other team members to create specific Moneybags–that is, bags of useful tactics that make you memorable to your prospects and that ultimately put money in your pocket. For more on the Moneybag concept, see Chapter 4: Gear.

Touch System:

- **Top 10 focus in each Basket**
- **Money Bag – immediate & personalized to Differentiate**
- **Other Touches made regularly**
  - **Other Influencers affecting the buy**
- **What high payoff touches can you make to advance your pipeline?**

Proactive Pipeline Mgmt. – Touch System
Inspect the Baskets

- Prospects
- Customers
- Clients
- Other

PERSONAL
GENERAL BIZ
FUN
9
YOUR COMPANY
INDUSTRY INFO & IDEAS
YOU

- F2F
- Call
- Email
- Vmail
- Mail
- Fax
- Social Media

STEP 4: SYSTEM OF ACCOUNTABILITY: SALES PROCESS SCORECARD

KPIs, Pipeline Management, CRM systems, Touch Systems—all of these aspects of a Goal Achievement Plan are vital to building a Sales Playbook for Hyper Sales Growth. While these are all functions that you'll need to keep up with—either personally or by allocating your non-HPAs to an assistant—a good Sales Manager will find ways to ensure that you and the rest of the team are using the best and most productive resources available.

A good Sales Manager will also have his or her own Touch System: a system of accountability that ensures all team members are doing well on their KPIs, that their pipelines are being managed well, their CRMs are up-to-date, and their own prospect-customer-client Touch Systems are on track.

This is best done through regular progress reviews using a Sales Process Scorecard, starting with the big-picture progress review once per quarter on what's working, what isn't working, and the best ways to move forward.

Sales Process Scorecards are for people who are serious about achieving their goals. Read more about the Sales Process Scorecard in Chapter 4: Gear.

When you don't write down a plan to achieve your goal, it simply becomes a "wish" that is easy to shrug off. Even with a written plan, a progress review becomes essential to help support and measure your efforts and encourage you to actually achieve your goal. Such reviews should be conducted once a quarter at a minimum.

Research shows us that people with (1) written goals, (2) commitment to action, and (3) regular progress reports and an accountability system produce 78 percent better goal achievement than people who just think about goals.[4] How much more do you want to succeed at your goals?

SCORING PLAY:

Take a minute to write down at least one of your goals and then answer the following questions:

1. **What is your goal** (period/year)?
2. **Where are you now** (current position, pacing toward goal)?
3. **Where do you want to be**/believe you will be for this period?

Minimum Standards of Performance

4. What are the Key Activities and skills required to achieve your goal?

High-Payoff Targets

5. Key account development of your top ten targets

Your High Payoff Activities

6. What key actions can you take to make this happen?

---

4   "Study Focuses on Strategies for Achieving Goals, Resolutions," Dominican University of California, http://www.dominican.edu/dominicannews/study-highlights-strategies-for-achieving-goals.

How can your Sales Manager and sales team help you improve sales? Remember, this is a team effort. Even Peyton Manning never won a game entirely on his own—the best players have a great team working with them, helping them win.

STEP 5: PLANNING YOUR HIGH-PAYOFF TARGETS

Whether you call it territory planning or determining your key account list targets, it's critically important to narrow your focus. Avoid the mistake of calling on too many customers and spreading too thin to be effective. The best salespeople focus on fewer targets that really matter. They increase the Quality and Quantity of calls on fewer people that are well-targeted. And they sell more.

Break down your territory plan into a four-week View and a two-week Focus.

What are the most important goals, the "big rocks," your team is planning for the coming quarter? How can you work together to improve your sales approach so that you are always well-prepared when speaking with prospects, customers, and clients? How can you plan ahead best to achieve the most, both as an individual and as a team?

Weekly Pre-Call Planner:

Big picture Quarterly view

- •   Plan the "big rocks"
- •   **4-Week View**
  - •   Territory Planning
- •   **2-Week Focus**
  - •   Pre-Call Planning your key accounts

Weekly Pre-Call Planner Review: WEST Territory ONGOING

4-Week View/2-Week Focus	JANUARY					FEBRUARY
	Dec 29 - Jan 4	Jan 5 - 11	Jan 12 - 18	Jan 19 - 25	Jan 26 - Feb 1	Feb 2 - 8
KEVIN MADISON	2-Week Focus		4-Week View		Longer View →	
Key Product-1 Presentations / Activities						
Key Product-2 Presentations / Activities						
Key Product-3 Presentations / Activities						
Promotional Activities & Support						
Prospecting / Lead-Gen Activities						
Special Activities / Projects						

PLAYBOOK RESOURCES:

SEE PROCESS, Weekly Pre-Call Planner

inSITE-app & http://leveragesalescoach.com/resources

That's where **Practices** come into play. At this point, you have the "magic" of a Goal Achievement Plan backed with accountability and should have a written plan based on the Five Steps to Creating Your Ideal Sales Process. You have begun managing your time to focus on HPAs, using CRM for Proactive Pipeline Management, and developing a consistent Touch System. With all those processes in place to set up your plays, now let's put them into action!

CHAPTER 3

PRACTICES:
WAYS TO TRAIN, PREPARE, AND PRACTICE

ON TRAINING, PROCESS & PREPARATION:

When players know that they have mastered the rigors of training . . . then their confidence leads to an unusual focus, free from distractions, doubt, or fear.

How we practice defines who we are. It is not only something we do in order to compete, but our practice is a competitive activity in and of itself. Practice is something we want to be the best at for its own sake.

A player who is fully prepared on the practice field will feel ready to meet whatever comes his way on game day and thus, feel more confident and able to minimize distractions of fear and doubt.

PETE CARROLL

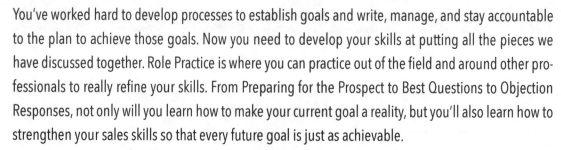

CHAPTER GAME PLAN

You've worked hard to develop processes to establish goals and write, manage, and stay accountable to the plan to achieve those goals. Now you need to develop your skills at putting all the pieces we have discussed together. Role Practice is where you can practice out of the field and around other professionals to really refine your skills. From Preparing for the Prospect to Best Questions to Objection Responses, not only will you learn how to make your current goal a reality, but you'll also learn how to strengthen your sales skills so that every future goal is just as achievable.

Every sports team practices before going into the game. Why would you go into the sales game without practicing how you would handle the toughest situations, like the unanticipated objection that could block your victory or a change in the company's decision maker?

The importance of practice should be obvious, but few do it. In the Hyper Sales Growth approach, all members of your team will work together to share the best ideas and perfect them by practicing with each other, not in the field. This type of preparation applies not only to practicing the HPAs of your top performers but also to learning as much as you can about your prospects, customers, and clients by asking the right questions, having answers ready to even the toughest objections, and understanding the value of Active Listening. More than just listening carefully, Active Listening involves showing attentiveness, such as by paraphrasing back what others have said.

MODEL THE MASTERS

Whether you are a rookie or a veteran, you can benefit by learning from those who do something best.

We call it Modeling the Masters. Identify your own shortcomings and what you need to make it in your company and industry, and then absorb all you can from the Top Producers. Go on sales calls with them, or sit in on their phone conversations.

LINKS in the SALES CHAIN

Where does *YOUR* sales chain break?

_____

Find the weak links & fix them.

_____

Work smarter. Earn more.

1. **Prospecting**

2. **Qualifying**

3. **Appointment Setting**

4. **Presenting**

5. **Objections Management**

6. **Closing**

7. **Follow-Up / Through**

- How do these masters describe things?

- How do they get the job done?

Observe how the top performers set their goals and pursue them. Be curious and ask as many questions as they will put up with:

- Why is this issue important?

- What matters here?

- Why are you doing that now?

Absorb as much as possible. Watch them intently, and be certain you do not miss a thing.

This may be especially valuable anytime you join a new company or a new sales team—when you want to ramp up as best you can and as quickly as possible. After all, much of your pay is based on how well you sell. But even if you are not new, if you are objective and honest with yourself, you will know that you are strong at some things and weaker at others. If you are avoiding HPAs because they are in your weak areas, you are missing opportunities.

Look for others on your team who are strong where you are weak, and swap insights and share Best Practices. Develop a relationship in which you can tell each other about the approaches that work best. Just as others will have strengths to offer you, you will have strengths to offer them. By communicating with one another, the whole team gets stronger.

Stretch yourself to reach your capabilities. Be willing to make mistakes. If you are not moving beyond your comfort zone, you are not trying hard enough. Then, when you do make mistakes, fix them immediately and try again. Once you've learned a new behavior, glue it into place. Make it part of your structure and use it from this day forward.

For example, stretch yourself to proactively manage common objections you know you will face later. If you know that "high price" will be their objection at some point, position your pricing structure connected to the unique strengths, services, specific solutions, and results that directly address your prospect's HVNs (Highest-Value Needs). Make sure your response is relevant to solving what matters most to them.

Do you actually have a proactive process you use consistently to ask for referrals—that is, after you have delivered strong value to earn them? Stretch yourself to make this work for you consistently!

PLAYBOOK RESOURCES:
SEE PRACTICE VIDEO, The Power of Leverage–Model the Masters
inSITE-app & http://leveragesalescoach.com/resources

PRACTICE WITH THE TEAM

Most of us heave a heavy sigh at the thought of sales meetings. They can feel like a waste of time, a long and tedious session that gets in the way of going out and making money.

Most sales meetings drag on with a lot of "housekeeping," as the leaders drone on about what's been happening, the latest sales data, who is running behind, and other updates. Most companies and salespeople admit to spending minor amounts of time at their sales meetings actually training, role practicing, and growing their teams' skills. With more focus on these types of learning and growing activities, you would likely find yourself looking forward to what you could learn and what you could contribute.

In advocating for more development-oriented sales meetings, consider urging your Sales Manager to host the following Sales Playbook practices or taking it on yourself to host these activities with other team members in order to grow your respective skills:

Playbook Practice #1: Role Practice
Role Practice is an essential element of training, as it helps colleagues identify and collaborate on the best sales methods.

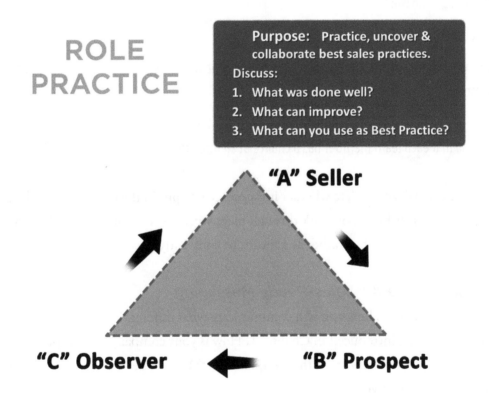

ROLE PRACTICE

Purpose: Practice, uncover & collaborate best sales practices.
Discuss:
1. What was done well?
2. What can improve?
3. What can you use as Best Practice?

"A" Seller

"C" Observer   "B" Prospect

SALES TEAM SCRIMMAGE
SELL ME

We encourage salespeople to do Role Practice in groups of three. Person A takes the role of seller, Person B takes the role of buyer, and Person C observes the interaction.

After A and B run through a sales scenario–focusing on price objections, for example, or on ways to differentiate the company–they discuss what happened with the observer. Much of the learning comes from this discussion. Often, it is the observer who gains the greatest insights. In offering feedback on the exercise, the observer should answer:

- What was done well?

- What could be improved?

- Can we extract anything from this interchange that we could use as a best practice for the company?

Ideally, the three-person team should switch roles three times, going through a different scenario each time so that each team member has a chance at all three roles.

Practice matters. Ask any athlete whether it is necessary to put in the extra hours at the gym, study the Playbook at home, or work through plays with the team and coach. They do not see that as a waste of time but rather as a means to constantly become better.

Playbook Practice #2: Sales-Ready Messaging

Sales-Ready Messaging is how you will communicate what differentiates your company, the Value Proposition we introduced in Chapter 1. How is your company, and its products and services, unique and different from the competition? You must get this core message across succinctly and clearly in your sales presentations.

The problem is that few salespeople take the time to develop a powerful, unique message. They may have a pitch they use, but is it really strong, does it really stand out, or is it just a spiel that they've become used to falling into?

When salespeople are not ready with a Value Proposition, we have found that they will stumble along and get it wrong or only partly right. But if they craft it together and practice it in-house, they will excel at delivering the message, and smooth delivery will pull in the sales.

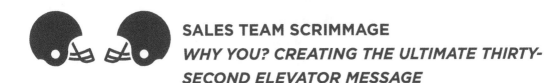

SALES TEAM SCRIMMAGE
WHY YOU? CREATING THE ULTIMATE THIRTY-SECOND ELEVATOR MESSAGE

As with any best practice in the field, coming up with the ideal approach is a team effort. During your next sales meeting, have each salesperson stand up and give their standard elevator message. Which ones stand out, and which ones fall flat?

Take the best lines, and work together to create one solid message that really stands out in both approach and content.

Having trouble coming up with a unique angle? Have your team dig a little deeper and start brainstorming on your products' or services' outstanding features and benefits. What makes you different than the competition? What makes you stand out to your ideal clients? What Success Stories and outstanding results can you share that will pique their interest?

Statistics are another way to turn your prospect from disinterested to curious. What are some positive stats you can share from other clients' results? Specificity sells!

The following **Value Proposition Template** can help you focus on some of the statistics and unique messages that can help you and your team hone your company's Unique Value Proposition.

Why Your Company?
Create Value that Differentiates Worksheet

"If you don't have a competitive advantage, don't compete."
Jack Welch, Former GE CEO

Why Your Company? The Problem: *It all sounds like everyone else*!

- Quality, Competitive, Friendly
- Good Customer Service, Responsive, Knowledgeable
- Trust, Convenient, Lots of Choice
- ME! Results, Save You Money

The key question: **What are _you_ offering that your _competitors aren't or can't_?**

- The best answers are the ones that are <u>sustainable</u> and <u>tough for competitors to duplicate</u> the benefits.

Why Your Company? The Opportunity

- Show buyers how you are **_unique, different and better_**!
- "Dazzle them with details." What do you or should you be offering to truly differentiate?

_____

_____

_____

Examples from **Creating Competitive Advantage** by Jaynie Smith

- We guarantee that your order will be confirmed and shipped within 3 hours of placement. Your calls will be returned within 20 minutes; our technicians will be on site the next day.
- Over 90% of our business comes from referrals.
- Last year, less than ½ of 1% of our customers returned one of our products.
- Our customer retention rate is 95%, twice that of our nearest competitor.
- After switching to our product line, our customers reported an average 25% boost in manufacturing productivity.

_____

_____

_____

Areas often overlooked or to be considered

- Terms, Materials, Delivery
- Guarantees, Inventory Turns
- Training, Information

Look for things _not claimed by the competition_. Start your list here.

_____

_____

_____

Brainstorm Exercise

1. What would **your competitors say** are their unique "Why their company" points?
2. What would you say to this question: **_"What's so special about your product/service?"_**
3. What **values add/extras**, beyond the basic product/services, do you provide? Spell it out.

_____

_____

_____

Additional Guidelines

- Strengths are important *but they are NOT differentiators*.
- If you *have the most options* for your customers, *say so*.
- *Show* customers how much you *save them*.
- What are you *measuring* (and not measuring) today in your company *that could give you differentiation*?
- *Review* your marketing and sales materials, as well as your website.
- What are you doing to *ensure that you will have a new list each year*?

_____

_____

_____

PLAYBOOK RESOURCES:

SEE PRACTICE, Why Your Company?

inSITE-app & http://leveragesalescoach.com/resources

PREPARE FOR THE PROSPECT

Now that you have practiced with the team, you still need to prepare yourself for a sales call by sizing up your prospect.

Personality Styles:

- **Be more effective with more people**
- **Identify the buyer's style and adjust accordingly**
- **Two Questions:**
  1) Are they MORE or LESS assertive?
  2) How do they tend to make decisions using LOGIC or EMOTION? (Facts or Feelings?)

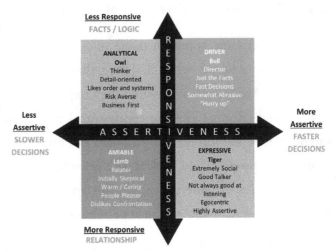

Personality Styles

As we discussed in Chapter 1, pretty much everyone's personality falls generally into one of the four Personality Styles: Amiable, Analytical, Expressive, and Driver. Do a quick personality assessment of your prospect by asking yourself two questions:

1. Are they more assertive, or less so?

2. Do they tend to make decisions using facts and logic, or emotion—their feelings about people and relationships?

Then determine where your prospect falls on the graph.

Once you have a good idea of their personality type, you can learn what "language" they prefer and tailor your approach accordingly. An Amiable might prefer more supportive language, for example, while an Analytical might appreciate a more systematic approach.

Top salespeople will figure out Personality Styles on their own and use that knowledge to their advantage. They will be able to identify whom they are dealing with and then adjust and respond accordingly so as to be more effective with more people.

For example, savvy sales professionals understand that when dealing with a decisive, Driver personality, this person "wants to decide" and is very comfortable making quicker, decisive decisions. So for this personality type, their sales approach would lay out several options for a solution along with the upside/downside probabilities attached to each. This approach is highly effective with a Driver personality, as it lets them buy in their own way.

However, that same approach made to a predominantly Analytical buyer would actually *slow down or stall* the decision. Using that same Driver approach would be a bad idea, because the Analytical buyer would then require gathering a lot more data to ponder about those several options. The sales professional understands that a proposal to an Analytical should reduce the number of proposed options and instead emphasize solid evidence to support this proposal and back it with reliable service after the sale. This ensures that what was promised is actually delivered. This approach, adjusted based on personality style, is highly effective with an Analytical personality and lets them buy in their own way.

Assessing Personality Styles is pretty simple to leverage in sales once you learn it well. But there are a few things you must keep in mind:

- It is important to know how you, as a salesperson, are wired—your strengths and the things that you are good at or not. You have to know your own personality style before you can adapt to someone else's.

- Learning how to quickly and effectively assess and respond to a personality type not your own requires study, preparation, and practice. You can get to the point where it becomes automatic and you adjust to whomever you are working with by second nature.

Note: Adjusting to your prospect/customer's personality style is not manipulation. Given that your product/service is bringing value in addressing the needs/opportunities/problems, it is going the extra mile for the benefit of the prospect/customer. You don't want personalities to get in the way of delivering value. It's the responsibility of the sales professional to adjust to the prospect/customer.

Once you have figured out a contact's personality style, you can establish a field in CRM by which any other people dealing with that contact will know at a glance what the better approach might be. Salespeople come and go, but hopefully your clients will stick around for the long haul. When the personality assessment is stored in CRM, the next salesperson can get a jump start in dealing with that client. This is true leverage and can be utilized ongoing.

PLAYBOOK RESOURCES:
SEE PRACTICE VIDEO, 4 Personality Styles, Chameleon Salespeople
inSITE-app & http://leveragesalescoach.com/resources

Pre-Call Planning

It is important to find out as much as you can about your prospects before you call on them. This is not so much to determine what you are going to tell them as to anticipate what questions you are going to ask them.

Remember that these calls aren't really about you—your prospects only care about their own problems and issues. They will pay attention only if they can see how what you offer might make life easier or better for them or their company. They want to solve their problem, not watch you beat your chest.

You can brainstorm to come up with questions and topics that will **make your call more relevant, meaningful, and important to them**. You cannot hope to do that effectively, however, unless you care enough to take the time to find out some things about the person you are addressing and the company that he or she represents.

Write down those questions, and consider how you will ask them. Make a list of things that you must find out so that you can talk intelligently to your target.

The "A" players already do this stuff. They do it instinctively. They go into a call with plenty of background information, knowing what they will ask, not just the "lines of the pitch." They anticipate the objections and are ready with a relevant response. When they see progress, they know just what they will do next. They have a plan—they do not just wing it.

If you want to improve your performance during sales calls, if you want to advance to Top Producer status, then you should do as the "A" players do. If you plan ahead and ask relevant and insightful questions, such as the ones that might be inspired by the next worksheet, you will see how quickly you build credibility with the people to whom you hope to sell your product or service. You will feel confident, and they will feel confident in you. When everyone on the team makes pre-call planning a priority, the results are obvious.

Pre-Call Planning Worksheet

3 Questions MUST BE asked before every call!

1. **What do we *KNOW*?**

   - INFO RESOURCES: What info do we already know or have access to better sell/grow this account?

   - Internal sources

   - Internet research

   - Their website/collateral

   - Vendors

   - Their Competition

   - Their customers

   - Your personal network

   - Their employees

   - Their sales dept.

2. **What do we *NEED TO KNOW*?**

   - What info do we need to learn to progress this sale?

   - Decision-Makers & Influencers

   - Decision making process

   - Business & Personal Objectives that drive the deal

   - HVNs: Highest Value Needs prioritized

   - Timeframe / Deadline

   - Budgets

   - Political agendas

3. **What do we need to *GET THEM TALKING ABOUT*?**

   - What do we need to learn to progress this sale?

   - Socrates → Collaborative discussion

   - They have the <u>Answers</u>, the <u>Reasons</u>, the <u>Motivations</u> for THEIR Buying Process

   - Need to Ask-Questions-And-Listen to learn it

Ask yourself this Question before every call!

What is the purpose of *THIS* call?

Never make a call WITHOUT a specific purpose!

PLAYBOOK RESOURCES:

SEE PRACTICE, Pre-Call Planning Worksheet

inSITE-app & http://leveragesalescoach.com/resources

BEST QUESTIONS AND ACTIVE LISTENING

Going into every sale, there are three essential questions to ask yourself, and they all center on one thing: What is the purpose of this particular call? You need to know what you hope to accomplish—and that is not always to win the deal and close the sale. If you are working on a long sales cycle, the purpose of the call might be to advance a step toward the eventual deal.

With that in mind, these are the three essential questions:

1. What do you know?

2. What do you need to know?

3. What do you need to get out on the table?

What do you know?

What do you know right now about the status of this particular customer or prospect? If you know very little, then you have much to find out. In Chapter 5 we go into more detail about why this is time well spent. A lot of information is available from the company's website, from the vendors, and from the competition. If you are new to the sales staff, check to be sure that somebody else does not already have some valuable history on the company. You are looking to learn as much as you can about this opportunity. If you're an ongoing client, the call should by now be a treasure trove of getting more information.

What do you need to know?

Then, look for missing information: What do you still need to know? How great is the buyer's need for what you are selling? What is the buyer's time frame for the purchase? Is there a budget, and if so, how much can they spend? Does the buyer have some other agenda or something else on the table that could influence the progress of this deal or change the way the decision will be made?

What do you need to get out on the table?

Is there anything yet to be identified, either by you or by the buyers themselves? What needs to get out on the table? Perhaps there is something they just do not want to talk about, such as a hidden motivation or a fundamental disagreement between partners. It may not seem relevant at the time, but it could loom large in determining the progress of the deal.

"SHOW UP AND THROW UP" SYNDROME

If you ask a silly question, you can expect a silly answer. If you ask a better question, you are far more likely to get a better response.

Why, then, would any salesperson ask an inconsequential question or ask no questions at all? That, in effect, is what often happens when salespeople go in and start spouting their spiel—the "show up and throw up" syndrome.

A better approach is the **AQAL principle: Ask Questions And Listen**.

When you ask a good question, you are compelling your listener to think and provide an answer, and through their response, you might very well gain the essential information that will lead to the sale.

Remember the axiom that **people buy for their reasons, not yours**. You already know why they should buy from you. If you want to find out *their* reasons for buying from you, it pays to shut up and hear what they have to say.

Your goal is to find out what truly matters the most to your potential customers. Help your customers prioritize their needs, opportunities, and problems in the best way that you can, even if that means losing the sale. **What are their Highest-Value Needs?**

If you ask questions sincerely, you will often get a clear answer. Sometimes you have to keep asking in different ways in order to understand what they want and need most and what they might fear about hidden issues or unexpected problems. Or perhaps they are looking for an opportunity that they have not expressed. If you can find out what that is, you can get it out on the table and answer it with your well-rehearsed Objection Response.

Our observations suggest that **top sellers ask six questions for every one statement they make**. In so doing, they learn far more than those who are only listening to themselves talk.

The victory goes to those who are prepared with the Best Questions. Through effective questioning, you can hone in on whether anything might be standing in the way of progressing toward the deal.

Building a **Best Questions Guide** with your team is a great way to get everyone focused on asking better questions to open up and engage customers, learn their situations, and understand their Highest-Value Needs.

Best Questions Guide
EXAMPLES

A Best Questions Guide has the most power and works best <u>WHEN it's collaborated and built with inputs from the entire sales team</u>. This has proven to increase results for companies that focus on building it. Below are sample excerpts from companies in a variety of industries.

Once a Question Guide is completed, training is essential to its successful implementation:

1) Prepare them for the answers they may hear.
2) Promote and reward the memorization of the questions.
3) Design prospecting calls using them.
4) Role practice in a variety of situations and styles.
5) Field coach using the guide before & after calls.
6) Coach them to develop the habits of pre-call preparation using the Question Guide as the focus on the "Purpose of *THIS* Call."

Example of Pre-Call Preparation

- What is the *purpose of THIS call*?

- What do we *KNOW*?

- What do we *NEED TO KNOW*?

- What do we *need to GET THEM TALKING ABOUT*?

RELATIONSHIP BUILDING

Excerpts from a company in the advertising industry

HOBBIES – OTHER LEISURE ACTIVITIES:

- What extracurricular activities do you enjoy outside of work?
    - What is your optimal work-life balance?
- How do you unwind after a long, tough day?
- What is your favorite sport?
    - Favorite team?
    - Do you golf? Where?
- What are your other interests outside of work?
    - Do you like to travel, and if so, where do you go?
    - What's your favorite type of music?

BUSINESS ACCOMPLISHMENTS:

- What accomplishments are you most proud of?
    - What kind of recognition have you received?

LAY OF THE LAND

Excerpts from a company in the contract packaging industry

VALUE ADDED / GIFT ITEM OVERVIEW:

- What seasons do you target?
    - Have you tried other holidays and discontinued them?
    - How do you evaluate how successful your programs are?
- What is your annual budget for these programs?
    - What are your goals for this type of marketing?
- What stores are you currently doing business with?
    - What other outlets are you pursuing?
    - When do you normally design products for the upcoming season?
    - What is your sourcing process?

PAIN

Excerpts from a company in the commercial plumbing industry

FINANCIAL:

- What has been the impact in the past when you have chosen a sub contractor on as the primary reason to award a job?
- How has a plumbing contractor or any sub contractors inability to meet a scheduled deadline affected you?
- What effects have the sub-prime mortgage industry had on your company?
- What experience have you encountered working with sub contractors that were not financially stable?

PLAYBOOK RESOURCES:

SEE PRACTICE, Best Questions Guide

inSITE-app & http://leveragesalescoach.com/resources

SCORING PLAY: SOCRATIC SELLING

Instead of positioning yourself as some sort of adversary—as if one of you will win and one of you will lose—think of yourself as a collaborator. The Socratic method gets all the considerations out in the open and starts the conversation on how to resolve matters. It is, by its nature, inquisitive and conversational. You ask questions to get the buyer to open up and talk about what truly matters in the decision.

Remember that customers buy for their own reasons, not for yours. If you ask questions and listen well, you can gain valuable insight. That's how you make progress. The bonus here is that the person who asks the questions is in control.

SUCCESS STORIES

Every company has its Success Stories. The best salespeople use those stories to enthrall prospects with the benefits of products or services. Success Stories help potential customers visualize themselves using the product or service to make life better for them.

Think of it as painting the picture. That is why so many salespeople fall into the Expressive personality style—good at using words and describing, good at connecting with people and talking. Sharing stories is where those of you who are Expressives can truly shine. But you have to be smart about how you do it—for a Success Story to be effective, you have to connect with the prospect's needs.

SALES TEAM SCRIMMAGE
WHAT'S YOUR STORY?

During your next sales meeting, ask fellow team members to share their Success Stories and compile them all into your Sales Playbook. Once you have a good collection going, share a few during the next sales team meeting and ask how each team member would frame a story around a common situation or problem that prospects face. It should not be hard to come up with several common problems that your prospects must deal with daily. Once you've done that, take turns telling those stories either to the group or in small teams.

Success Stories will lead prospects to expect the same thing, and they will want to give your product or service a shot. Practice your storytelling so that you can make it as powerful as possible. 🏈

Two Amazing Success Stories
Hyper Sales Growth Success Story #1: How a two-hotel group added $200,000 per-year profit

This story involves a company with two one-hundred-room hotels. Small, independent operators like that company use a national buying group to pool their purchasing power and get supplies at lower prices. But Jim, who manages the hotel properties, didn't have sufficient budget to sign a contract with the buying group we were coaching. Getting Jim's hotels to sufficient profitability to afford the contract became an important Success Story for us to sell to other buyers in similar situations.

For about two years, Jim's nearby competitors were outperforming his occupancy and room rates significantly. "My parking lot is always emptier than the guys across the street. They're consistently fuller, and we're stagnant. We're not growing," he complained. Jim figured he was missing out on more than $150,000 in profit every year. Jim's hotels were clean and provided a good value but were still not competitive. He was serving what he thought was a good complimentary breakfast that was built into the room rate, but it was just adequate. He wasn't getting complaints in his customer feedback, but the revenue shortfall led him to realize he needed to compete better with the national brands located within a mile— Hampton Inn and Holiday Inn Express—that offered complimentary, full, hot breakfasts. Jim struggled with how to afford to upgrade his breakfast offerings.

Our buying-group client recommended that Jim needed something to WOW his customers, especially core customers—business guests and those with longer stays. To be competitive, he needed to offer two hot breakfast items, some rotating items, and fresh fruit. It had to be high quality, simple to provide, plentiful, and easy for the guest to consume. Jim knew he had to try something like this but could not see how he could pay for it. The buying group showed Jim its product guide with items identified. Jim saw the rebates being offered and how it was possible to make the math work: The new food would cost just under $3 per room, triple the less than $1 per room he had been paying. But after the upgrade, he was able to increase his average room rate by $10 per night.

- Jim's profit increased by $200,000 per year.

  - **Room rate** increased by $10 per night gross, and net revenue increased $8 per night, resulting in a **net gain of $8 per night.**

  - **Occupancy increased 5 percent.** He is averaging 70 rooms per night. (70 rooms per night = 25,000 room nights per year X $8 = $200,000 gain.)

The national buying group was able to show Jim how he could afford to compete with the national brands and actually increase his profitability using their service. Now when Jim sees his parking lot fuller than before and competing much better with his competitors, he's happy to have learned how to compete more successfully and profitably.

Hyper Sales Growth Success Story #2: How a yacht crane manufacturer reorganized its sales organization to become a very strong global competitor

At our company, Leverage Sales Coaching, we worked with a yacht crane manufacturer that was much newer and had significantly smaller resources than its top five, well-established, competitors in North America. This manufacturer had designed a high-quality product line with numerous advantages but struggled to increase sales, especially among the largest shipyards globally, which didn't take this young company seriously.

The solution we offered was stronger sales leadership and a more effective, more efficient Sales Process. Hiring two top-gun salespeople played a big role in doubling sales growth each year for three years. But what transformed the company into a formidable competitor in its industry was that it focused its sales efforts on four key target channels and developed a distinct sales message that increased preference for the brand.

Differentiating itself and streamlining its Sales Process helped the company expand into new markets around the world. It squeezed one direct competitor out of business, a second competitor stopped making yacht cranes, and its largest US competitor, a fifty-year-old company, was greatly weakened. Eventually, the newer company tripled the size of its factory to keep up with sales demand, and—because of its powerful brand position, value, and preference in the marketplace—it was purchased by a large marine industry conglomerate.

OBJECTION RESPONSES

The last—but just as important—element of sales-call preparation is getting ready to respond to objections that the prospect brings up.

You can look at an objection as a stumbling block preventing the sale from going forward. When making their Sales Playbook, the best salespeople look at Objection Responses as a call for more information: those who raise an objection just don't know enough yet. They don't see enough value, but that's almost always because they have not been educated sufficiently on what you're offering.

What are some of the biggest objections you've heard from prospects? How have you handled them? Did you stumble through a response or did you have a practiced, confident, game-ready reply?

When it comes to objections, the more confident and clear you are with your response, the more likely it is you'll get your prospects past their concerns and well on their way to becoming customers and clients. But perfecting your Objection Response is not something you want to practice in the field. Instead, look to your team to help you prepare and improve.

An added advantage of knowing key Objection Responses is the increase in our personal confidence, comfortability from being prepared and ready, and greater conviction that sells!

 **SALES TEAM SCRIMMAGE**
CHALLENGE THE RULING ON THE FIELD

You may have an idea of how you deal with objections in the field, but how do your other team members handle them? Someone may have a much better response to one objection, while another salesperson has a great reply to another.

During a sales meeting, have each team member write down the five toughest objections they've ever heard, and then share with the team. Chances are, a lot of them will overlap. Write down the top five or ten, and then ask how everyone has responded to each objection and how their prospects responded.

Eight Types of Common Objections:

1. Price
2. Competition
3. Company issues/Bad experience
4. Time
5. Satisfied
6. Financial constraints
7. Stall/Indifference/Brush-off
8. Wrong person/Not decision maker

Which responses were the most effective?

Collect the best responses and then separate into teams to practice them. This can be done during the meeting or between team members when they're not in the field. Either way, the objective is to learn the best responses and practice them until they're game ready.

See the example Objection Response Guide for some examples here and in Part III.

Objections Guide:
Best Responses to your Top Objections

An Objection Response Guide works best <u>WHEN it's collaborated and involves the entire sales team</u>. It is dynamic! Commit to constantly improve it by listening to the responses of the top performers.

Objection Responses Foundation

There's hardly anything that goes on in a sales call that couldn't be anticipated before one's arrival. So it's wise to prepare and practice for the objections and tough questions that you know you will need to deal with!

The primary reason your customer does not buy is his or her FEAR of making a bad decision.

Why do we get Objections?

- People **don't like change**
- People **don't trust you or your solution**
- Previous **bad experience/bad reputation**
- **Shortfall in developing HVNs (High Value Needs)**

Managing Objections Guidelines

1. Managing Objections is selling and good communication: "Seek first to understand, then to be understood."
2. Selling is easy if there is a true need.
3. Qualify any objection so the focus is on the primary reason preventing the prospect from moving ahead.

4. "No" does not mean "No, I don't like you", but "No, I'm not comfortable with going ahead with a decision yet."
5. Think of objections as the details that need to be worked out.
6. Once you have effectively answered an objection, continue your presentation and...ask for the business!

Special Note:
One size does not fit all! Generalized objection responses rarely are specific enough to be effective. Every company needs to customize their Objection Guide to their specific business and industry to optimize the winning!

Actions to take:
Identify the top 3 to 5 most common, and difficult objections and start there. Go around the room and get everyone's best objection responses to each, one at a time. Capture those responses, improve them. Then circulate those best responses and practice them in-house regularly!

How many Objections?

Many people think there are dozens or hundreds of objections. The reality is there are very few. Brainstorm your top 5 or 10. Define the best responses and practice them!

Types of Objections out there:

- *PRICE:*
    - *Your price is too high.* / I need a better price.

- **COMPETITION:**
    - *We are using a competitor. / We only use (certified; approved; etc..) vendors. / You do not have enough experience.*

- **COMPANY ISSUES**
    - BAD EXPERIENCE with this solution or your company. / The last time we used your company, the service was terrible. / Your way of doing business is too cumbersome.

- **TIME**
    - *I'm too busy right now. / I don't have time. / It's not the right time.*

- *SATISFIED:*
    - *I don't need your service. / I'm happy with my current relationship/provider. / We are using a competitor. / We do that inside our company.*

- **FINANCIAL CONSTRAINTS**
    - *We have no budget*

- **STALL/ INDIFFERENCE/BRUSH-OFF**

    o *Let me think about it. / Decision making put off 'til later. / Send me some information.*

- **WRONG PERSON/NOT DECISION-MAKER:**

    o *I don't know the answer. / I don't make this decision.*

EXAMPLES: 3 Objections and Responses

STALL

Buyer: *I like what we discussed, but let me think about it. / Put off decision making until later.*

- **Note: A classic stall. Any response that stops the sale from moving forward is <u>a decision not to make a decision</u>.** The best sales people won't leave until they know WHY the prospect can't make a decision (or is unable to).

<u>Qualify their level of Interest</u>:

- *(Seller Q1:) On a scale of 1 to 10 where 10 is high... where's your level of interest?*

    o Their answer: 5 or 6 = Not interested; 7 or 8 =   Maybe; 9 = Very interested

- *(Seller Q2:) What would it take to get you to a "10"?*

    o Their answer: 9 =   You're real close. They may need you to address a concern or make a minor concession. (You've QUALIFIED the GENUINE PROSPECTS)

    o Their answer: 7 or 8 = You have the real opportunity to close a lot more genuine prospects.

        ▪ They like what you've discussed... but they believe there's still   __(ISSUE)__   and they don't want to   __(ACT TOO SOON / STILL UNCOMFORTABLE / UNANSWERED QUESTIONS)__ .

    o The key is, now you know what's in the way and you can better deal with it. (You've learned what SPECIFIC CONCERN is holding back a genuine prospect)

    o Their answer: 5 or 6 = You're miles apart (unless they're being cagey). If they can't tell you what it'll take—mark them for a "call back" or put them in your touch system and move on. (You've DIS-QUALIFIED the NON-BUYERS)

PRICE

Buyer: *Your price is too high/higher than I'm paying. I need a better price. It's more than I can afford.*

Clarify the Objection–

- **Our price is too high? Why do you say that?**

- Get clear on what they're comparing you to, then deal with it.

Framing the True Cost

- We agree. **I wouldn't expect you to buy from me if we are a truly higher cost for your company.**

- But savvy buyers know that it's important to **consider ALL the cost factors**—not just the initial cost/pound.

- They look at all the factors that go into the mix on costs and a good working supplier relationship.

    - **Cost of irregular Quality**

    - **Cost of inconsistent product**

    - **Cost of lack of Control of supply chain**

- That's exactly why savvy buyers know that it's important to consider ALL the cost factors—not just the initial cost/pound. They look at all the factors that go into the mix on costs and a good working supplier relationship.

Your True Costs – **Do you know how much you're really paying?**

- Ask deeper questions to find out what they know OR point out "hidden" costs.

- Difference between TOP LINE PRICE and BOTTOM LINE PRICE.

- **How price, sales & bottom line profit tie together (Hidden cost)** – It's not the price you pay that matters most... isn't it the price & profit margin that becomes your bottom line gain that matters most? Would you agree?

- **Sales Cost of Lower Quality, weaker service and other factors** – How much in sales and profit could you be losing due to...

    - Consistent quality product? Service? Response time? Knowledge and advice?

        - (Cost of irregular Quality, Cost of inconsistent product, Cost of lack of Control of supply chain)

    - Give success stories/case studies that illustrates the point. Examples of how much sales and profit can be lost buying lower quality product that is lower price on the supply side.

SATISFIED

Buyer: *I don't need your service. I'm happy with my current relationship/provider. We are using a competitor. We do that inside our company.*

You're dealing with a "satisfied" objection—one of the most challenging to overcome.

If you're getting this early in the conversation, often they're just hoping you'll go away. They don't see enough reason to continue or don't want to go to the effort.

If it's after you've had some good Q&A dialog, it still could be a brush-off or be more legitimate after they've considered your value proposition.

Either way you need to get them talking and get more info. You can easily challenge their "all-OK" assertion with questions like...

- **"So you're happy with your_____...**

    - **Current pricing** that is at or below   %?;

    - **Level of customer service, attention and care** to make sure you're fully maximizing all the support you need for your operation to run smoothly, and avoid slowdowns?

    - **Level of innovation** to locate new ideas that match-up well to your needs as they change? (You're looking for an opening of "I'm really not that satisfied")

- The better you probe to uncover their needs, opportunities or problems that they're experiencing... the better you expose new needs and opportunities for your solutions.

At Leverage Sales Coach, we coach sales managers to train their teams to sell more effectively using powerful sales tools like a customized Objections Response Guide. This guide is most powerful when it is *developed with and through your team in a process to develop their buy-in*.

Sellers and sales managers produce more when they train and practice using clear, focused selling tools. Practice using them in-house or you're practicing on your customers!

Dan Larson, Leverage Sales Coach

Customize Your Play: One size does not fit all! Generalized Objection Responses are rarely specific enough to be effective. Every company needs to customize their Objection Response Guide to their specific business and industry to optimize the winning!

PLAYBOOK RESOURCES:

SEE PRACTICE, Objections Guide

inSITE-app & http://leveragesalescoach.com/resources

When you respond to an objection from a prospect, it should not be the first time those words are coming out of your mouth. If you put in the necessary practice but find that you are still struggling to close a sale, you need to work on it some more. You need to find a better way to overcome the objections. In sales, you learn very quickly whether what you are doing is working or not.

As we discussed in the section on Best Questions and Active Listening, half of your time with prospects should be spent on identifying needs, problems, and opportunities. Does the prospect see a true need for your product or solution? If not, do not be surprised if you hear a lot of objections. The fundamental objection that you must overcome is, in essence, "I am just not sure I need this." Take the time to craft the most reassuring response, and once you have that out of the way, work on the other objections that could arise. Think about the ones that are toughest to overcome and that you hear most frequently. Focus on nailing down those Objection Responses, and you're well on your way to overcoming one of the most difficult hurdles in the Sales Process.

A WORD FROM DAN . . .
WHAT IS STANDING IN THE WAY?

Sometimes it just takes a simple question to get to the bottom of what potentially could hold up a deal. Even when the sale seems to be going well–a good fit between what you have to offer and what the customer needs–it pays to ask: "Is there anything else standing in the way that would prevent us from moving forward?"

Let's say that you are dealing with a business owned by two partners, but they are not in alignment and they do not want to admit that or talk about it. Moreover, they are equal partners, and so the decision is stymied. This is a common situation, and it can be daunting to try to figure it out if it is not on the table. Still, you may get the sense that something is not quite right, that there is something unsaid, and so you ask about it.

This is what you might hear: "Here's the deal. My partner and I do not see this the same way. I want to make this happen. I am gung ho about it, and I think it is our top priority. But my partner just flat out does not want to spend the money right now."

Any number of reasons can explain the difference of opinion. Perhaps the reluctant partner is older and ready to retire and does not feel energetic about the opportunity. He does not want to invest the time, money, and effort that his younger partner is more than eager to expend. The two partners are at a different place in life, with different interests, and so the partnership is getting in the way. But if no one asks the question, that information does not get out on the table.

You can bump along and struggle and fail to get a decision from anyone—all because of a hidden objection that you did not even know about. You could spend hours trying to sell a widget to a couple of partners like that, when actually you never had a chance because one of them was not going to budge and neither had the voting power to decisively say, "This is what we will do."

An even worse situation is when the majority stockholder is the one who does not want to do the deal. The minority holder, who has 49 percent or less, is the go-getter who really wants to make it happen. He sees the deal as a worthy investment, and frankly, in another several years he likely will be taking over. But the majority owner has other plans and aspirations.

Those scenarios are classic cases of how things can go wrong when you do not have all the decision makers in the room. If you are not paying attention and do not recognize what is happening and get it all out on the table with questions, you are likely to be left in the dark, wondering what happened. Just ask: "It seems as if something is holding you back. Do we need to talk about something?"

So many other situations can come up. It may be that the partner you have been talking with is only a 35 percent owner. That's something you are going to want to know. Perhaps a spouse wants to quash the deal. Perhaps somebody in the leadership has a health issue that is weighing heavily on whether the decision should move forward. Or perhaps people have family issues that distract them, justifiably or not, from focusing on the deal you want to strike with them.

Until you identify what could be standing in the way, you risk getting nowhere. Once it is out in the open, you can all get a perspective on it. Yes, it might mean that the deal is not going to happen. But it might also turn out that the problem is not as severe as the owner perceived it to be.

DAN LARSON

EQUIPPED FOR THE JOB

You now know *how* to practice before you go out on the field, whether through Role Practice in sales meetings, by Modeling the Masters, or by sharing with colleagues what works best. In this chapter we also covered the importance of identifying and using your prospects' Personality Styles, the value of being prepared with the Best Questions and Active Listening, Objection Responses, Sales-Ready Messaging, and Success Stories.

ON PREPARATION:

The partner to anticipation is preparation. The question that inevitably comes up in my line of work is this: Is it possible to over prepare? My answer to the question is no. You can always prepare more. All told, we probably devote a hundred hours a week to preparing for a Saturday game. And it is not enough.

NICK SABAN

You have your best people, you've determined the best processes, you've practiced before the game to the point where you can answer just about any objection or paint a picture with a Success Story in your sleep. Now there's only one thing you need before you hit the field: your gear.

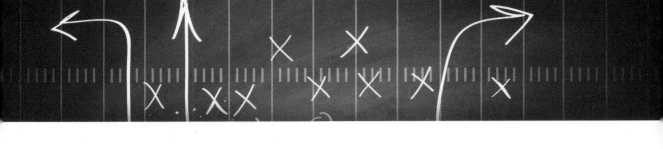

CHAPTER 4

GEAR: WHAT YOU NEED TO LEVERAGE WINNING PLAYS

 **CHAPTER GAME PLAN**

Think of this chapter as the duffel bag or locker where you'll find your game gear. Dig in and pull out whatever you need to succeed in the field. Worksheets for People, Processes, and Practices discussed in the previous chapters can all be found here.

A football team needs more than its Playbook. It needs helmets, cleats, pads—all the gear necessary for achieving victory. Likewise, a winning sales team needs the tools of its trade. Many of the tools that we have mentioned in previous chapters are here, as well as new ones.

Whether you are a player or a coach on the sales team, do you feel your team is equipped for success? We believe wholeheartedly that you cannot possibly perform to your potential unless you have all the necessary tools at your disposal. A sports team cannot practice without its gear—and neither can a sales team.

A WORD FROM DAN . . .
PUTTING ON THE GAME GEAR

Our coaching firm was hired to help a company selling training to employees of large manufacturers. We were hired to bring in the right processes to a start-up that didn't already have systems in place.

First, we identified the firm's core Value Proposition and how it was different from the competition. Other companies were offering employee training that was considered the best available, and along came these folks with a much better and unique Value Proposition, which we turned into a powerful Sales-Ready Message.

Once we identified that message, we were able to build the presentation that salespeople could use with prospects. We came up with questions and answers. What would be the best way to open up a dialogue with customers, to qualify them, and to reassure them that we would serve them well? We built out the best responses to the top five objections that the team anticipated or had experienced.

That start-up was selling to some of the biggest manufacturers on the planet—Fortune 100 and Fortune 500 companies—and its close rate in the early going was 100 percent. The team did not miss, and it was selling to people with whom it is not easy to close a deal. Eventually the salespeople did lose a few, but the close rate continues to be high. Why? Because from the start they were properly equipped, including having one clear, convincing, and unique Sales-Ready Message.

The following is a summary of the client's early Value Proposition that became the core of their very effective sales presentation. It accurately engaged prospects with their three main problems then actively illustrated how the company's solutions effectively solved these problems better than anyone else.

MANUFACTURER PERFORMANCE AND PROFITABILITY:
THREE BIG PROBLEMS THAT REDUCE EMPLOYEE PRODUCTIVITY AND INCREASE COSTS—
AND HOW TO SOLVE THEM

1. **Limited domain knowledge**
   - Conventional employee training / no training
     - The only thing costlier than conventional training is *no* training for employees.

□ Employee training is largely insufficient, ineffective, and painfully expensive in time and money.

2. **Value decisions**

- Employees make poor choices in value decisions due to lack of knowledge, lack of experience, or missing previous history.

- Production costs increase while efficiency and productivity decrease.

3. **Institutional knowledge**

- The company's collective experience is scattered and mostly unorganized.

- Company know-how (experiences and knowledge) is ultimately lost when employees leave or retire.

THORS: The Helpful Online-Resource Site

- The ultimate online, on-demand learning environment

    □ Accelerate learning.

    □ Apply it.

    □ Increase productivity.

Solving the Three Big Problems through Better Learning and Collective Intelligence

1. **Accelerate learning** utilizing domain-specific knowledge that is applicable to each organization.
   - **Climb the learning curve.** Drastically shorten the time required for an employee to build an on-the-job knowledge base.

2. **Make better value decisions** by applying the learning to baseline the knowledge across departments and functions.
   - **Efficient communication and improved decision** making result from the increase and uniformity of technical know-how.

3. **Institutionalize knowledge**: capture, preserve, and access your collective experiences and knowledge.
   - **Harness your in-house expertise**. Build a foundation of "tribal" knowledge to ensure that the next generation of talent has the tools and information required to succeed.

THORS: eLearning Solutions

- **Interesting to learn**

  - Holds their interest, keeps them motivated to continue

- **Contextual**

  - In a context that relates to their job

- **Layered & interactive**

  - Relates to the big picture–see the trees *and* the forest

- **Easy to understand**

  - Complex information explained simply and succinctly

- **Easy to remember**

  - Higher recall using multisensory learning

- **Easy-to-apply learning**

  - Learning-management solutions that measure progress, report results, and are designed for total scalability

- **Boundaryless and multidisciplinary**

  - Experience-based or "tribal" knowledge covering a wide variety of manufacturing-related subjects

What Has the THORS Value Proposition Produced in the Last Five Years?

- The Value Proposition still holds true. It remains the core of our initial discussion with potential customers.

- We have continued growth of our content. The quality of the content has delivered on the Value Proposition, which has helped maintain an extremely high renewal rate from existing customers.

- THORS has experienced a CAGR (compound annual growth rate) of 135 percent in revenue growth over the past five years. This compares with corporate eLearning market growth estimates of around 20 percent.

With the right gear, your people can accomplish more than you might imagine.

DAN LARSON

GOAL ACHIEVEMENT PLAN (GAP)

Goal Achievement Plan

1. **Focused Goals**	Backward Thinking
2. **Written Action Plan**	Key Activities
3. **System of Measurement**	Tracking Performance
4. **System of Accountability**	Progress Reports

When you have a goal, the best way to make it happen is with a clear plan. What do you want, why do you want it, when do you want it, and how will you get there? By writing these down in your Sales Playbook, you're mapping out your path to success, as explained in the Goal Achievement Plan discussion in Chapter 2.

Your GAP game gear pushes you to answer the questions that help you establish and reach your goal by developing systems of measurement and accountability and encourages you to report your progress to someone who will keep you on track.

 **Goal Achievement Plan Summary**

Goal Achievement Plan Overview

The Goal Achievement Plan (GAP) is an underlying foundation to the very purpose of a successful sales organization. If you are serious about achieving your goals, then you should want to create a serious plan to make it happen. We know that "Winners keep score!"

The crux of a Goal Achievement Plan is to consistently perform the high payoff activities on the high payoff target accounts to drive bigger results. Below are the key elements needed to create a GAP that works.

Goal Achievement Plan	
1. **Focused Goals**	Backward Thinking
2. **Written Action Plan**	Key Activities
3. **System of Measurement**	Tracking Performance
4. **System of Accountability**	Progress Reports

Goal Achievement Plan

- **1) Goals in Writing   Backward Thinking**
    - Break down your goals "back to front" (Annually → Quarterly → Monthly → Weekly → Daily)
    - Using your specific Key Measurements. Some examples below
        - \# Existing_____Sold (accounts, units, etc)
        - \# New_____Sold (accounts, units, etc)
        - Revenue \$ per_____(period)
        - Average \$ per_____(sale \$, margin, etc for your key measurements)
- **2) Written Plan   Key Activities**
    - What Key ACTIVITIES *really matter* to drive results?
        - \# Prospecting calls to target accounts → \# Qualified leads
        - \# Appointments set → \# Presentations to key decision makers
        - \# Deals won → \# Relationships advancing
        - \# Referral partners developing
        - Marketing visibility: \# Networking events; \# Trade Shows, etc.
        - Other? _____
- **3) System of Measurement   Tracking Performance**
    - How you are pacing toward your goal?
    - Use your CRM, pipeline reporting, pacing report or other system to track your progress & pacing toward your goal
- **4) System of Accountability   Progress Reports**
    - What adjustments do you need to make?
    - Look for ways to adjust activities, targets or effectiveness to be sure to stay on track

 **Goal Achievement Plan Summary**

Goal Achievement Plan driven by Backward Thinking

Below are several keys to implement an effective Goal Achievement Plan using Jack Daly's "backward thinking." The end result is to develop an effective action plan to know what you need to achieve your goals.

Principles/Concept:

- **The "funnel" concept** of "begin with your end $$ needed" (e.g. $1,000,000 revenue)

- **Sales Process Steps & Key Activities**: Then backward think/reverse engineer the activity plan. Break down the amount of Key Measurements and Key Activities required at each step.

- **Three related factors affect the amount of activity you need to achieve goal:**

  - **1) High Payoff Targets** = The right best-fit targets must be the focus

  - **2) Key Activities** = Amount of Activity required to be sure to hit your goal?

  - **3) Conversion Rate** at each step is determined by how effective you are at each step?

  - Achieving your goal requires having enough leads & best-fit target opportunities in the front end of the funnel that are sufficient to reach your goal.

  - Your Conversion Rate at each step helps determine if you have sufficient target opportunities in the front end or if you need to get more.

Top 10 Best-Fit Account Rating Steps

The steps below will help you identify your **Best-Fit Target Accounts** for your highest payoff activities.

 **Goal Achievement Plan Summary**

Identify your Top 10 high payoff accounts for Existing and New Accounts:

1. Begin with your broad list of all Existing accounts and New target accounts.
2. Use the ratings steps below to identify your Top Account targets. It's recommended doing this in an Excel spreadsheet so that it can be easily sortable.
3. Identify the Best-Fit Targets using the criteria below or choose your own. Determine the most productive Top 10 Accounts to pursue and grow.

Best-Fit Account Ratings Tool used to focus your high pay-off activities on the best key account targets

Purpose: Be more objective about identifying the best target accounts to grow your business. Create a system and process that helps you target better to work smarter.

Rate your list of Prospects and Customers according to the following:

VOLUME OF BUSINESS account is doing <u>in the marketplace</u> (not with you)

- **A**   X-Large $____/ yr or more   (<u>**set your own rating thresholds**</u>)
- **B**   Large $____/ yr
- **C**   Med $____/ yr
- **D**   Small $____/ yr

YOUR **SHARE** OF CUSTOMER

- **1**   Does most/all buying thru your company
- **2**   Does some buying thru your company
- **3**   Does no/little buying thru your company
- **4**   Good potential as a Referral source

Best-Fit Account Rating for Top 10 Targets:

- **A2 & A3:**   Focus greatest mktg/sales effort
- **B2 & B3:**   Focus strong mktg/sales effort
- **C2 & C3:**   Focus medium mktg/sales effort
- **A1, B1 & C1:**   Maintain good relations & ensure good contacts and service

Top 10 Accounts Activities Goal:

1. Use Best-Fit Account Rating to identify the best targets for focused sales & touch program effort.
2. Sellers schedule follow-up communication plan based on progress and Best-Fit Account Rating.

Top 10 List Forms

 Goal Achievement Plan Summary

PROSPECTS Best-Fit Target List:

Focus precedes success. What accounts deserve your biggest focus in order to greatly increase your income?

PROSPECTS: Top 10 Best-Fit Target List					
List your best prospect targets according to your ratings & sales potential. What will each account be worth when successful?					
Target #	Company	Best-Fit Acct Rating	Account's Total Purchase Vol./Yr.	Your Current Purchase Vol./Yr.	Your Target Purchase Vol./Yr-1
1			$	$	$
2			$	$	$
3			$	$	$
4			$	$	$
5			$	$	$
6			$	$	$
7			$	$	$
8			$	$	$
9			$	$	$
10			$	$	$

 Goal Achievement Plan Summary

CUSTOMERS Best-Fit Target List:

Focus precedes success. What accounts deserve your biggest focus in order to greatly increase your income?

CUSTOMERS: Top 10 Best-Fit Target List					
List your best customer targets according to your ratings & sales potential. What will each account be worth when successful?					
Target #	Company	Best-Fit Acct Rating	Account's Total Purchase Vol./Yr.	Your Current Purchase Vol./Yr.	Your Target Purchase Vol./Yr-1
1			$	$	$
2			$	$	$
3			$	$	$
4			$	$	$
5			$	$	$
6			$	$	$
7			$	$	$
8			$	$	$
9			$	$	$
10			$	$	$

 **Goal Achievement Plan Summary**

CLIENTS Best-Fit Target List:

Focus precedes success. What accounts deserve your biggest focus in order to greatly increase your income?

	CLIENTS: Top 10 Best-Fit Target List				
	List your best client targets according to your ratings & sales potential. What will each account be worth when successful?				
Target #	Company	Best-Fit Acct Rating	Account's Total Purchase Vol./Yr.	Your Current Purchase Vol./Yr.	Your Target Purchase Vol./Yr-1
1			$	$	$
2			$	$	$
3			$	$	$
4			$	$	$
5			$	$	$
6			$	$	$
7			$	$	$
8			$	$	$
9			$	$	$
10			$	$	$

PLAYBOOK RESOURCES:

SEE PROCESS, Goal Achievement Plan

inSITE-app & http://leveragesalescoach.com/resources

SALES PROCESS SCORECARD

From start to finish, the Sales Process Scorecard spells out the steps of the Sales Process. What are the Key Activities that really matter and that drive each step? How do we identify the Best Practices so that we can sell well for a better close-and-conversion rate?

Sales Managers and salespeople can both use this scorecard to evaluate progress using the same one-to-three measuring system. If progress scores for different tasks vary between the manager and salesperson, the disparity can help bring light to issues that otherwise might not have been addressed. Together, Sales Progress Scorecards from Managers and team members can pinpoint weaknesses in the game plan and identify plays that need more practice.

Sales Process-Scorecard Example

Below are examples of HPAs (High Payoff Activities) that really matter to drive results in each step of a sales process. Note the following attributes of the HPA descriptions:

- **Succinct, Clear, Useable:** "Bite-size" description that's still clear enough to know exactly what to do
- **Specific:** Specific actions to be taken and key questions or reminders of best sales practices
- **Quantifiable:** Wherever possible, add an amount of activity to establish Min Stds for sellers

SALES STEPS & HPAs	Tools & Training
Step 1: Prospecting << KPI: # CONTACTS >>	
Target Prospect List Prep & Planning: Prep weekly Top 10 List for prospects, customers, clients from Target List based on Pre-Qualifying Checklist	• Master Target List • Top 10 List • Pre-Qualifying Checklist
Networking/Trade Shows: Goal = 8 or more pre-qualified leads; Give cards to sales asst.; Complete a trade show recap; 24-hr follow-up touch on leads	• Networking Best Practices
Social networking: Post blog update & insights post at least 1x per week	• Social media marketing
Calling-Warm/Cold: Min 5 hours blocked/week for directors and above, inside sales calling your top 20 list	• Calling Best Practices • Top 10 List TODAY • Pre-Qualifying Checklist • 10 Tips Better Voicemails
Leads Tracking & Follow-Up: 24 hr or less follow-up, track in CRM	• CRM
Step 2: Qualifying Phone Call/Meeting << KPI: # QUALIFIED >>	
Advance prep work on target: Identify Decision-makers & key influencers	
Qualifying Checklist: Questions List to determine deeper Qualifying criteria; Current buying program; Questions list; Consultative selling training	• Qualifying Checklist • Questions list • Consultative selling training
Step 3: Appmt Setting << KPI: # APPMTS that STICK >>	
Appointment setting: "Calendar handy?"; Suggest specific time/date; Ensure right people will be there; Outline agenda for meeting-1; Meet/exceed Appmt activity Success Goals each month	• Appmt Setting Best Practices • Success Goals
Opportunity Brief: Create and review Opportunity Brief with Mgr	• Opportunity Brief
Meeting Reminder/Confirm: Send reminder & confirm 24 hrs in advance	
Step 4: Needs Analysis: Mutual-Fit	
Role Practice Tough Questions: Anticipate prospect's tough questions. Who will answer (if team selling)?	• Role practice training
Needs Analysis meeting: Get prospect talking; Understand their needs & priorities; Probing questions to learn business objectives & core issues; Identify HVNs; Reason to proceed/Solution awareness/End results/Value we deliver	• Qualifying Checklist • Questions list • Consultative selling training

Step 5: Presentation << KPI: # PRESENTATIONS >>	
Presentation Prep meeting: Focus on HVNs (High value needs) = Know their 'end zone' (what matters most to client)	
Create Presentation: Focus on THEIR needs and smart solutions, discuss measurable value, relevant success examples	• Presentation templates
Role Practice: Practice Q&A and buyer's tough questions	• Role practice cheat sheet
Solution Presentation: Customer-focused presentation, interactive questions, Focus on THEIR reasons/HVNs	• Presentation notes cheat sheet
Follow-up: Recap next steps who-what-when for all, Send calendar to all	• Calendar invitation
Step 6: Closing / Won or Lost << KPI: # WINS >>	
Negotiate with Buyer/Mgr: Negotiate terms, discuss & confirm	
Closing: Recap solution plan that meets their needs, terms, and timeline	
Agreement Signature: Get signature or follow up to secure signature	
Submit signed order & process it: Alert Mgr, fulfillment or operational team	
Win/Loss ratio: 50% or higher?	
Success Review: What worked? What didn't? What can we learn? What needs to be improved?	• Success Review tool
Step 7: Follow-Up / Follow-Through	
Follow-up/Follow Through: Recap actions; Who is doing what by when? Calendar follow-up actions and follow-through	
KEY ACTIVITIES	
Total Score	

PLAYBOOK RESOURCES:

SEE PROCESS, Sales Process Scorecard

inSITE-app & http://leveragesalescoach.com/resources

PRE-CALL PLANNING TEMPLATE

With the Pre-Call Planning Template, you can effectively plan your sales calls in a way that allows you to always know where you need to focus next and to feel equipped for the task. Planning a month out will show you what's coming up in the five or six key areas that drive business, while helping you define your upcoming two-week Focus.

Pre-Call Planning Worksheet

3 Questions MUST BE asked before every call!

1. **What do we _KNOW_?**
   - INFO RESOURCES: What info do we already know or have access to better sell/grow this account?
   - Internal sources
   - Internet research
   - Their website/collateral
   - Vendors
   - Their Competition
   - Their customers
   - Your personal network
   - Their employees
   - Their sales dept.

2. **What do we _NEED TO KNOW_?**
   - What info do we need to learn to progress this sale?
   - Decision-Makers & Influencers
   - Decision making process
   - Business & Personal Objectives that drive the deal
   - HVNs: Highest Value Needs prioritized
   - Timeframe / Deadline
   - Budgets
   - Political agendas

3. **What do we need to _GET THEM TALKING ABOUT_?**
   - What do we need to learn to progress this sale?
   - Socrates → Collaborative discussion
   - They have the Answers, the Reasons, the Motivations for THEIR Buying Process
   - Need to Ask-Questions-And-Listen to learn it

Ask yourself this Question before every call!

What is the purpose of _THIS_ call?

Never make a call WITHOUT a specific purpose!

PLAYBOOK RESOURCES:

SEE PRACTICE, Pre-Call Planning Worksheet

inSITE-app & http://leveragesalescoach.com/resources

SALES SUCCESS GUIDE

The Sales Success Guide combines the Sales Playbook's Three Game Gear Essentials. We discussed these three equipment essentials in Chapter 3: Practices. They are the Best Questions and Active Listening, Objection Responses, and a Success Story Guide.

Game Gear Essential #1: Best Questions and Active Listening

When developing a lead, what are the Best Questions for opening up a new prospect? What are the team's best qualifying questions? What are the Best Questions for setting appointments with key decision makers? During calls, how can you effectively use questions to draw people out, rather than just subject them to a spiel? As explained in Chapter 3, listening actively is your best play to advance your position in the field.

Best Questions & Active Listening:

- **Do you prepare and ask effective Questions?**

- **Do you ask deeper, probing questions to learn the underlying reasons?**

- **Do you listen actively as much or more than you talk?**

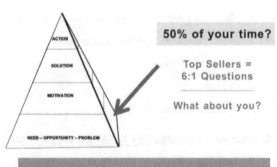

50% of your time?

Top Sellers = 6:1 Questions

What about you?

Victory Goes to Those Best Prepared

Do your Homework – Deeper / Taking control!

- Best questions to <u>uncover THEIR Needs</u>? Surface hidden issues?
- Best questions to <u>uncover THEIR Problems</u>? Unexpected problems?
- Best questions to <u>uncover THEIR Opportunities</u>? Possibilities?
- When it comes to decisions like this, how are they decided?
- Would you like to know our points of difference?
- Is there anything else prohibiting you from going ahead?
- What question should I be asking that I'm not asking?

Game Gear Essential #2: Objection Responses

How do you handle the tough questions and objections that you might get in return? Can you anticipate them? If you commonly hear them during sales calls, Chapter 3 explains how you can have practiced responses. Use this worksheet to collect your team's best responses to those tough questions, narrow them down to the few best ones, and practice with one another how you will deliver those best responses.

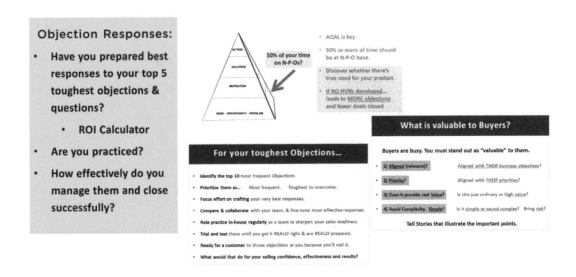

Objection Responses:

- **Have you prepared best responses to your top 5 toughest objections & questions?**
  - **ROI Calculator**
- **Are you practiced?**
- **How effectively do you manage them and close successfully?**

- AQAL is key
- 50% or more of time should be at N-P-O base.
- Discover whether there's true need for your product.
- If NO HVNs developed— leads to MORE objections and fewer deals closed

50% of your time on N-P-Os?

For your toughest Objections...

- **Identify the top 10** most frequent Objections.
- **Prioritize them as...** Most frequent. Toughest to overcome.
- **Focus effort on crafting** your very best responses.
- **Compare & collaborate** with your team, & fine-tune most effective responses.
- **Role practice in-house regularly** as a team to sharpen your sales readiness.
- **Trial and test** those until you got it REALLY right & are REALLY prepared.
- **Ready for a customer** to throw objections at you because you'll nail it.
- **What would that do for your selling confidence, effectiveness and results?**

What is valuable to Buyers?

Buyers are busy. You must stand out as "valuable" to them.

- 1) Aligned (relevant)? — Aligned with THEIR business objectives?
- 2) Priority? — Aligned with THEIR priorities?
- 3) Does it provide real Value? — Is this just ordinary or high value?
- 4) Avoid Complexity. Simple? — Is it simple or sound complex? Bring risk?

Tell Stories that illustrate the important points.

Game Gear Essential #3: Success Story Guide

On your own, you may have one or two Success Stories that can help nudge your client toward a sale. But what if you had several or even dozens to choose from? Chapter 3 shows how pooling all the Success Stories from your team gives you a wealth of real examples that illustrate to potential clients how you and your company have been able to solve problems like theirs. Pool your stories and practice your storytelling, and you'll be amazed at how powerful your presentation becomes.

- **Categorize Success Stories by common situations & problems**

- **Match relevant stories to prospects**

- **Sell results and outcomes**

- **'Paint the picture' – make memorable**

- **Collect them & share with team**

- **Practice them, be sales-ready**

Build your Success Stories Guide:

- **Keep a notebook**

- **Capture your stories**

- **Use them with buyers in similar situations**

Role Practice

This part of your game gear will go far in helping you and your team improve actions and responses during sales calls in the field. Look for actions to avoid in these team scenarios, as well as Best Practices that can help you greatly improve your game on the field.

Role Practice

Role Practice:

- **Deliberate practice on specifics**

- **1) Set-up Purpose & Situation**

- **2) Seller Presentation**

- **3) Observer Feedback**

  - 1) What was done well?

  - 2) What can improve?

  - 3) What can you use as a Best Practice?

  - 4) Discussion – What did we learn?

ROLE PRACTICE

Purpose: Practice, uncover & collaborate best sales practices.
Discuss:
1. What was done well?
2. What can improve?
3. What can you use as Best Practice?

"A" Seller

"C" Observer　　　　**"B" Prospect**

And remember, if you don't schedule it, it will not happen. Lastly, how often do sport coaches cancel practice? Model that!

Sales-Ready Messaging

Sales-Ready Messaging delivers your Value Proposition; it's how you as a company and you as an individual stand out from the competition. How are you selling yourself? Are you able to reassure the customer that you will be right on top of things, responding consistently and quickly? So much of what you are selling is your competence in servicing this account. Your combined unique Value Proposition and your attention and consistent support of the customer is the core message that you must get across succinctly and clearly in your sales presentations. Are you sales ready with your powerful message? If you have not already completed Playbook Practice #2 in Chapter 3, here again is the worksheet you will need for an effective Sales Playbook.

Sales-Ready Messaging

EXAMPLE: Why Leverage Sales Coaching?

The only coaching & sales development company that wrote
the book with Jack Daly on creating a Hyper Sales Growth Playbook

- **Deliverable Results:**
  - A manufacturing client grew their results by 108% in 32 months. Their sales process became 40% more time-efficient so they could close more business more effectively in much less time
  - We helped a distributor client sell-through 71% of their slow-moving inventory. They cut their fixed overhead cost by $3.5 million per year & realized a huge boost in profits
  - We helped another client change one sales closing process that increased their close rate from 20% to 85% in the first 30 days. It remained over 80% closing for years. They got paid 4x better for doing the same amount of work
- **Guarantee:** We guarantee you'll grow results with 2 commitments from you. 1) **Be Coachable** – open, teachable and willing to accept new ideas 2) You and your team **Take Action** on ideas consistently to get the work done, implement, and execute
- **Customized Playbook:** We help you develop a Hyper Sales Growth Sales Playbook that gets your team focused on their HPAs (High Payoff Activities) to drive reliably bigger results. Train, practice and improve while using the best in People, Processes and Practices. Customized to your industry, company and culture

- **Experience & Know-How:** We've been working closely with Jack Daly since 2003. Our experienced coaches know how to implement these hyper sales growth ideas to get your team producing more
- **Implement Quicker:** We help you Build, Coach and Manage proven sales growth systems and processes quicker and better. Choose top priorities for greatest impact. Speed up building using templates, coaching help and know-how. We help the Sales Manager and sales team Train & Practice to change behavior to grow & scale results
- **Delivery:** Sales development coaching is done onsite or online to increase effectiveness and efficiency
- **Action:** Get your Sales Managers and sales team focused on consistently taking action on their HPAs. We are always agenda-driven and focused on driving change and improvement
- **Terms & Options:** Easy to start. We offer customized solutions to create the right-fit coaching and training plan for your needs

We help you implement better and faster.

SALES MANAGER
MULTIPLIER
EFFECT

Touch System

Staying in touch with the contacts in your target list and pipeline should be done at least monthly. Decide the mix of types of touches, whether face-to-face, phone call, snail mail, e-mail, social media, or text, and how frequently you touch them.

Use your CRM system for this and keep it updated. Indicate the personality style of each contact. Look for a way to make this time efficient. Can you involve an assistant? Making the touches valuable, personal, and memorable can become a huge competitive advantage for you when you install it and use it as an ongoing system to set yourself apart. So a natural part of your Touch System can be using a Moneybag. Those ideas next!

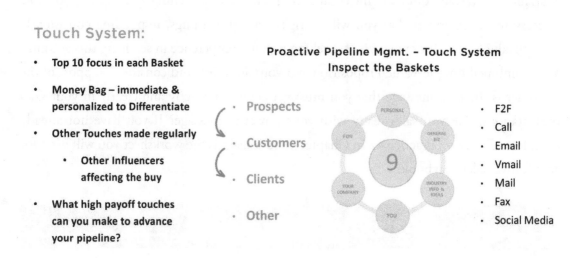

Touch System:

- Top 10 focus in each Basket
- Money Bag – immediate & personalized to Differentiate
- Other Touches made regularly
  - Other Influencers affecting the buy
- What high payoff touches can you make to advance your pipeline?

Proactive Pipeline Mgmt. – Touch System
Inspect the Baskets

- Prospects
- Customers
- Clients
- Other

- F2F
- Call
- Email
- Vmail
- Mail
- Fax
- Social Media

Moneybags

Similar to those zippered bags that merchants use to carry cash or checks to the bank for deposit, salespeople should have a bag of useful tactics that can make them memorable and put money in their pockets. These tactics can be most effective after the first contact with a prospect. What do you do next? What's your follow-up touch? It could be a simple e-mail or a handwritten note, but by doing something unique and memorable after an otherwise routine contact, you're vastly improving your impact and impression with your potential client.

Here are some suggestions for personal touches or gestures that will help you stand out as memorable with your contacts. What are they really passionate about? What do they talk about with vigor? Send them personal notes, articles, news stories, magazine clippings, videos, or other points of interest on their favorites, such as:

- Favorite sports team(s)

- Family's, spouse's, or kid's interests or activities

- What they like to do as a hobby or special causes they support

- Personal or professional events or achievements

- Topics they are passionate about

- Entertainment they enjoy: books, movies, food, wine, travel, past or future favorite vacation spots

- Dreams of the future: what they want and are working toward personally or professionally

- News or stories in their town or community

- Points of interest of any type that matters to them

PLAYBOOK RESOURCES:
SEE PRACTICE VIDEO, The Importance of a Money Bag
inSITE-app & http://leveragesalescoach.com/resources

Personality Styles

Knowing how you're wired as a salesperson—where your strengths and weaknesses are—and knowing how to respond to your client's personality style can certainly work to your advantage. As we noted in Chapter 3, evaluating and correctly adapting to Personality Styles takes study, preparation, and practice, but in practicing it at sales meetings and with coworkers, you can develop it into a powerful advantage.

Personality Styles:

- **Be more effective with more people**
- **Identify the buyer's style and adjust accordingly**
- **Two Questions:**

  1) Are they MORE or LESS assertive?

  2) How do they tend to make decisions using LOGIC or EMOTION?

  (Facts or Feelings?)

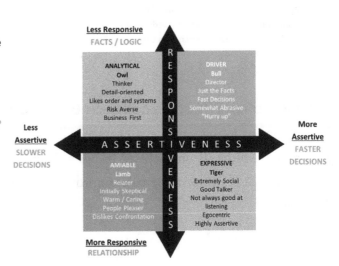

Modeling the Masters

Modeling the Masters is a critical piece of game gear. A team of any size will have some players who are stronger than others, and by leveraging their talent and experience in various mentorship and training activities, you strengthen all members of the team.

This can be done through something as formal as a panel discussion with the top three performers in a particular niche, allowing the entire team to conduct a Q&A, or it could be a simple, informal tag along between Top Producers and weaker players.

Remember that respect is the top thing that employees crave. How better to show respect than to let someone know that others need his or her expertise? Remember, if it doesn't get scheduled, it doesn't get done.

Model the Masters / Mentoring

- Know your *personal strengths* (what you can offer someone)

- Know *your weak spots* (help needed)

- Look for resources on your team to "trade strengths" or mentor with

- Observe intently who you can learn from

- Role practice what is learned. Collaborate often

- Practice deeply: 1) Stretch your self Make mistakes 2) Correct immediately 3) Fix it and repeat 4) Anchor in the correction

LINKS in the SALES CHAIN

Where does *YOUR* sales chain break?

Find the weak links & fix them.

Work smarter. Earn more.

1. Prospecting
2. Qualifying
3. Appointment Setting
4. Presenting
5. Objections Management
6. Closing
7. Follow-Up / Through

The Multiplier Effect: Excellence Builds on Itself

The equipment in this game gear chapter will dovetail. The more gear you use, the better your results will be. If one activity brings a 20 percent improvement to one task, that's great, but what if two or three tasks improve by 20 percent? **The results multiply across the board**.

Results from a truck-lighting manufacturing client's sales team showed that a 10 percent improvement in three steps of their Sales Process produced a 31 percent improvement in overall conversion rates, while the same percentage improvement in seven steps of their Sales Process produced a 78 percent improvement.

Excellence builds on itself. That Multiplier Effect is a lesson for sales as much as it's a lesson for life.

"Perpetual optimism is a force multiplier," Colin Powell said when he was secretary of state. "The ripple effects of a leader's enthusiasm and optimism is awesome, and so is the impact of cynicism and pessimism. Leaders who whine and blame engender those same behaviors among their colleagues.

"I am not talking about stoically accepting organizational stupidity and performance incompetence with a 'What? Me worry?' smile. I am talking about a gung-ho attitude that says, 'We can change things here. We can achieve awesome goals. We can be the best.' Spare me the grim litany of the realist. Give me the unrealistic aspirations of the optimist any day."[5]

---

5   Oren Harari, "Quotations from Chairman Powell," 1996, http://govleaders.org/powell.htm.

CHAPTER 5

TIME TO MAKE MONEY

 CHAPTER GAME PLAN

In order to successfully implement any plan, time management needs to be an absolute priority. When you waste time on activities that have little payoff instead of focusing on those all-important HPAs, you're throwing out earnings potential. This chapter focuses on the Four Ps: Planning, Preparation, Practice, and Profit. When you have the first three in place, then you have everything you need for the fourth: Profit.

Pay attention to what matters. Focus on what gets results. That's what time management is all about. It should be self-evident that salespeople should concentrate on the high-payoff stuff. What brings you the greatest gains? How will you set yourself up to make the most money?

When it comes to time management, remember two things:

1. **If you don't have an assistant, you are one.** The key here is focusing on High Payoff Activities (HPAs), which are different for each business. Anything else should be delegated to an assistant. We know of several Top Producers who are leveraging five or more personal assistants, enabling the focus of the top performer to stay front and center on HPAs.

2. **Know your hourly rate.** Every person who works and gets paid, even if it is 100 percent commission, has an hourly rate. Simply track the hours you work every day in your business, add them up for the month, and divide the money you make in a month by the hours worked. Let's say it comes to $50 an hour. Knowing this number will help you cut down on calls that have no promise so that you can focus on those that do. Knowing the hourly rate can rationalize paying an assistant who enables you to work on things that will best generate sales.

Time management enables the Four Ps:

Planning + Preparation + Practice = Profit

As a salesperson, if you are not planning and preparing and practicing before you get out onto the field, then you're essentially practicing on the customer. You risk fumbling the deal simply because you didn't refine your presentation, failed to really learn the Best Practices of Personality Styles, or muddled your way through a half-learned Success Story. Those who are better prepared, and who know how to do a better job of differentiating themselves and their company, will be the bigger winners.

Preparing for that profit gain starts with you. What is your focus? Is your emphasis only on what you must sell and what you must do to make your quota today, or are you looking two weeks, four weeks, a quarter, or even a year ahead? The most common reason that salespeople fail is that they focus their efforts on themselves and their own immediate needs instead of how they could build better results by planning for far greater gains in the future.

TIME FOR PLANNING

Before you start preparing to sell to any particular customer, take time to research your prospect target list. Are you putting a lot of time and effort into a prospect with not much liquidity, poor purchasing history, or little margin for new purchases? If so, then the value of your potential sale likely does not warrant the time you're putting into it. But for a more qualified purchaser, that extra research and effort may make all the difference.

A lot of companies segment the types of targets to whom they are selling. For example, they may use a simple alphabetical scale—A for "large corporation" and D for "microindustry" or "very transactional"—to quickly identify the size, scale, and scope of the potential deal so that the salesperson can readily calibrate how much time to devote.

It makes sense. Why would you invest hours of research on a small, transactional sale? By contrast, why would you do little preparation for a big deal, one that you and the company might find lucrative for many years? In other words, plan to match your effort with your expected return. Focus your preparation and planning on the biggest opportunities worth pursuing.

TIME FOR PREPARATION

Now that you have a plan in place, the next step is to assess your prospect's buying process and to determine what factors inside and outside of the business may affect your sale. As we noted in the section on "Prepare for the Prospect" in Chapter 3, you have to start by asking yourself what you know. For example, do you know—really *know*—the answers to the next three questions?

1. **Who is the real decision maker?**

Let's say everything is going well for you in a sale. You have targeted and qualified the customer, identified the decision makers, and set up the appointment. As far as you know, you are focused on the one calling the plays. You might not understand, however, that this particular leader is inclined to involve various other people in the company, particularly when it comes to major purchases. He needs to know that the team is on board. He wants everyone to have a say.

In other words, some players you have never seen can easily trip you up from the sidelines. The person who seems to have the authority is actually deferring to others. In fact, such decision by committee could be in the company's nature. You need to know the buying process, and to do that you need to ask questions—sometimes the same ones asked a few different ways to make sure you have a clear understanding of the company's system.

Preparation for a sales call or presentation should also include a look at the prospective client's purchasing history.

- Have they purchased from you before?

- Are they buying from your competitors?

- What are they buying, and how much of it?

These are the questions that can reveal what you are up against and what you have to overcome to get this piece of business.

2. Is the buyer facing any political or economic issues?

This could involve a major change such as upheaval in the health-care system or changes in financial-planning law. Or it could be alterations to state or local regulations that affect their business, either pro or con.

No matter what, it pays to understand the trends in the marketplace. You need insight into what is happening both in your industry and in the buyer's industry. Not only does this show that you care about their business enough to be knowledgeable on the subject, but that same knowledge can likely be applied to several more if not all of your potential clients.

3. Who else is the customer buying from?

Why is your prospective customer buying from a competitor? Do they have some deep relationship that you will have trouble rooting out? Has the competition been doing a better or worse job lately in delivering value and service? Has it raised its prices? Lowered them? You need clarity on who else is getting the customer's business and why that is the case.

TIME FOR PRACTICE

You have your plan and you've prepared and gathered your information, but before you hit the field, you have to *practice*.

You may have all the helpful information in the world on how your product or service will benefit your potential client, but if you stumble all over your words, or if you pour too much information on them at once, you might lose that prospect before you finish your introduction.

Practice. Following the guide in Chapter 3, work with another team member and do some Role Practice on how best to use your knowledge of your prospect's industry and business structure. Work on your Objection Responses and flesh out the Success Stories that apply well to your prospect's situation. Refine your Sales-Ready Messaging until you could say it in your sleep, and even consider asking a Top Producer at your company how he or she might approach your prospect. Lastly, if you don't schedule it, it won't get done.

ON TRAINING:
Under pressure, we do not rise to the occasion; we rise or fall to the level of our training.
URBAN MEYER

TIME FOR PROFIT

You have everything you've been able to gather about your potential client. You've practiced your approach, and once in the field, you asked questions that got them to open up about their processes and needs. You've shown them that you're there to collaborate with them and help them, not win a sale; that your brand "gets it" and sees them as unique from any other potential client. You've sold to their reasons for buying, not your own. So what's next?

If you've successfully applied every factor of the Four Ps equation, then your answer is "Profit."

Because you have learned to make time for Planning, Preparation, and Practice, you have stayed focused on the High Payoff Activities in your Sales Playbook, and you are ready for

Hyper Sales Growth. The next part of the book is aimed at Sales Managers but should also interest salespeople who have leadership aspirations or want to better understand sales team dynamics.

PART II

SALES MANAGER PLAYBOOK:
MULTIPLIER EFFECT

A Sales Manager's job is not to grow sales; it's to grow salespeople in Quantity and Quality. A Sales Manager leads salespeople in the process of developing and increasing their—and the company's—sales, growth, and income.

No matter how good your Top Producers may be, they're still limited by the hours of the day. Recruiting more Top Producers and ensuring that they're following and building on your company's winning systems, processes, and Best Sales Practices can help excellence build on itself. This Multiplier Effect can boost the results of the whole team as you incorporate new recruits' personal Best Sales Practices into your company's Sales Playbook.

At the same time you're building your sales team in Quantity, you're likely also dealing with the inevitable and unfortunate gap between your sales team's current and desired performance: the issue of Quality.

There are many problems that prevent salespeople from achieving desired performance, some of them related to selling techniques and practices, and others related to how the team is managed. But no matter where they originate, all of these challenges are the responsibility, and opportunity, of the Sales Manager.

WHAT ARE YOUR HPAs AS A SALES MANAGER?

Just like each of your team members, as a Sales Manager you have your own list of High Payoff Activities that will help you leverage the Multiplier Effect and build up and improve your team, both as a whole and as individuals.

My Sales Management HPAs Checklist

Key Area	My Sales Mgmt HPAs	An important HPA	I'm Performing well	I'm OK at this	I need to Learn or Improve
Team Development	Ranking of Sales Staff	☐	☐	☐	☐
	Recruiting & Upgrading Talent	☐	☐	☐	☐
	Culture & Team-Building	☐	☐	☐	☐
Mgmt Process	Sales Strategy Improvement	☐	☐	☐	☐
	Sales Org. Planning, Strategy & Org	☐	☐	☐	☐
	Sales Game Plan Building & Execution	☐	☐	☐	☐
	Prioritization / Focus	☐	☐	☐	☐
	Territory Strategy/Planning	☐	☐	☐	☐
	Goal Achievement & Key Activities Tracking	☐	☐	☐	☐
	Minimum Standards of Performance	☐	☐	☐	☐
	Inspect Expectations/Accountability	☐	☐	☐	☐
	Sales Process Build, Train, Practice & Perform	☐	☐	☐	☐
	Use of CRM & Reporting Tools	☐	☐	☐	☐
	Pipeline Mgmt – Inspect the Baskets	☐	☐	☐	☐
	Touch System Inspection	☐	☐	☐	☐
	Follow-Up & Follow-Through	☐	☐	☐	☐
	Sales Data Tracking & Interpretation	☐	☐	☐	☐
	Profit Analysis	☐	☐	☐	☐
Training & Development	Sales Mgmt Skills Development	☐	☐	☐	☐
	Sales Success Guide Building & Training	☐	☐	☐	☐
	Effective Sales Meetings	☐	☐	☐	☐
	Sales Process Build, Train, Practice & Perform	☐	☐	☐	☐
	Role Practicing Leadership	☐	☐	☐	☐
	1:1 Development & Progress Reviews	☐	☐	☐	☐
	Field Coaching Calls to TGD	☐	☐	☐	☐
	Mentoring	☐	☐	☐	☐
	Empowerment & Leader Development	☐	☐	☐	☐
	Career Path Planning & Communication	☐	☐	☐	☐
	Effective Communication – Team & Upper Mgmt	☐	☐	☐	☐
	Continuous Learning	☐	☐	☐	☐

The Profession of Sales is for Sales Professionals

Raising performance is driven by HPAs... high payoff actions.

1) Learn

2) Practice

3) Perform

4) Improve

PLAYBOOK RESOURCES:

SEE SALES MANAGER PLAYBOOK, Sales Management HPAs Checklist

inSITE-app & http://leveragesalescoach.com/resources

SCORING PLAY:

Ask yourself two key questions to help you focus on your HPAs and how to improve them:

1. What end results are you measured on?
2. What leading HPAs really matter to drive your performance, which, in turn, leads to your results?

Use the **Sales Management HPAs Checklist** tool to sort what you do well and what you could improve on.

- In the "I need to improve" list, how many of those activities could be improved by changing your approach or by getting training to improve those activities?

  - Can you strengthen those weaknesses so that they result in more sales?

- For your "I'm performing well" list, consider what you're currently doing and how you can strengthen those activities to improve results. Instead of "making field calls," for example, you could say, "making regular field calls with a specific growth plan and purpose for each salesperson."

COMMON SALES TEAM CHALLENGES

Companies suffer from numerous challenges within their sales teams. Here's a breakdown of the most common.

Challenges with salespeople:

- **Poor prospecting:** not hunting enough new business, not enough of the right activity

- **Slow or no closing**: missing easy sales opportunities, weak sales presentations, struggling with objections

- **Selling value:** struggling to communicate your product or service's value, struggling with lower priced competitors

- **Not hitting goals**: lacking focus, poor time management, not getting a big enough share of customer dollars, lack of accountability, poor reporting of activities

- **Poor sales skills:** talking too much, asking too few questions, poor follow-up, lacking sales-skills training, not practicing

- **Losing accounts:** increasing attrition

Challenges with sales management:

- **Lacking leadership**: sales management is part time or not effective, unsure how to grow, team morale and energy and activity are down

- **Lacking a real sales game plan**: sales strategy and game plan is outdated/needs a better approach

- **Selling value:** reacting to low-priced competitor, discounting too much to sell

- **Results lagging/goals not achieved:** team not achieving sales goals, KPIs not identified/tracked, struggling to hit sales targets

- **Lacking processes:** no logical Sales Process that can teach and ramp up sellers, no reporting or management of sales pipeline, targeting the wrong client targets/segments

- **No real sales training plan:** no plan to train/grow/develop in order to improve skills; lacking team and individual development; sales presentation not strong enough; Best Questions and Objection Responses are not captured, practiced, and used by entire sales team

- **Recruiting/hiring poorly:** not hiring Top Producers

All of these challenges fall under the purview of the Sales Manager, and each can be addressed with a solid company Sales Playbook. The Playbook can incorporate activities such as Modeling the Masters mentorship programs (introduced in Chapter 3) and the entire team's winning systems and processes. A Sales Manager with such a Playbook can focus on coaching, leading practices, and driving his or her team to success.

The fact is, **there aren't thousands of best ways to sell; there are only a handful.** Solid coaching focused on those winning ways will build exceptional performance. **A proven Sales Playbook is the basis for a winning sales team, but it takes a great coach to take those game plans from paper to practice to success.**

In this section, we introduce the Sales Manager's Top Six Plays to Achieve Hyper Sales Growth. The following six chapters further explore how sales teams can execute each play consistently. This is a different organizational structure from Part I of this book, but Part II draws on the concepts defined in Chapters 1–3 and the "gear" provided in Chapter 4.

THE SALES MANAGER'S TOP SIX PLAYS TO ACHIEVE HYPER SALES GROWTH

1: Developing **processes and tools** that equip the team to win

- Create a collection of the Best Sales Processes and most effective tools from your top performers provides everyone with the same training so that you can coach up and ramp up quicker and better.

2: Capturing and using **Best Sales Practices** to create an unfair competitive advantage

- Create change through an effective team-training program that focuses on Best Sales Practices as well as measurement standards, elevating your efforts to create the change you need for Hyper Sales Growth.

3: **Coaching and managing** to elevate success and results

- A Sales Manager needs to use all of the tools available in the Playbook to drive results and company success. This includes strengthening your People, Processes, and Practices with systems such as Key Performance Indicators (KPIs), Goal Achievement Plans, Pipeline Management, and Touch Systems, as well as hands-on coaching through individual development and team-training meetings and field calls.

4: Promoting a productive **culture and team building**

- The Sales Manager sets the tone for the team's culture for "how we get things done" on this team. This includes setting goals and priorities to achieve them; who you have on the team and what you do to train, grow, and upgrade your players; and how you work together to collaborate, problem-solve, and share Best Practices. The Sales Manager sets the pace for ongoing recognition, communication, personal and professional development, and empowering team members to equip them to sell better.

5: Putting key **people** in key spots and developing your talent pool

- Without working to develop productive people, all the great Sales Processes in the world aren't going to help you. Process improvement can only go so far without the right people behind it. Recruit to build the team you need to win. Rank the team members you have now, and deal with the underperformers.

6: Using **time** to make money; Implementing **tools and practices** to regain Sales Manager sanity

- Time is one of your most valuable assets, and managing it well is vital. Ideal Sales Manager calendars are based on the what, why, how, when structure of decide, prioritize, plan, and schedule. And meetings—from one-on-ones to culture-building activities and standards assessments—should be the heartbeat of your organization, with each beat as effective and efficient as possible.

Each of these key areas is discussed in depth in the following chapters. While it's not necessary to do them in order, each key is a powerful component of a Playbook that will benefit your company for a lifetime. The first step is finding out what works, the second is making it happen. The last step? Making sure you have it all in one place and clearly explained so that every new sales team member and Sales Manager can look to it, learn and practice it, implement it, and keep the business growing.

CHAPTER 6

PROCESSES AND TOOLS:
SALES MANAGER'S PLAY #1 TO ACHIEVE HYPER SALES GROWTH

 CHAPTER GAME PLAN

There aren't dozens of best ways to sell what you sell; there are only a few that have been proven, time and again, to have the strongest impact and the best results. To effectively implement a Sales Playbook, you need your team members to study and practice the written processes that have been tested and proven over the years. You need your sales team to collaborate and share what they have learned in order to continually improve on your company's Best Practices.

This chapter provides a higher-level view of many of the processes and tools already discussed, moving the focus from individual implementation to how these processes work in a team construct, and using them to drive success.

Our coaching company once worked with a wealth-management firm that was looking to improve its Sales Processes. We helped the firm quadruple its rate of closed sales without extra work. We merely showed how the salespeople could change one small piece of their process–something they had overlooked for years.

Company salespeople would spend time with a potential client who would end up saying, "Yes, I am going to switch my portfolio to you." These new clients would receive the paperwork to make it happen but often would never return signed documents.

"How often does that happen?" I asked. When they told me that the paperwork came back only 20 percent of the time, I dropped my pen. My jaw may have dropped too. "Are you kidding me? How could it be that low after they have already said yes?"

We changed only one thing, and within thirty days, the close rate rose to 85 percent–where it has remained to this day. Within two years, during very challenging markets, the firm tripled its assets under management.

What was that change in their Sales Process that led to such momentous results? We specified the date that the FedEx package would arrive, and we made sure that the decision maker would personally be present that day to receive it. We made crystal clear the simple steps of signing and returning the documents. We asked the recipient to commit to a time for getting the package back out for a pickup, telling them that we personally would arrange for FedEx to come by at precisely that hour. "Any questions, just call," we told the recipient. "We just want to make sure it is ready for the FedEx pickup at that time, so we can get right to work for you."

Closing the sale simply meant getting the paperwork signed and returned. But when the paperwork went out as regular mail, it would end up on a corner of someone's desk, gathering dust while people attended to more urgent matters. We just added that missing sense of urgency and removed the chance for the potential client's fervor to fade.

The owners had looked at me cross-eyed at first when I identified the sales-process issue. Why would I spend so much time on this one little aspect? It was as if they accepted the 20 percent return rate because it had always been that way. They wanted to move on to the big stuff. But it was not the big stuff that was causing the big problem.

Solving this problem was mind-numbingly simple, and yet people overlook solutions like that all the time. The solution took all of half an hour to identify and implement. A fourfold increase in results is quite an incentive to work smarter.

DAN LARSON

Collaboration is essential. When the sales team works together, participating and contributing in building your best practice processes and tools, then the salespeople's buy-in and usage of it all will increase. These elements are key to creating a winning Playbook. With them, you have what you need to practice and prepare for the big win.

In Part I, we discussed five essential processes and tools needed to promote success, including:

1. A Goal Achievement Plan

2. A Sales Process Scorecard

3. A Customer Relationship Management (CRM) system, including a method of managing contacts

4. Proactive Pipeline Management

5. A consistent Touch System

GOAL ACHIEVEMENT PLAN

In Chapter 2: Processes, we discussed Goal Achievement Plans for the salespeople on the front line. Here, we need to talk about how you can use those GAPs to track your sales team's progress and hold them accountable for achieving each step.

By now, you probably know what a Jack Daly–style process involves: asking yourself some fundamental questions, establishing goals, putting them in writing, and developing systems of measurement and accountability.

Annual Goal Worksheet (Backward Thinking / Goals Back-to-Front Plan)

| | Name: | | Dated updated: | | 1/1/2016 |

GOAL LEVELS		Minimum	Realistic	Stretch
		Minimum results I commit to this period no matter what the conditions.	What I realistically expect to produce this period.	Results I expect this period, if favorable, better than expected conditions.
Annual Goal (example)		$750,000	$1,000,000	$1,300,000
Quarterly (Consider seasonality or variables)	Q1			
	Q2			
	Q3			
	Q4			
	Total	$0	$0	$0
Monthly (Consider seasonality or variables)	1			
	2			
	3			
	4			
	5			
	6			
	7			
	8			
	9			
	10			
	11			
	12			
	Total	$0	$0	$0
Weekly The minimum I need to produce every week to achieve my goal.				
Daily The minimum I need to produce every day to achieve my goal.				
My High-Payoff Top Targets				
My Key Activities that really matter most to drive results				

PLAYBOOK RESOURCES:

SEE SALES MANAGER PLAYBOOK, Annual Goal Worksheet

inSITE-app & http://leveragesalescoach.com/resources

You need to be able to assess whether each salesperson is on pace toward his or her goals. The salespeople need to regularly track and measure their progress with you to help them achieve their personal best.

Your Goal Achievement Plan should make sure that each of your players maintains a serious commitment to his or her own written GAP on what needs to be accomplished personally for the year, for the quarter, for the month, and for the week. Review your salespeople's plans with them regularly, helping them measure their progress toward goals.

The Funnel – Goal Achievement Plan – ACTIVITIES

The Funnel – Goal Achievement Plan – ANNUAL

SALES PROCESS SCORECARD

In coaching clients over the years, we often ask Sales Managers, "How strong is your Sales Process now?" Usually they answer, "Well, it is pretty good." So we ask them to send it to us. Often they don't really have one they can send—only about half of them have something written down and defined. But if they do have a Sales Process, it is usually rather lightweight. To be strong, it would have to clearly define the steps and activities that really matter to drive success—the HPAs. Most of the written sales-process documents we see fail to include Best Sales Practices or even minimum standards of success.

In short, there is no Sales Process Scorecard that helps the manager and salespeople frame and train success.

To improve your Sales Process, make a Sales Process Scorecard. Start by asking yourself:

- Do you have anything that resembles an effective scorecard?

- Do you have clearly defined steps, Key Activities, and Best Practices spelled out?

- Is everyone clear on the standards? And if so, can you identify where someone is falling short, so that you know exactly where to work with that person?

- Are you scoring your people so that they know where they stand?

Note: The specifics here are dependent on the industry, company culture, and history of proven success initiatives.

The Sales Process Scorecard is valuable both for improving the skills of your players and for training new hires. You can measure, track, and pinpoint areas that need improvement because it spells out, in writing, the steps from prospecting and lead generation to closing, negotiating, follow-up, and follow-through.

In essence, a scorecard is your best tool for unlocking the enormous upside performance potential on your sales team. **Your scorecard will:**

- **Provide clarity on where team members can improve;**

  - Know exactly where to go to work with each salesperson to improve their performance. Identify their strong and weaker areas.

- **Leverage performance;**

  - Help them "work smarter" to get paid at a higher rate for the work they do, to make more money more efficiently.

- **Help create an Action Plan for improvements**; and

  - Look for ways to build in "wins" for them to make improving more interesting.

- **Serve as a vehicle for regular updates.**

  - Encourage team members to report back to you on their progress, and monitor results—once per quarter and *more frequently (monthly or weekly) for new people ramping up or those underperforming.*

SCORING PLAY:

Conduct a regular series of evaluations on the progress that has been made in the Key Activities on each of your salespeople's scorecards, and ask them to do their own self-evaluation. At each progress-review meeting, compare notes and discuss what is working well and what areas need more work. If one person sees the need for more work and the other thinks all is well, you can be sure that will open up a productive discussion. You exchange the reasons that you evaluated as you did, and that should help you both see where to go to work on improvements. This isn't a "right-wrong-gotcha" session. Rather, it's an opportunity to work together and pinpoint what needs to be done to map out an individual plan for improvement.

What's Working?	What's NOT Working?
▫	▫
START Doing This:	STOP Doing This:
▫	▫

CUSTOMER RELATIONSHIP MANAGEMENT SYSTEM

A Customer Relationship Management (CRM) system must be managed well and made important to produce results. A CRM is indispensable for tracking your team's pipeline opportunities and measuring how everyone is pacing toward their goals.

Most critical is that a CRM must maximize real-time clarity and focus on the health and advancement of your team's sales pipeline. Key measurements in a CRM are having the right Quantity and Quality of opportunities for any person and the team to be on track to achieve their goal. With this in place, it should track their leading metrics for pacing against their goals. You want to know and track in real time the status, what is needed, and the next step of each opportunity in order to get them closer to closing.

Setting up a CRM effectively requires defining the stages of pipeline advancement: the milestones of how an opportunity progresses through to closing. (For more on helping your salespeople develop their ideal pipeline, see Chapter 2: Processes.)

The main point of a CRM is for it to become a powerful tool for your sales team but not to become an all-consuming task that anchors people to their desks, monitoring their screens. Some companies have a CRM fully in place and are making great use of it. Others try and fail. The system may be simple or more complex—but nothing about its design matters unless it gets used.

If CRM is to thrive in your company, it must be "cheer-led and butt-kicked" from the top. Unless the company executives and leaders make CRM important, and communicate this often, it will be perceived by the team as not that important and a "flavor-of-the-month" project that will fade away over time.

It needs to be used on the front line, and Managers and executives need to use it as well. Unless everyone is on board, the potential will be wasted.

Sometimes the best way to get people on the front line embracing CRM is to somehow tie part of their compensation to using it. Remember, what gets measured and paid gets done! Also, leveraging the assistant concept can go far here and result in handsome dividends.

PROACTIVE TEAM PIPELINE MANAGEMENT

Proactive Pipeline Management is very closely tied to CRM, as that system is what makes the pipeline visible and manages it, organizing the contacts and letting you and your salespeople know at what point each prospect, customer, and client is in the pipeline.

In Part I we explained how salespeople benefit from a dashboard view of where they stand in relation to their goals. As a Sales Manager, you have to make sure the goal lines and line markings are clearly visible:

- Have you defined and assigned a value to each stage of your team's pipeline process?

- Can you clearly identify where the opportunities lie in each of your salesperson's pipelines?

- Are you helping call the plays to advance those opportunities to the next stage?

SCORING PLAY: DEVELOPING YOUR TEAM PIPELINE

Your Team Pipeline represents all of the revenue that could be projected from current accounts and those prospects your sales team has in their individual pipelines. By developing this real-time Team Pipeline and keeping it active, Sales Managers can help salespeople take actions to increase the probability of realizing the revenue in their individual pipelines. Here's what the Sales Manager should do:

Step 1: Create a list of opportunities and the valuation and probability in each team member's pipeline. This should include a list of account opportunities, deal sizes, stages of pipeline, current status, and next steps.

Step 2: Analyze and discuss the sales data and momentum in the pipeline frequently, weekly at a minimum, with each salesperson. Questions you should consider asking include:

- Does this individual's pipeline have a sufficient number of opportunities, sufficient in deal size?

- Is the salesperson clearly aware of status and next steps?

SCORING PLAY CONTINUED

- Is there sufficient action being taken to advance each opportunity?

- At what pace are the opportunities advancing? What, if any, problems, slowdowns, or challenges are there? (More on momentum of opportunities is in Chapter 10.)

- What's needed to get it moving/make advancements?

- What is their Action Plan? By when?

- What additional resources do they need to advance each opportunity?

What's Working?	What's NOT Working?
☐	☐
START Doing This:	STOP Doing This:
☐	☐

Rate on a scale of one to ten, how well you and your people are managing your current pipelines. If it is anything less than eight, nine, or ten, ask yourself how much more in sales and profit you could bring to your company just by improving that a couple of notches. Then, get busy by taking action.

PLAYBOOK RESOURCES:
SEE SALES MANAGER PLAYBOOK VIDEO, Proactive Pipeline Management
inSITE-app & http://leveragesalescoach.com/resources

CONSISTENT TOUCH SYSTEMS

For your sales team to effectively maintain contact with the people in their pipeline and advance their prospects through the stages to becoming clients, the salespeople need a Touch System.

In Chapter 2: Processes, we offered a Scoring Play for salespeople to develop their unique Touch Systems. The next step is for you as a Sales Manager to hold them accountable for keeping up with that system, as well as checking in to make sure it's effective and, worst case, not driving potential clients away.

The Sales Manager should be inspecting and evaluating each salesperson's Touch System at least once a month. Weekly is better. How can it be improved? Consider these questions:

Proactive Pipeline Mgmt. – Touch System
Inspect the Baskets

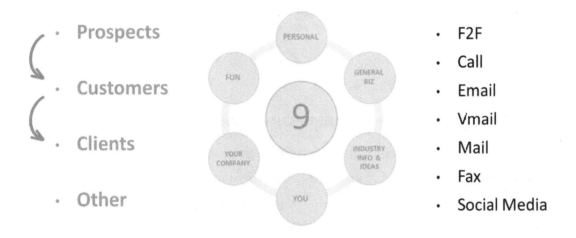

- Prospects
- Customers
- Clients
- Other

PERSONAL
GENERAL BIZ
FUN
9
INDUSTRY INFO & IDEAS
YOUR COMPANY
YOU

- F2F
- Call
- Email
- Vmail
- Mail
- Fax
- Social Media

Do they have separate baskets for Prospects, Customers, Clients, and Referrals? Have they identified their top ten or twenty target accounts in each basket? Have they rated their A, B, C, and D targets, with more frequent, valuable, and different touches going to their As and Bs? Are they mixing up the variety and type of touches, beyond just e-mails and voice mails to include things like snail mail, articles, and social media? Are they managing this in the CRM system? What are the company and you doing to support their Touch System?

PLAYBOOK RESOURCES:
SEE SALES MANAGER PLAYBOOK VIDEOS, How to Build your Touch System, Tools to Touch inSITE-app & http://leveragesalescoach.com/resources

HOW MEMORABLE ARE YOUR SALESPEOPLE?

Sometimes the personal touches that your salespeople develop become part of the company culture. Southwest Airlines is known for doing special things. For example, it sends some of its customers a birthday card every year, sometimes with drink tokens in it. Does the card bring tears to their eyes? Well, probably not, but they do remember. How many airlines sent you something on your birthday? The company is showing its desire to make a connection—and that alone speaks volumes.

Ask yourself:

- *How memorable are your salespeople?*

- *How often are their messages replied to?*

- *Are their prospects engaged, or do they seem bored or neglected?*

WHAT'S YOUR TOUCH SYSTEM FOR YOUR SALES TEAM?

Hold your salespeople accountable: regularly check in with them on the frequency and quality of their Touch System to ensure that they not only are making their touches unique but are not driving off potential clients in the process. Make those touches memorable, too! What can your sales team members take away from each check-in? How can you keep your advice, reminders, or encouragements fresh in their minds?

When you have a good Touch System in place, both for clients and for managing your sales team, the results can be highly profitable.

A WORD FROM JACK . . .
TRULY "TOUCHING"

I once spoke to a company's sales team of 180. After arriving home from ten days of travel, there was a large box waiting for me at my home. As a thank-you, one of the sales reps sent me tools from his company to help in my business, along with personal goodies like golf balls, towels, tees, wine, and other things he learned that I enjoy (displaying good listening skills). A year later, I completed my first Ironman, and the sales rep sent me a note of congrats and a gift bottle of wine to celebrate. On another occasion, he noticed that I was presenting to another company in his city and arranged for a tin of holiday cookies to be placed in my hotel room. Over the years, many more touches took place.

One day I received an e-mail from him, letting me know the company had been sold and he was uncertain about his fit with the new owners. I stated I could refer him to three nearby clients of mine if he'd like. I couldn't help the other 179 sales reps. Why? Well, I didn't know who they were, as I had never heard from them.

One rep realized I could be a Center of Influence (COI) and maintained an effective Touch System. Now that's profitability!

PS: This rep was regularly in the top 5 percent of his company. Top reps follow a system, a process, a Playbook.

JACK DALY

GEARED UP AND READY FOR PRACTICE

You've run through your winning plays and equipped your team with the best gear—that is, the methods, stories, and tools that have served your Top Producers well. Now it's time to put them into **Practice**.

CHAPTER 7

PRACTICES:
SALES MANAGER'S PLAY #2 TO ACHIEVE HYPER SALES GROWTH

 CHAPTER GAME PLAN

The method of in-your-face, old-school selling is dead. In an oversaturated marketplace, people choose to buy for their reasons, and salespeople who try to force their own vision, their own "why" for buying, are immediately rejected. The answer, then, is to stop selling and focus your team's strategy on mastering a higher level of sales. In this chapter, we'll go over methods for learning your customers' "why," how to sell with a relationship rather than a product, and how to extract the best selling practices from your Top Producers so that every team member is equipped with the best plays possible for the game.

We'll also dig into Best Practices for Sales Managers, explaining how they can most effectively ingrain these Best Practices in their team, how to provide their team with the ideal Playbook for tackling any sales situation, how to be highly effective and constructive during team and individual meetings, and the value of continuous coaching.

STOP SELLING

The reality is that people do not want to be sold to, and any salesperson who is still trying that old tactic needs to stop. Instead of focusing on your company and your own "why," you and your sales team should be focusing on the customer.

In Part I we admonished salespeople to shut up and listen to the customer, to ask good questions but talk less. Sales Managers must understand the rationale—the difference between the *company-focused* sales approach and the *customer-focused* sales approach.

Remember: People buy for *their* reasons based on what's relevant, meaningful, and important to *them*. They buy what aligns with and helps them achieve their personal and business goals. Therefore, to sell effectively, you need to answer your potential clients' "whys," and make it easier for them to say yes.

 **SALES TEAM SCRIMMAGE**
TIE TO YOUR CUSTOMERS' WHYS

At your next sales meeting, ask team members to answer the following questions from the perspective of a potential client. This is a Role Practice set in your prospect's office after their people have heard a presentation from your company. They are asking themselves:

- *Why your company?*

- *Why you, personally?*

- *Why should I buy?*

- *Why is this a benefit to me?*

- *Why does it make my life, my business better?*

- *Why is this a problem solver?*

Then discuss how your salespeople should answer the customer's "whys" as opposed to giving them theirs. The answers to these "whys" are your customers' End Zone Benefits, and when those answers speak to *their* reasons in a direct, powerful, compelling, relatable, and connective way, it resonates. This is the foundation for becoming known. 🏈

BECOMING KNOWN: CUSTOMER MESSAGING THAT RESONATES

Look for opportunities to leverage these End Zone Benefits to the customer, and then message these benefits consistently and thoroughly with your sales team and throughout your sales materials: written, online, and otherwise. Selling is easier when you're able to lift your brand so that it penetrates the marketplace's plane of consciousness—when everyone finally "gets it" and starts to see you differently.

The discipline is that you must stay committed to consistently messaging over what seems like forever. You'll think, *Everyone gets this by now,* but in order to penetrate a crazy, busy, all-about-me buyer marketplace, it takes more effort than we'd like to think.

The good news is that if you have made the connection to what is **relevant, meaningful, and important to your customer,** you will Become Known in the marketplace.

THE VALUE OF LEARNING FROM YOUR PROSPECTS

It is the Sales Manager's challenge to impress upon his or her salespeople the nature and importance of this customer-focused approach. Naturally, the salesperson and Sales Manager are focused on the deal, but first they need to learn why the prospects would want it.

So let's learn THEIR reasons, then speak to those reasons in the most direct, powerful, compelling, relatable, and connective way that we can.

When a salesperson cares more about the customer than about the deal, he or she will sell more than anyone else out there. Help your customers with their needs, opportunities, and problems in the best way that you can, even if that means losing the sale.

A WORD FROM JACK . . .
RARE AIR OF SELLING

I am totally blessed with a robust pipeline and calendar, often essentially booked a year in advance. Of that, more than 80 percent is repeat and referral business. Yet, we send out/refer about 20 percent of inquiry calls to our company to others that will provide a better fit or solution.

Examples include help with compensation-plan designs, personalized coaching, and general speaker needs. This then builds trust by putting the customer's needs above my "need to sell," and it's this trust that generates the healthy pipeline.

Such a caring approach is so rare out in the selling world that it sends a message of real value. Salespeople who take this approach find that their reputation quickly grows in the marketplace and that they receive a flood of referrals and repeat business.

JACK DALY

SELLING THE RELATIONSHIP

In Part I, we introduced the concept of building trusting relationships as a key to selling, a concept that we have advocated for years as a powerful way to differentiate yourself. You achieve top results by building relationships based on caring more about your customers' needs than about "selling" them something. So, how are you encouraging your salespeople to care more about helping potential clients make the right decision, even if this time it's not you? How are you driving them to become a resource to clients and a potential partner in building their success?

A WORD FROM JACK . . .
THE VALUE OF HONESTY

My wife, Bonnie, and I were looking to "move up" in class and size with our personal residence. We engaged Doug, a highly touted Realtor familiar with the area. Doug spent considerable time with us, getting a clear picture of what we were seeking, before ever going out and showing us homes in the area. He then studied the available inventory and set up an efficient tour of potential homes. After a solid weekend, none of what we visited made the cut. Doug then spent more time with us, narrowing in on the pluses and minuses. Another day of house visits took place. Again, nothing hit the mark. At this point, Doug sat us down and said there were two brand-new developments close by, and he felt that they would probably be best for us, given all he learned and what was available in resales. He then suggested we independently take the new-home tour, as he had no value in the process (note, also no upside commission either).

Doug was correct. Bonnie and I loved the houses, and we sure did consider them. The only challenge was having to go through years of waiting for the softscape and hardscape improvements needed on the new property to come to life. It just wasn't something we were willing to take on, having done so with several homes in our past. We returned to Doug, reported our findings, and told him to continue to keep us in mind while we were going to stay put and do some home improvements with our existing home.

Since then, we have gone on to buy not one, but two, resale residences with Doug. He earned our trust by putting our needs above his sale. Not only did he win us over personally, but we have been a referral source on several more house sales for Doug. Now that's selling!

When you become a trusted advisor to your customers, you also become their resource and partner in building their success. You present them with ideas and insights that help take them to new levels. You are, in effect, teaching them how to improve their business in ways that are linked to the solutions that you are selling.

 JACK DALY

A useful tool in establishing a trusting relationship is learning how to understand and relate to your prospect's personality style.

THE POWER OF PERSONALITY ASSESSMENT

In Chapters 1 and 3, we discussed the four Personality Styles that each of us mainly falls into:

1. Amiable

2. Analytical

3. Expressive

4. Driver

How well do your salespeople and you as a manager understand these Personality Styles?

 Remember that the Sales Manager will be more effective knowing the style of each member of the sales team and adjusting to his or her style. It's the job of the Sales Manager to adjust to the style of each salesperson, not vice versa.

While this powerful knowledge is pretty simple once learned, it requires study, preparation, and practice. Encourage your sales team to try identifying different styles of personalities at sales meetings or among your coworkers, urging them to practice it to the point where adjusting their personality style to be compatible with whomever they are working with becomes second nature.

SALES TEAM SCRIMMAGE

During a sales meeting, try an in-house practice for identifying different styles of personalities. Let team members draw a personality style from a hat and have other team members try to guess what style they are. Then have the team members try to speak their language in order to land a sale.

REVIEWING THE PLAY

How good are you and your team at selling the relationship?

- How well do you and your sales team understand these four Personality Styles?

- Do you provide training and encourage practice in sales meetings?

- What tactics would you use to match a personality style other than your own to leverage a sale?

- Do you and your team identify, note, and adjust to the personality style of the primary buyer for each account?

- What gains can you and your team make by improving this best practice?

- Be sure to have the team update the CRM with such style identity. Beyond the obvious value to the sales rep and company-support team, the bonus is that we have it system captured should there be a change in sales reps.

LEVERAGING CENTERS OF INFLUENCE

Some of those "right people" may actually never buy or use your product or service, but they can connect you with those who do and send you a wealth of business. We first discussed this type of contact, called a Center of Influence (COI), in Chapter 2, in the section on Proactive Pipeline Management. These people do not necessarily need what you have to offer, but they certainly see the value and are willing to send others your way.

Few salespeople target COIs, despite the incredible opportunity they offer for leveraging the growth of your business. It is the responsibility of the Sales Manager to focus activity on this rich opportunity.

Salespeople need to hear from their Sales Manager that they should care more about the customer than about the sale and that they should consider what noncustomer Centers of Influence might be rich sources of referrals. Who are these important COIs? What are the plays in the Playbook to win over their referrals?

A WORD FROM JACK . . .
A CENTER OF INFLUENCE

I often speak to representatives of companies in the staffing industry, who recruit workers for businesses. "In my company," I tell them, "I do not have any employees, and I do not want any. And therefore, I cannot be a customer or client for you, and you would not consider me a prospect.

"However, I am certainly what we call a 'Center of Influence' for you. Why? Because in my business I deal directly with the C-suite—and those are the same people who are engaging you."

If a salesperson working for a recruiting firm networked with me on LinkedIn, I explain, he or she would find that most of my contacts there would be C-suite people. The salesperson could look through that list to see if anyone there could help set up a meeting with a hard-to-reach prospect. If so, the salesperson could ask me for an introduction.

That's a step toward building a great relationship with me—even though I am not a person who will ever use that salesperson's service. Nonetheless, as a Center of Influence, I could be responsible for bringing a wealth of business to the company.

JACK DALY

PLAYBOOK RESOURCES:
SEE SALES MANAGER PLAYBOOK VIDEO, Swim Coach Steve, Who Are Your Swim Coaches? inSITE-app & http://leveragesalescoach.com/resources

BEST PRACTICES: THE BEST SALESPEOPLE ARE "CANNED"

No doubt, any Sales Manager has often heard and used the term "Best Practices." But are you doing more than just talking about them? Have you captured those practices? Specifically, what are you advocating in the way of lead generation, qualifying, presenting, handling objections and tough questions, conducting the closing, follow-up and follow-through, and all the other elements so essential to solid sales?

The biggest challenge of harnessing the Best Sales Practices of your Top Producers is that, in most cases, these practices live only in their heads. That is, if you were to ask them what their Best Practices are, you'd more than likely get an underwhelming response of "I don't know, I just do what I do."

Top Producers usually aren't very good at articulating exactly what it is that they do so well. It takes a diligent effort to extract and capture their magic. In our sales coaching, we often ask them the same question several different ways to discover the more subtle nuances of what they do that really differentiates them from the herd.

Imagine that you're managing a thousand salespeople. Each of them probably has heard the objection "Your price is too high," and although there certainly aren't a thousand best ways to respond to that objection, you would probably find that they have a wide variety of answers. Out of those responses, you likely could identify two or three best ways to answer that tough question for your company. So why not get all of those thousand people responding with the answers you know work best?

SALES TEAM SCRIMMAGE

The Best Sales Practices for most sales teams typically reside in the minds of several Top Producers, so to extract and capture those practices, you need to collaborate. Convene a roundtable discussion of Best Practices in a key area of your Sales Process. Lead the discussion but don't command and control it. Ask key questions, get input from all players, and let the best ideas get recognized, rise to the top, and get agreed on. This allows your team to simultaneously learn and buy into using the Best Sales Practices.

REVIEWING THE PLAY

- As the leader of your team, are you doing more than just talking about your team's Best Sales Practices?

- Have you captured those practices?

- Specifically, what are you advocating in the way of:

  - Lead generation;

  - Qualifying, presenting, and handling objections and tough questions;

  - Identifying key questions to be asked;

  - Conducting the closing;

  - Follow-up and follow-through; and

  - …All the other elements of your Sales Playbook?

Be sure to capture these Best Practices on paper and share them with everyone on your sales team. Then practice those Best Practices. Do it in-house, practicing on one another so that your salespeople aren't trying out new responses for the first time on prospects. You don't want to risk losing a deal because a team member doesn't have his or her answers down pat.

Most salespeople—easily 90 percent of them—do not practice in-house, which means that they are engaging in the expensive default of practicing on the customer. Instead, they should be defining each of the plays, getting them into a Playbook, and scheduling regular scrimmages so that they can reach and maintain excellence.

Can you imagine a sports team not practicing? And how long do you predict that coach would last?

PRACTICING SALES STRATEGIES IN-HOUSE

Practicing out on the field is not the path to victory. Anybody on a professional sports team understands this, which is why they practice against each other until they get the plays down right. In-house practice works the same way. Sales teams practice against each other, trying out your company's messages until they can say them in their sleep.

Now, as we did with the Processes and Tools, let's revisit those Best Practices that we described in detail in the Playbook for the front line, but this time, from the Sales Manager's perspective.

In-house practice can take many forms, but we chose two to highlight that work well for just about any size team: Role Practice and Modeling the Masters.

ROLE PRACTICE

The sales meeting is an opportune time for Role Practice, as discussed in Chapter 3: Practices, in which the group breaks down into threesomes with one taking the salesperson role, one being the prospect, and the third observing, then switching roles and trying it again with a different scenario so that each team member gets a chance at every role.

How can you help your team members evaluate what they've learned during this practice? Consider asking them some of the following questions:

- On a scale of one to ten, how did you rate? If less than ten, what was lacking?

- Which scenario did you feel most comfortable in?

- Which scenario was the most awkward? Why?

SMART Selling Role Practice: A-B-C Method

A-B-C Roles   Responsibilities

- A = **Seller** – goes through key steps of presentation (condensed for time)
- B = **Prospect** – prospect plays desired role for type of FOCUS practice (below)
- C = **Observer** – make notes of observations
  - Strengths and Weaker areas to improve

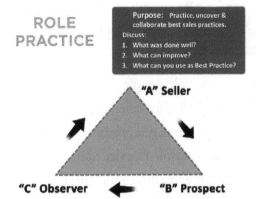

Steps:

- **15 minutes total**   (time may vary but keep it focused on ONE main area to practice)
  - 1 min set-up/agree on situation. GOAL is a Realistic buyer/seller situation; Constructive learning experience to help everyone be more effective
  - 5 min to present / role practice
  - 4 min for Observer feedback
  - 5 min Discussion

- **1) Set-up Purpose & Situation**
  - Type of Selling Practice to FOCUS on   _____
    - What do you want to work on? General? Questions? Objections? Closing? etc.
  - Call type – 1st call, Follow-up, Service call, etc.   _____
  - Situation
    - Type of account? – Relevant to selling situation?   _____

- **2) Seller Presentation**

- **3) Observer Feedback**
  - 1) What was done well?
  - 2) What can improve?
  - 3) What can you use as a Best Practice?

- **4) Discussion – What did we learn?**

- **5) Repeat 2 more times rotating A-B-C roles. Total time approximately 45 min.**

Of course, salespeople do sometimes moan and groan about doing this exercise, but it is invariably a highly valuable practice that leaves most team members feeling energized. Then, when they see that it produces results—and money in their pockets—they feel motivated to continue the Role Practice training. Schedule them in your calendar. Make them mandatory. Never cancel them. Think "sports coaches" here!

MODELING THE MASTERS

A team of any size will have some players who are stronger than others, with more experience, better techniques, and greater knowledge. You can leverage that strength by pairing salespeople with a master—or mentor—so that they can learn as much as possible. (See more about how your salespeople can benefit during the mentoring process in Chapter 3: Practices.)

Participation in this type of training doesn't have to be limited to new salespeople. For example, it's likely your Top Producers are talented in only a few niche areas. One might be excellent at handling objections, while another is the most effective at relating Success Stories. Allowing all of your team members to shadow with others who demonstrate exceptional skills in areas where they know they're lacking is an excellent way to create a well-rounded and effective team.

Modeling the Masters not only helps weaker players get up to speed, but it also offers the side benefit of making the mentors feel valuable and privileged when they're able to help someone who is struggling. Remember that respect is the top intangible that employees crave. How better to show respect than to let someone know how much others need his or her expertise? Again, put these sessions on the calendar!

A WORD FROM JACK . . .
MODELING THE MASTERS

In my many speaking engagements around the world, I often have addressed the top salespeople of large organizations in such balmy getaways as Hawaii or the Caribbean or Mexico. The company leaders invite their best performers and significant others to fine resorts to honor them as members of their President's Club or Chairman's Club.

Recently, a client invited me to speak in Cancun to help his people learn how they could enhance their game. This particular client's company has more than four hundred salespeople. Before I spoke, the chairman of the company addressed the group. With a big screen behind him, he said that he wanted to announce the Chairman's Club winners for the coming year–the cream of his four hundred-plus crop.

Each year, thirty-three to thirty-nine of those people make it into the club. And of those, about thirty are the same people year after year. Now, imagine that you were a man from Mars who just happened to land in Cancun that day. "Wait a second here," you might say. "Everyone has the same product, the same price, the same service, the same competitors, and the same economy, but it is always mostly the same people who get the reward. How can that be?"

Well, here's the answer, for Martians and Earthlings alike: those thirty folks must be doing something different. Everyone else should be focusing on figuring out what that is, and then they should be doing it themselves. That's how you build on success. You can create a great Playbook by Modeling the Masters.

When I was thirteen years old, I spent the summer interviewing two hundred business owners on how they had found success. I wanted to learn how to start developing my own game plan so that I, too, could become a successful entrepreneur.

That summer I got a job as a caddie at a private country club. I soon noticed that I was carrying clubs for people who were driving fine new cars. They were able to take off time midweek to golf. I learned that they lived in big estate homes. I did not live in such a home, and though my dad worked extremely hard, he did not play golf during the week, and our car was a nine-passenger station wagon with well over a hundred thousand miles on it. I think our mechanic had it in his garage more often than we had it on our driveway.

I wondered how these men had created such a life for themselves and their families. This was a marvelous opportunity to find out. I would never have been able to stroll into their offices or knock on the front doors of those fine homes, but here I was, as a caddie, at their side for hours on end. And so I peppered them with questions. I asked them all about how they had become successful, and whether they would have done anything differently, and what advice they might offer a thirteen-year-old. Imagine the conversation later back at the clubhouse when that golfer ran into a couple of friends at the bar. "Hey, did you ever have that Jack Daly kid as your caddie?" I am sure they laughed, but I am also sure that I caught their attention. "You know, the next time that boy caddies for me," the conversation no doubt continued, "I am going to see if he took me up on my advice."

And they did. That summer, about two hundred successful business people helped me to grow at an exponential rate. That summer was a turning point for the rest of my life. I was learning from those who had been where I wanted to go, who had figured it out and proven themselves. I was Modeling the Masters.

It is a mistake to rush out onto the field without the proper preparation. Modeling the Masters is one of the easiest ways for salespeople and Sales Managers to increase the probability of success and to build a Playbook that will position them to win. It results in generating more business with less work.

I have long been a voracious reader and remain one to this day. Among the many materials I consume are twenty to thirty business books every year. Studying others' books is my lifelong pattern: I am trying to learn from people who have already demonstrated their success in a rapidly changing world. By coming to understand how those authors are going about the pursuit of excellence, I can find ways to enhance the systems and processes by which I conduct my own life. Learning does not stop with school. It must be a lifelong endeavor.

JACK DALY

A WORD FROM DAN . . .
A TRAINING ISSUE AT THE ROOT

Several years ago, I consulted with the regional vice president of a company that had been experiencing high turnover. He recently called me with an update. He said that after working with me, he had been able to retain 70 percent of his top performers. Other Managers like him average 30 percent.

We talked about how he had achieved that. At the time when I was called in, the company had been doing a lot of hiring, filling seats quickly. They were focused on Quantity rather than Quality.

We zeroed in on his capacity to train well. You need to hire right, getting the players who are the best fit and the best equipped for the job. Then you train them well for early success. A lot of time goes into hiring the right people and teaching them the company's systems and processes.

However, we made it clear that with such a high turnover, hiring several people a month, he did not have sufficient time for training. That would inevitably result in their failing at a much higher rate. In other words, his training capacity limited his hiring capacity. It is important to be clear about your training capacity in advance of hiring.

We took the approach of focusing on his strongest performers and having them serve as mentors. We created the compensated position of training leader, starting with one and then adding a few more. This built up his training capacity—which in turn expanded his capacity to hire competently. He could bring people on board and ramp them up quickly, no longer suffering the massive turnover.

The lesson for Sales Managers is this: To hire smarter, you must know your training capacity. If you are able to spend only a little time with one new salesperson and you are hiring several, you are setting most of them up for failure. It is hard to succeed with anemic and fragmented training.

That regional vice president came to understand that he had a training-capacity problem before he had a hiring problem. We went to the root of the issue, priming and motivating his existent talent. He got the fundamentals in place, and he has continued that pattern—resulting in the impressive retention rate he enjoys today.

DAN LARSON

BUILDING YOUR SUCCESS GUIDE

Another key to training and developing your team is building a Sales Manager's Sales Success Guide. The Sales Manager cannot leave it up to the individual salespeople to build such a guide, because it is really a compilation of the Best Practices among all the team members. The concept is this: **There is hardly anything that goes on during a sales call that cannot be anticipated before arriving on that call.** As such, there is no reason to not be prepared before the call.

We have long noticed, for example, that Top Producers tend to say the same things the same way each time they encounter a particular situation. You might say that their presentations are "canned," but the beauty of it is that they do not sound that way. The top salespeople make it sound as if it is the very first time they have ever presented it.

A Sales Manager's Sales Success Guide should be a combination of three practices that sales team members can use time and again in the field to effect a solid sale. They should be compiled from the best of what was learned in the in-house sessions in which salespeople collaborated to "extract and capture" Best Practices, as well as your Role Practices and Modeling the Masters efforts. The three practices in your Sales Success Guide are:

- Best Questions and Active Listening

- Objection Responses

- Success Story Guide

Best Questions and Active Listening

When your salespeople listen intently and ask incisive and insightful questions, they are far more likely to acquire the critical information that will result in a deal. As we discussed in Part I (sections on Prepare for the Prospect and Best Questions and Active Listening), too many just spout out what they think they know while the prospect looks at the clock and waits to escort them from the room. Good questions elicit revealing answers. The best way to strong sales results is to find out why the prospects believe they should buy, not why the salespeople think they should.

To determine what you need to help your team learn, ask yourself:

- How effective is your team at Active Listening?

- Do you train your people to ask careful questions and show they are listening to the answers?

- Do they understand and practice Active Listening?

- When developing a lead, what are the Best Questions for opening up a new prospect?

- What are the team's best qualifying questions that will cut to the chase?

- What are the Best Questions for setting appointments with key decision makers?

- During presentations, how can you effectively use questions to draw people out, rather than just subject them to the spiel?

All the way through the Sales Process, great questions are important. Help your people learn what to listen for and what to ask about, and watch the results improve.

Building an Effective Best Questions Guide

The Sales Manager's Sales Success Guide can include a cheat sheet to help your salespeople ask better questions that produce better answers.

You want them to ask questions that engage potential clients, get them more psychologically involved, and develop a stronger connection with them. The focus and precision of the questions increases the prospect's perception of your competency. The right questions help the prospect clarify his or her thinking and will guide a more successful sales conversation.

Remember that people often speak in generalities, so your questions need to be more focused to uncover better, specific, more useful answers that will advance the selling conversation.

The following structure helps to create a Best Questions Guide that defines productive questions to be used throughout the selling process.

Six Main Areas of Questions:

1. **Relationship building**

   □ Purpose: Open up and develop stronger relationships. Learn more about your buyer's head and heart.

2. **Decision making**

- □ Purpose: Understand their buying data and information—what, when, and how they buy.

3. **Pain**

   - □ Purpose: Identify current problems. Learn the issues, challenges, and frustrations that they're dealing with now. Learn their priorities and HVNs (High-Value Needs).

4. **Fear**

   - □ Purpose: Identify their concerns about the future and what's weighing on their mind.

5. **Desire**

   - □ Purpose: Identify what goals and opportunities they are pushing for in the future. Where are they heading?

6. **Deficit**

   - □ Purpose: Identify a relevant, important area that they have trouble answering or can't answer. It positions you as an expert or useful advisor.

Developing questions and practicing them with your team will help your salespeople better steer and guide effective conversations with buyers.

For more on how to create a Best Questions Guide, see the section on Best Questions and Active Listening in Chapter 3, and the resources in Part III. And remember to customize to your business and get inputs and buy-in from the sales team—this will increase the number of people actually using it!

OBJECTION RESPONSES

How does your team handle the tough questions and objections that they get out in the field? How can they learn to anticipate them?

SALES TEAM SCRIMMAGE

Objection Responses are an inevitable part of the Sales Process; it's how your team members handle them that will often make or break a sale. During your next team meeting, compile and categorize the best Objection Responses for as many objection types you can think of, including:

1. Price

2. Competition

3. Support/Service

4. Decision making

5. Company issues

6. No time

7. Financial constraints

8. Miscellaneous

Note: Your sales team will likely feel like there are hundreds, thousands, and even infinite objections. The reality is that less than fifteen will cover more than 90 percent of what is encountered. This we've learned from more than a decade of helping our clients build their Success Guides and Playbooks.

This is one of those activities that your team should practice regularly–at least once a month–so that they can stay fresh and sales ready with their responses. Refer to these responses often and even throw in a pop quiz now and then just to keep them on their toes.

Objection-response practice doesn't just have to be in a team format, either–they can also be practiced during one-on-one meetings. Remember, you're either practicing in-house or you're practicing on your prospects and customers!

What's Working?	What's NOT Working?
☐	☐
START Doing This:	STOP Doing This:
☐	☐

In Chapter 3, we discussed how sales team members can turn to each other to collect successful Objection Responses. Encourage these Sales Team Scrimmages during sales meetings by asking team members how they've dealt with specific or general objections in the past. Collect the best responses and compile them into your Sales Playbook, practicing these responses regularly and from different angles so that salespeople are well prepared when similar objections come up in the field.

SUCCESS STORIES

Every established company has had successes. Your company has stories about how it has solved problems for its clients. Unfortunately, many of these stories are locked up in the minds of Top Producers. They are not written down and go unshared.

Take the time to **identify a few of your company's best successes** by speaking with the CEO, or upper management, and your Top Producers, and asking:

- What was the customer's situation and problem before your company entered the picture?

- What did your company recommend, and what was the result?

- What was achieved, or overcome, or avoided?

That Success Story will be highly relevant to anyone experiencing a similar situation to the one your company addressed. Prospects can picture themselves getting the same results. Your salespeople will have tapped into what your target finds most meaningful. Success sells!

SCORING PLAY:
Make sure everyone on your team keeps a notebook in which they capture the elements of their stories, and those notes should be stored so that they are available to all. Also, the stories should be categorized based on the situation that was addressed and the problem that was solved. That way you can easily find the ones that your prospect will be most interested in hearing, the ones that will help to score the sale.

SALES TEAM SCRIMMAGE
SPOT CHECKS

Wherever you see the need for improvement in your sales team's use of Best Questions, Objection Responses, or Success Stories, do something about it. In sales meetings, regularly try some spot checks.

"So, Jim, tell me what you would ask prospects to find out why *they* would want to buy from us instead of the competition when they have so many choices?"

Or: "Tell me, Linda, what would you say if someone told you that our widget just costs too doggone much?"

Or: "Fred, let's hear about one of our big successes that you might share with a prospect who seems to need some reassurance."

If you find that Jim, Linda, Fred, and the others are giving you some vague answers, that's not good enough. It is time to raise the bar and provide some specific training.

REVIEWING THE PLAY

Each of your sales team members should be:

- Ready with the Best Questions to identify the prospect's "why";

- Able to efficiently handle the many forms of objections that a prospect could raise as a reason for not buying; and

- Fully versed in Success Stories–their own and others–that they can relate to their prospect.

SALES-READY MESSAGING

As we discussed in Chapter 3: Practices, Sales-Ready Messaging is your ideal thirty-second elevator message—it's how your team communicates what makes your products and services unique and different from the competition's. This is the core message that you must get across succinctly and clearly in your sales presentations.

Ask yourself whether all of your sales team members are clear on that core message and can convey that message succinctly in a sales presentation.

Some Sales Managers expect their people to somehow be able to come up with the perfect Sales-Ready Messaging on their own, with little training or direction. They assume that everyone on the team is speaking from the same page about the right things, and they do not even bother to check whether that is true.

Are all the members of your sales team speaking the same language? If so, is that language the best, most effective language they could use?

In Chapter 3, we provided a Sales Team Scrimmage for brainstorming the best Sales-Ready Messaging for your team using your unique Value Proposition. Once you have your Sales-Ready Messaging ready, it's your job to make sure your team is not only rehearsing it but also implementing it clearly and convincingly in the field.

As with all the other Best Practices tools, the key with this one is to work on it consistently, practicing in-house until your team has it mastered.

Salespeople need to sell more than what the company has to offer—they have to sell what they themselves have to offer, too. They have to reassure the customer that they will be right on top of things and will respond consistently and quickly. We often hear clients complain that salespeople promise the moon and then are never seen again. So much of what you are selling is your competence in servicing the account. And that, too, needs to be an element of the Sales-Ready Messaging.

TAKING YOUR TEAM TO THE PLAYING FIELD

As you get your People, Processes, and Practices into your Playbook, you will be better equipped to elevate your team's performance. And with these key areas in place, coaching and developing your team and individual players with your new Playbook is the vital next step. The focus of the Sales Manager's job is to grow salespeople in Quantity and Quality, so they can grow and scale results. With that in mind, let's look at effective ways to **Coach and Manage** your team.

ELEMENTS OF EFFECTIVE SALES-READY MESSAGING

Sales-Ready Messaging should have the following elements for responding to that critical question on most buyers' minds, *Why should I do business with your company (and you) versus any and all of your competitors?*

- What is your company promise—and your promise?

- What is your unique Value Proposition (see template on page 57)?

- Why do your best customers start with you *and* stay with you?

- What are your personal competitive advantages that set you apart as unique and better?

- What specific things make you **unique and well-qualified** to be a great choice for them to do business with?

- What's special about you and what you do to get great results for your customers?

- In what ways do you add value for them that sets you apart?

CHAPTER 8

COACH AND MANAGE TO GROW SUCCESS

 CHAPTER GAME PLAN

The processes, such as the salesperson's Pipeline Management and Touch System described in Chapter 2, should be regularly inspected and evaluated by the Sales Manager for ways they might be improved. In this chapter, we discuss the necessary frequency of those evaluations for established team members and salespeople just starting out with your company who need to be trained for success. How do you manage and coach every member of your team effectively without overburdening your own workload? Read on to learn more about our Best Practices for coaching the team.

Congratulations! The Processes and Tools and Practices gathered from your team can now be considered your basic Sales Playbook. There are plenty of other elements that can and will be added over time and to each individual's custom Sales Playbook, but your essential Playbook core is in place. With it, you can effectively **Coach** your team on Best Sales Practices and help **Manage** their Goal Achievement Plans, holding them accountable for accomplishing the Key Activities necessary for achieving their sales goals.

Every business will have a specific list of Key Activities that a salesperson should be doing. It is the Sales Manager's responsibility to hold team members accountable for performing those activities adequately. Managing this performance for Hyper Sales Growth begins with making sure they're aware of those activities by building them into the Playbook for their particular territory.

Once those expectations are clear, you are ready to focus on the important work of training new hires, coaching your salespeople as both a team and individuals, creating a one-on-one progress-review regimen, and getting away from your desk to coach and train in the field.

NEW HIRES: TRAINING FOR SUCCESS

Imagine for a minute that you are coming aboard a sales team with a few dozen members, and you tell your Sales Manager this is how you expect to spend your first month:

"I do not want you to put me in the field or have me working in my territory yet. In fact, I do not want you to hold me to any production numbers. I do not want any sales quotas. I am telling you I do not want to be in front of a prospect or a customer for my first thirty days. I do not want to be on the phone with them. I will do nothing that would normally be expected of a salesperson in most organizations.

"What I intend to do in my first thirty days is this: I am going to spend the first week on the job attached to the hip of the number-one salesperson. I am going to find out what led that person to become number one, and I'm going to ask questions such as the following:

- 'What did you do, and why did you do it?'

- 'What did you not do, and why did you not do those things?'

- 'What was your Pipeline Management like?'

- 'What were your Key Activities like?'

- 'Do you have an assistant? If so, what does that assistant do?'

- 'What do you do with regard to objections that you run into in the field?'

- 'What is your Touch System like?'

- 'How do you go about creating perceived value?'

- 'What are the five biggest potholes that you went into in your career that I could identify now so that I can drive around them rather than drive into them?'

"In week two, I am going to do the exact same process with the number-two salesperson. In week three, I'll focus on number three. Week four, I am going to sit down and take everything I learned from those three, plus everything that I have learned to date in my own personal experience. I am going to sit down and build a Playbook. I am going to build the written systems and processes that will enhance my probability of being successful. I am going to practice those systems and processes. Then I am going out onto the field with the intention of winning."

How would your Sales Manager react? Imagine if you were taken seriously and your plan accepted. Would you be a better salesperson by virtue of learning and studying and practicing the Playbook with the pros on the team? That's what all professional athletes do before heading out onto the field. If they did not, it would be absurd to think they could win.

Why, then, shouldn't the sales professional do likewise?

BEST COACHING PRACTICES

To effectively coach a winning sales team, a Sales Manager has to be able to coach well on both an individual and group level, as well as provide consistent messaging across the board. The Sales Manager should have a consistent Touch System with his or her team, making sure processes and messaging are clear and no one is dropping the ball.

The many duties of the Sales Manager—the field calls, team Playbook building, and other HPAs introduced at the beginning of Part II—must be scheduled. Sales Managers need to be disciplined in attending to all these elements of the job. All too often this does not get done, as the Sales Manager rushes to the urgent at the expense of the important—in effect, being reactive instead of proactive.

Let's look at a sample month of focus and time demands for a Sales Manager of ten people who is committed to growing his or her team in Quantity and Quality.

SALES MANAGER MONTHLY TIME DEMANDS (TEAM OF TEN)

Example	Time
PEOPLE: Team Development	
• **Ranking** salespeople; **minimum standards** of performance	4 hours
• **Recruiting and upgrading** the sales team	8 hours
PROCESSES: Management Processes	
• **Goal Achievement (GAP) & Key Activities**: inspect	10 hours
• **Sales Process Key Activities & Best Practices**: inspect and rank	4 hours
• Proactive **Pipeline Management**: inspect the baskets	20 hours
• Prospecting **Touch System**: inspect	10 hours
PRACTICES: Training and Development	
• **Sales Success Guide** building and training	6 hours
• Effective **sales meetings** that train and develop	6 hours
• **Sales Process Key Activities & Best Practices**: train and develop	4 hours
• **Role Practice** process	8 hours
• **One-on-one** sessions	20 hours
• **Field calls** that train and develop ("Three Types of Field Calls," page 162)	40 hours
Total time **each month**	**136 hours**

This activity breakdown requires committing time to the HPAs for a Sales Manager that really drives growth and performance. For example, a Sales Manager should be spending a minimum of four hours per week in the field with each salesperson just conducting coaching, training, and joint calls, which we speak to later in this chapter.

Think about that. If a manager is responsible for ten people, that is forty hours per month that should be spent on just that one particular line item. As you can clearly see, Sales Managers simply do not have time to be riding a computer screen in the office, whiling away the day with less important matters. They need to be out in the field, engaged with their salespeople for the necessary personal development to take place.

SALES TEAMS: BETTER BY THE DOZEN

What is the size of a team, then, that a Sales Manager can reasonably be expected to handle? The answer will vary from business to business, but it is hard to imagine that the manager can do an effective job if he or she is leading more than twelve salespeople. Even a dozen may be a stretch, when you consider the weight of all those duties and the responsibility owed to each of those individuals. If the Sales Manager has twenty people, for example, then it's almost certain that all twenty are being shortchanged in some way. What is being sacrificed is sales excellence, and that's a high price to pay when you consider what it does to the top and bottom line.

If you rank the team, where will the Sales Manager spend the most time? In business, we ignore the top quartile. We leave them alone. In sports, the coach invests the most time with the first team. What is your approach? If change on your part is needed—how and when?

COACHING THE TEAM

We often hear salespeople complaining that they hate sales meetings because, frankly, they tend to just be a monologue. The Sales Manager drones on and on, yakking about policies and procedures, when all the salespeople really want out of the meetings is personal development. They want to learn ways to be better at what they do.

Sales Managers should ask themselves: "At the end of this meeting, will my team be thinking that this was worth their time, that what they heard will bring them more success and more money?" If so, then the Sales Manager truly did a great job of conducting the sales meeting. Unfortunately, salespeople often leave meetings feeling that they have been deprived of time that they could have spent in front of prospects and customers.

The ultimate goal of the sales meeting should be, quite simply, to enhance sales. Anything else that Sales Managers feel they need to communicate should be done through some other venue, such as e-mail or a report on a CRM dashboard.

At the meeting, let the focus be on personal and professional development so that the salespeople can do a better job in the field.

SCORING PLAY: LEADING CONSISTENT AND EFFECTIVE MEETINGS

The End Zone Benefit of all meetings, whether team or individual, is to drive the activities and progress needed to achieve your sales goals. Regularly setting the focus, behavior, expectations, and actions necessary is the best way to help your team members reach their personal and company goals.

The most effective meetings should do the following:

- Be held in an established sequence of quarterly, monthly, weekly and one-on-one progress meetings

- Have time dedicated to developing greater skills in your team

- Be planned, with the agenda sent in advance, so that you can stay on course and keep it productive

- Keep everyone educated, aligned, and accountable to deliver the performance necessary to achieve their goals

- Reach conclusions and assign action items

- Repeat your core message regularly

- Have a main purpose

- Be short, purposeful, and structured with time limits–end on time

- Recap the main action items: distribute notes, action items, and timelines to all attendees after the meeting

- Follow up on action items

SCORING PLAY CONTINUED

- Start with recognition of individuals or the team

- Include a pop quiz on the team's sales knowledge, skills, and messages they should know

- Have a Role Practice: it's best to calendar these regularly and vary the topics

- Brainstorm and problem-solve issues that are common to the team

- Work on building or adding to your Sales Success Guide

- Touch on at least five, if not more, of the following topics: prospecting, questions, Active Listening, time management, Goal Achievement Plans, e-mail, voice mails, qualifying, opening, presenting, closing, follow-up, differentiation, creating COIs, RFPs, differentiation, product training, objections, reaching and selling to the C-suite, gatekeepers

Team members should leave each meeting feeling energized, educated, and ready to take their selling to a higher and more effective level.

REVIEWING THE PLAY:

- What is the nature of your sales meetings?

- How frequently do you hold them, and what content do you cover?

- Does each seller do goal and status reviews with the team?

- How much time is spent on training to develop greater selling skills?

- Do you discuss case studies/Success Stories?

- Do your people "get to go" to sales meetings, or do they "have to go"?

Attitude is everything. You want your people to feel energized as they go into a meeting, not dragging and wishing they were elsewhere.

Therefore, think about what you might do to keep their eyes from glazing over. For example, housekeeping items such as number crunching, reporting, and the like, could more easily be handled via CRM or e-mail.

SCORING PLAY CONTINUED

On a scale of one to ten, with ten being "all the time," how much of your sales meetings are currently being spent on training and growing your sales team? If your answer is anything less than an eight, you really need to take a hard look at how you can improve those meetings. Focus on skill development and High Payoff Activities. You will soon see the results, and the meetings will not be such a drag.

COACHING THE INDIVIDUAL

"How do I motivate the people on my sales team?"

We are asked that question everywhere we go. The simple and only answer is "Hire them that way!" We can create an environment—a company culture—that unleashes a salesperson's motivation, but motivation is intrinsic to each individual. When you do something that you *want* to achieve as opposed to it being *required*, when you accomplish a personal goal, then you feel motivated. You get more done because you've achieved your "why."

A Sales Manager must have a development plan specific to each team member that speaks to their "why," their motivation, and then consistently follow up with that plan with regular one-on-one meetings.

Salespeople come to organizations with a variety of backgrounds and experiences, therefore a cookie-cutter approach will not work. It is important to sit down with each individual and talk about his or her personal goals. Satisfying the personal goals of the salespeople will also motivate them to be more interested in pursuing the organization's business goals.

Personal Action Plans, covering one-month, two-month, and quarterly spans, should be drafted with specific aims, and reviews need to be scheduled. Refer to these as progress reviews, not performance reviews. At least once a quarter, sit down for a couple of hours with each individual and talk about what worked and what did not work and what should be done going forward. Examine every team member's sales pipeline and Touch System. Take a close look at territory planning and management. Minimum standards need to be negotiated and agreed on with each individual to secure buy-in. Customization is the key.

CREATING A 1:1 PROGRESS REVIEW

One-on-one meetings are focused on how to train, grow, and develop individual members of the sales team and are primarily forward-looking, pivoting off of the individual's recent performance history. A constructive meeting should leverage the Sales Manager's note file for each salesperson, which should include his or her Sales Process Scorecard progress history. (Read more on the Sales Process Scorecard in Chapter 2.)

Progress reviews are for people who are serious about achieving their goals.

Progress reviews are designed to help support, measure, and encourage each of your sales team members to achieve their goals. By conducting these meetings a minimum of once per quarter, you are actively holding them accountable for turning those goals from wishes to reality.

Research shows us that people with:

- Written goals,

- Commitment to action, and

- Regular progress reports and an accountability system

produce 78 percent better goal achievement than people who just think about goals.[6] How much more do you want to succeed at your goals?

6   "Study Focuses on Strategies for Achieving Goals, Resolutions," Dominican University of California, http://www.dominican.edu/dominicannews/study-highlights-strategies-for-achieving-goals.

SCORING PLAY:

Take a minute to write down at least one of your goals and then answer the following questions:

1. **What is your goal** (period/year)?
2. **Where are you now** (currently/pacing toward goal)?
3. **Where do you want to be/believe you will be** (period/year)?

Minimum Standards of Performance

What are the Key Activities and skills required to achieve your goal?

Key Targets

- Key account development of your top ten targets

Your High Payoff Activities

- Key actions you can take to make this happen

It requires a lot of time and commitment on the part of both the manager and team member to keep these meetings on track and Sales Process Scorecards up-to-date, but effective sales management is a hands-on job. Those Managers who do commit to maintaining these tasks see remarkable improvement in their salespeople. The real key is that Managers commit to a robust management plan and then have the discipline to follow through and get it done.

COACHING IN THE FIELD

Being actively involved with the development and scaling up of team members doesn't stop with in-house meetings. Sales Managers need to be engaged with their people in the field where they meet customers and prospects, as well. One of the ways that they can do that is through what we call the Three Types of Field Calls:

1. Joint

2. Training

3. Coaching

The Joint Call

The Sales Manager and the salesperson participate equally in a joint call, after which they have a debriefing on what went right, what went wrong, and what could have been done better. Then together they come up with a design for how they will handle such a call the next time out. This is a highly valuable type of interaction, and it is the joint call that we tend to see whenever we observe Sales Managers out in the field with their salespeople.

The Training Call

In this type of call, the Sales Manager accompanies the salesperson onto the field, but it is the manager who actually conducts the call. The purpose is for the salesperson to observe how the manager handles matters. After the call, they talk about how the presentation went: Did the salesperson fully understand the procedure? What might be the next steps in winning over the account?

The Coaching Call

The coaching call can be the most difficult call of the three. Again, the Sales Manager accompanies the salesperson on the call, but this time the salesperson conducts it without any assistance. No matter how that call is going, whether very well or dismally, the manager does not intervene. Managers can find it difficult not to jump in for the save when a call is going south, but they must remember their role: it is not to grow sales but to grow salespeople. The manager might want to come in like some great white knight to save the day, but what does that really accomplish? What happens the next day, on the next call, when the salesperson is alone and has not learned from experience? The manager needs to be willing to lose a sale to help the salesperson grow.

Debriefing the Three Calls

On the first two types of field calls, the debriefing comes right after the call. However, on coaching calls, the Sales Manager should let the salesperson know that the debriefing will not be conducted until the end of the day. By maintaining silence and not immediately evaluating the salesperson's performance, the manager will get a clearer picture during successive calls of how that salesperson operates in the field. The manager will more readily pick up on weaknesses that need to be corrected.

CONTINUOUS COACHING

Coaching is not something you do a little here and a little there. It's a continuous process that requires regular check-ins. Much of this is covered in the team and one-on-one meetings, but a good Sales Manager and coach should be able to address the following 10 Key Areas for Continuous Coaching on an ongoing basis:

1. **Goal Achievement Plans**

   □ Have specific goals been set for the year with a "backward-thinking" plan of action created to achieve them?

   □ Have they been updated to reflect the market and company momentum?

   □ Are they set at Minimum, Realistic, and Stretch levels?

   □ Have minimum standards of performance needed to hit the goals been negotiated and agreed on with each salesperson to secure buy-in?

2. **Ongoing Feedback**

   □ Are suggestions for improvement communicated in such a way that the salesperson will be receptive and collaborate?

   □ Have you offered to help the salesperson develop and grow?

3. **Two-Way Communication**

   □ Have you developed an effective working relationship with each salesperson, and is it uniquely suited to each person?

   □ Is communication truly open? Can salespeople disagree or explore without anxiety?

4. **Day-to-Day Coaching**

   □ Is some portion of each day spent asking questions of your sales team?

   □ Is it planned? Does this activity include note taking?

   □ Is follow-up action being taken as discussed?

- For each salesperson, can you point to an instance when day-to-day coaching paid off? Do you note what they best respond to?

5. Team Meetings

- Do you conduct regularly scheduled training meetings, dedicated solely to developing stronger selling skills in your team?

- Does each salesperson do goal and status reviews with the team?

- Do you discuss tough Objection Response situations, challenging case studies and Success Stories?

6. Personal Improvement Plan

- Can you name two developmental experiences for each salesperson over the last six months?

- Do you have a specific personal improvement plan for each salesperson, negotiated and agreed on between the two of you?

7. Personal Growth

- Do you know the aspirations and ambitions of each of your people?

- What motivates each one? Are you delivering your part toward making those things happen?

8. Empowerment

- Have you practiced asking, "What are your thoughts/opinion?" as opposed to solving the problem?

- Do salespeople have the ability to make commitments on the spot? If mistakes occur, are the salespeople supported and the experiences viewed as learning opportunities?

9. Recognizing Results

- Are sales-production reports distributed and discussed?

- Does each salesperson know his or her standing?

- Are the top performers rewarded, while encouraging others to achieve at higher levels?

10. Assistance

- Are you there for your salespeople—proactively?

- Are you regularly reviewing goals, plans, and performance?

- Are you providing regular encouragement and suggestions to improve?

- Are you actively looking for ways to reduce your salespeople's time on low-payoff tasks that an assistant can do?

The Playbook needs to encompass just how this will all happen, personalized to your industry, company, and culture. But in every case, whether you are meeting one-on-one to review progress or coaching in team meetings or in the field, you are actively engaging with your salespeople around goals you agree on—growing sales and getting great results for the company. Your team's shared goals are part of your company culture, which we cover next.

CHAPTER 9

CULTURE AND TEAM BUILDING

 **CHAPTER GAME PLAN**

To build a winning culture, you need to start with yourself as the Sales Manager. Are you committing one of the Three Sins of Sales Management? Are you committed to embracing and developing the three key roles of a Sales Manager? In this chapter, we share how Sales Managers can best position themselves to lead their teams for maximum results, as well as the four systems proven to build a winning team and culture.

THE THREE ROLES OF A SALES MANAGER

Sales Managers play three distinct and important roles: Manager, Coach, and Leader.

The **Manager** role is to help the team be efficient and stay on task. Managers monitor the workflow efficiency from marketing and lead generation through sales and into customer-fulfillment operations. They look for slowdowns and obstacles and remove them so that salespeople can stay focused on their High Payoff Activities of actually selling. Managing includes measuring, tracking, and reporting useful sales data.

As a **Coach**, you are a developer of talent, working to grow the Quantity and Quality of the team. Coaches develop individuals into stronger performers. They identify what's working well and what is not, and what improvements can be made and how to do it. They connect with salespeople one-on-one and know they need to stretch and grow people beyond their comfort zone to become more productive.

We also believe the Sales Manager needs to be a true **Leader**. An essential role, it begins with vision for the sales team that aligns directly with the company's one-, three-, and five-year vision and beyond for its strategy, direction, and growth. As an effective leader, where do you want your team to grow and go—in the next quarter, the next six months, the next year? What needs to be in place to get there? People want to be a part of something bigger than themselves. Invite them to be a part of it, and show them how they are needed to contribute. Give them a compelling opportunity worth pursuing.

We have mentioned company culture throughout the book in relation to building a sales team. The connection is vital because a unified culture helps make it possible to get things done in a company and keep things on track in the Sales Process. An effective sales team stays on the same page, and **if there is no clear leadership and established culture, the rest of your job will be so much harder**.

As the Sales Manager, you set the tone for the culture, energy, and pace of the team. You can energize, motivate, and build excitement around the sales team by making your work culture fun and empowering. Allow people to show what they can do. Turn them loose. Give them autonomy to prove themselves and how they can contribute to the team's bigger vision. It takes a strong leader to nurture a team that way, but you reap an abundance of energy and drive.

You as the Sales Manager are dealing with the same elements as the people on the front line, but your perspective is much different. The salesperson is out making plays while **you are building a plan and strategy for the game, the season, and beyond.** You want the right people in the right places doing the right things. If you can accomplish that, you will have a winning team.

Let's take a look at how you can grow your team to greater heights as manager, leader, and coach by examining how those roles relate to the Sales Playbook element: People, Processes, and Practices.

But first, can you say what kind of a Sales Manager you are today?

PLAYBOOK RESOURCES:
SEE SALES MANAGER PLAYBOOK VIDEO, Sales Manager's Job
inSITE-app & http://leveragesalescoach.com/resources

ARE YOU A MULTIPLIER OR A DIMINISHER?

In Liz Wiseman's book *Multipliers: How the Best Leaders Make Everyone Smarter*, she describes two types of leaders. The "Multipliers" and the "Diminishers." The Multipliers lift performance of the team by making the team around them smarter, sharper, and more productive. They describe a clear vision for their company and team and invite each person to step up to contribute to make it happen. They challenge everyone to be better by asking provoking, tough questions that deserve, even demand, them to deliver better answers. They lead to engage people at a higher level through their head, heart, and guts, which drives greater performance. The Multiplier leader makes people on the team want to do more, work smarter, perform better, and achieve more.[7]

Applying this idea to growing your business, if the Sales Manager is primarily focused on "growing sales," often by doing the selling himself or herself, there is no Multiplier Effect. However, when the Sales Manager focuses on and is successful at training, growing, and developing a sales team to perform better, their efforts are multiplied together.

---

7   Liz Wiseman, *Multipliers: How the Best Leaders Make Everyone Smarter* (New York: HarperCollins, 2010).

A WORD FROM JACK . . .
THE THREE SINS OF SALES MANAGEMENT (AND HOW TO AVOID THEM)

In the two decades I've been traveling the world teaching sales and sales management, I have seen so many small-to-medium companies struggling. Why? Because they are guilty of committing one or more of what I call the Three Sins of Sales Management:

1. THE CEO IS ALSO THE SALES MANAGER.

Being a CEO is a demanding, full-time job, and so is the role of a Sales Manager. It is impossible for one person to fulfill both roles effectively. When the CEO also serves as a Sales Manager, it's the same as having a part-time person in both roles. That is, every moment you spend doing your CEO duties, you are by definition holding back the growth of your business.

If you want your business to grow, you must grow your sales, and to do that, you need to have a manager who can make that a priority. Given all that we've covered so far in this book, the job of a Sales Manager is clearly a full-time job that is crucial to your revenue growth. With the right person in this role, the position should pay for itself in a year or less. I've never known a businessperson to say, "I am so excited about my company's prospects that I am going to go about it part time."

2. THE BEST SALESPERSON BECOMES THE SALES MANAGER.

Making your best salesperson the Sales Manager can work, but it often doesn't. In fact, it's a prime example of the Peter Principle, where employees are raised to their level of incompetence. The most common result is that you lose your best salesperson and wind up with a mediocre Sales Manager.

It's not that the newly elevated salesperson is poor at his job; it's just that the role of Sales Manager requires an entirely different set of skills. The salesperson prospects for new business and maintains contacts and customer relationships; the Sales Manager recruits, hires, trains, coaches, develops, manages, and builds both individuals and the team.

By moving top-performing salespeople away from that role, you're essentially doing them a disservice by placing them in a position that they neither know how to do nor want to do. In the end, you may end up losing your best salesperson altogether–and maybe to the competition!

One other note: We encourage you to stop calling it a promotion. This creates a sense among all on the team that they should strive for this role. We like saying it this way: "Protect them from themselves, they know not what they ask."

3. THE SALES MANAGER *HAS* TO SELL.

This is likely the worst of the Three Sins of Sales Management. It's a variation on the second sin, but worse because the Sales Manager is forced to divide his or her time between managing the sales team and selling in order to generate personal income. Not only does the sales team wind up largely ignored or left as a lower priority, but the manager often winds up competing with the sales team for business.

How do you avoid these Three Sins of Sales Management? You make **growing your sales team in Quantity and Quality** the Sales Manager's full-time job and number- one priority.

JACK DALY

PLAYBOOK RESOURCES:
SEE SALES MANAGER PLAYBOOK VIDEO, The 3 Sins of Sales Management
inSITE-app & http://leveragesalescoach.com/resources

A WORD FROM JACK . . .
PROACTIVE SALES MANAGEMENT

NEW LIFE AT THE WORKSTATION

As I looked out over the room, I could see the problem at a glance.

The company had brought me in to see if I could improve the conversion rate of its salespeople. They were all together under one roof at an internal sales center, also known as an inside-sales call center.

The workstations were arranged in rows. It appeared that there were twelve teams, with Sales Managers at the head of each row of ten stations. In my first day there, I observed that the Managers were sitting at their desks all day long. There was little interaction with the salespeople.

We set about to make a big change there. We taught them the systems and processes that Sales Managers should use to increase the capability of their salespeople. We directly tied the Sales Managers' compensation to the team results. Within one week, we doubled the conversion rate overall. All we had to do to enhance the salespeople's productivity was implement a successful Playbook that got the Sales Managers away from their desks and actively engaged with their teams.

JACK DALY

BECOMING A SALES *LEADER*: SETTING THE VISION, GOALS, AND EXPECTATIONS FOR YOUR TEAM

As a Sales Manager, being an effective leader is one of the most important components of your role. You need to be able to lead your team in the direction of success by setting clear goals and standards, establishing a compelling Vision that everyone can get behind and excited about, by building a winning culture.

Planning Your Vision

Every Sales Manager needs a Vision for the sales team that reflects not only the Vision of the company but also a Vision that is relevant to the team and gets them energized. A solid Vision makes everyone *want* to get involved and ask how they can help make it happen, while at the same time raising the bar on team performance, encouraging team members to achieve higher and higher goals.

PLAYBOOK RESOURCES:
SEE SALES MANAGER PLAYBOOK VIDEO, Vision, Communicate the Vision
inSITE-app & http://leveragesalescoach.com/resources

How to Communicate an Effective Vision:

- Define your overall Vision, goals, and expectations for the year, including

    □ This year's budget expectations; and

- Goal Achievement Plan expectations.

- Commit to a culture ("how we do things around here") that centers on setting and achieving goals and has a tone of "work hard, smart, and have fun doing it!"

- Include the Sales Manager's clear Vision with strategy, direction, culture, and goals with an Action Plan to reach them, as well as new Processes and Tools to drive greater success. This helps to outline a team-growth game plan.

- Build team buy-in to want to work smarter.

- Set a productive tone in the role as the Sales Manager where you

  - Execute on their expectations; and

  - Energize your people about **where** you're going and **why** they would want to be on board.

- Focus on what matters to elevate the team.

FOUR SYSTEMS PROVEN TO BUILD A WINNING CULTURE

A truly *energized* sales culture is the most important, most impactful, biggest leverage play that a company can use to grow its sales performance, yet it's the least understood and least acted-on area in the entire sales arena. Jack Daly built six companies to national success driven by an energized sales culture in each. What can we learn from this?

> *If you get the culture right, everything becomes easier. If you don't get it right, all is hard.*
>
> **JACK DALY**

Whether it's the Super Bowl or the World Series, when the winning team celebrates in the locker room, the players often say something like this: "**What made the difference for us is that we're a family**. We care about each other. It doesn't feel like anything is out of the ordinary to go out of our way. We don't have an attitude like 'I'm a guard and I don't play a forward position.' We help out wherever we can for the benefit of the whole."

That kind of attitude is what companies need to develop. You want people who don't isolate themselves by role or team but instead look for the **overall success** of the organization and the customer. That's when the magic happens.

> *If company and team leaders make culture a high priority, the people in our companies will willingly come in early, stay late, work weekends. They will see their work as far more than a job.*
>
> **JACK DALY**
>
> *Culture eats strategy for breakfast.*
>
> **PETER DRUCKER**
>
> *The two resources your competitors can't copy are people and culture.*
>
> **ERIC FLAMHOLTZ**

A WORD FROM JACK . . .
MOTIVATING FROM A YOUNG AGE

When I was twelve years old I took over a newspaper route from a previous newspaper boy. It was forty-two customers. In the two days of working together before he passed the baton to me, it was obvious to me that he was satisfied with the money he was making and stopped selling. After he left, I put in a focused selling effort that resulted in building the route to 275 customers in one year. Not wanting to deliver 275 papers in the night and cold of the Philadelphia area, I hired five kids under twelve years old to deliver the papers. I went on to be recognized as newspaper boy of the year. I then convinced the company to let me coach five kids each Saturday at a rate of $100 for four hours of coaching. That was 1962, and very few people were making that kind of money back then, let alone a thirteen-year-old.

So do you really think you need to "motivate" a person like that to sell in your company? All you need to do is build a winning culture that unleashes such enthusiasm. The key is to get your new-hire salesperson candidates to cite and discuss similar Success Stories in their lives. No one has ever had to "motivate" me; I came into this world rip roaring and ready to go! Find those people while interviewing, and watch your revenues grow!

JACK DALY

As you work to motivate your team, how do you develop a strong culture that will promote performance? That's the challenge. You want a culture that is compelling and energizing, unified, and collaborative. You want to promote a healthy competition among your people, while also encouraging them to contribute ideas and support to one another.

We've found that creating this culture of motivation and success in your sales team can be done with the use of **Four Proven Systems**: Recognition, Communication, Empowerment, and Personal and Professional Development.

System 1: Recognition

Your people are starving for recognition, so why not feed them? Recognition doesn't have to be done with money; small gestures go a long way. These could include a handwritten note from time to time, letting them know that you appreciate their efforts and accomplishments, or popping a congratulatory e-mail to a salesperson who has just closed a deal. Recognition can be done systematically on the company dashboard, where you recognize the go-getters and the winners, or you can offer recognition at weekly or monthly meetings and in your internal newsletters. Once a week or month or quarter, you could praise your Top Producers or your most improved ones, calling out specific successes that were exceptional. To learn more about these recognition strategies, read through the methods Jack covers in Hyper Sales Growth in Chapter 4: Culture by Design, Not Default.

Sound good? Then implement it. No one on your team feels "overly recognized" for their work. In coaching, we find that personal recognition is often more motivating than money. Be prompt and timely to recognize people for the actions and results you want more of. Just be sure it's legitimate praise that has been earned and is not perceived as superficial or meaningless. How about starting a meeting with a standing ovation for someone who did something exceptional? It costs little or nothing to offer genuine recognition, but the return on investment is tremendous. When your people know that your eyes are open and that you appreciate that they're doing the right things and exceeding expectations, they will want to step up to perform at that higher standard.

System 2: Communication

Communication, too, is essential for a healthy culture. People perform far better when they feel informed and included.

We know a group that gets together for a ten-minute huddle every day at 10:55 a.m. Anyone who has anything to say that is relevant and beneficial to the group is welcome to speak up. We recently participated in that huddle to see what it was all about, and fifteen contributors mentioned things that were going on at the company and issues that needed to be addressed. Some people offered recognition to others, as the group applauded and cheered. Everyone knew that the entire session needed to be concluded within ten minutes. After that brief interlude, they headed back to their desks feeling energized and aware.

How does your team communicate on a regular basis? Certainly there is no shortage of methods. You can communicate at the sales meetings, of course, but you can also keep in touch through phone calls and e-mails and snail mail and texting. You can post on your website. Perhaps you could speak one-on-one at the end of the day with someone who has been struggling.

The biggest complaint that Managers are likely to hear is that people feel as if they do not know what is going on. It is the classic breakdown between the left hand and the right. Just as with recognition, it seems that there can never be enough communication.

By keeping your team members informed and including them in the decision-making process, you can vastly improve their performance and motivation.

System 3: Empowerment

Salespeople should feel empowered to make decisions on their own. Few things are more frustrating to both salespeople and potential customers when the regularly recurring answer is "Let me talk to my manager and I'll get back with you." If you don't trust your salespeople in the field, then you need to bring people on board that you do trust.

Giving team members this autonomy in the field not only helps them feel empowered, but it takes more off of the Sales Manager's plate by eliminating the need to check off every little decision so that a team member can take action.

If you have the mindset of a leader, you know that your number-one job is growing talent so that your salespeople become more productive on their own.

Trust your people to do the right thing. Give them the systems and processes they need to do the job properly, and then let them do it. You will see the results.

System 4: Personal and Professional Development

All team members need to understand what is expected of them to help the company be successful, as well as what the company will do to help them become more successful as individuals.

This calls for concerted and consistent efforts in personal and professional development. It is part of the Sales Manager's duties to make sure that the team and all of its members are generously offered opportunities to hone their skills so that they can become the best that they can be.

A WORD FROM JACK . . .
VOICING OPPORTUNITIES

At twenty-eight years old, I was reporting to the president and CEO of a national financial company. Now, my goal since I was a teenager was to be the CEO of such a firm by the age of thirty. One day I got a call from the CEO, who told me that I was one of the finest he had ever had as a direct report, and he asked whether I ever thought of what I wanted to be when I grew up.

Since he was in his midforties at the time, I decided to tell him the full story. It was a risk, but since I was already job searching for that CEO role, I thought why not "go for it." The CEO told me to stop searching, and we would sit down and craft a succession plan. In the process, he said that if I learned the areas I was soft or weak on by the time I was thirty, he would toss me the keys and move on to other things. By thirty that is exactly what happened.

From that day on, I knew the value of showing my team the opportunities and working with them to achieve such opportunities, and the culture throughout the company always benefited.

JACK DALY

Have you talked about a career path with each person on your team and mapped it out? Have you talked to your people about what they really want, both professionally and personally? Some people might want to be president of the company, but most will have less ambitious but quite honorable goals. When you are clear about what they want, you are better able to support them, and in doing so, not only are you offering them recognition and appreciation, but you are showing them respect.

Employees feel respected, for example, when you send them to a seminar or workshop that is relevant to their goals. They feel energized and motivated. Help your people to explore their career ambitions, and also help them to see any weaknesses where they might need further development. Show that you care. Give them the opportunity for growth. They will appreciate it, and performance will increase.

PLAYBOOK RESOURCES:
SEE SALES MANAGER PLAYBOOK VIDEO, 4 Legs to a Strong Culture
inSITE-app & http://leveragesalescoach.com/resources

TEAM CONTESTS: RECOGNIZING AND CELEBRATING ACHIEVEMENTS AND SUCCESS

Holding sales contests is a healthy and exciting way to motivate team members, reward them for their successes, and drive sales at the same time. Check out what this client of ours did to drive revenue up almost half a million for the year!

Successful Sales Contest Set Up:

A manufacturing client wanted to create an exciting contest for its nationwide sales team in February 2014, themed and timed around the 2014 Winter Olympics in Russia. To challenge the sales team to drive extra business for the month, individuals could win prizes of Gold (a one-ounce, pure-gold coin), Silver (a twenty-ounce bar of silver), and Bronze (a bronze statue). Other individual winners achieving certain levels could win a five-ounce bar of silver.

Management and Leadership:

The director of sales organized it and built real excitement around the Olympics and excellent performance, the contest and prizes, and the company's desire to generate a big kick start on new business for the calendar year. The director and Sales Managers promoted the contest kickoff and progress to the team often. The management team gave it life, energizing it with fun banter in sales meetings and e-mails and working with team members to help get deals closed. Plus, they kept real-time tracking and communication of the standings and progress in a team dashboard.

Results:

The sales team overdelivered big time! In the month of February alone, they added over $400,000 for the year in booked new revenue, far more than what was anticipated. Both individuals and regional teams surged with stellar performances that were emphatically recognized, rewarded, and publicly celebrated. It proved to everyone on the team the high importance of the culture and team-building elements covered in this chapter: focus, motivation, and commitment to achieve a goal; the power of fun, excitement, and teamwork; and the real benefits of Proactive Pipeline Management practices to help them advance and win more business in the future.

Go to http://jackdalywebcastseries.net/ to see a one-hour webcast for many more ideas and suggestions for street-proven contests and prizes.

Next, we return to the subject we started with in Chapter 1: People, but this time from your perspective as a Sales Manager who already has learned to be not only a manager but also a coach and leader.

CHAPTER 10

PEOPLE:
DEVELOPING YOUR TALENT POOL

CHAPTER GAME PLAN

Do you have the right people, in the right seats, doing the right things?

If your company has low turnover, that's not necessarily a good thing. Low turnover of Top Producers is great, but you also need to weed out the poor performers until your team consists entirely of top performers—"A" players who are on top of their game and willing to contribute consistently.

Creating this team, however, is not something you can do overnight or even quickly. There is a cost to not having all of the seats on your team filled, but the cost of having the wrong people in those seats can cost you far more.

THE TRUE EXPENSE OF A HIRING MISTAKE

According to an article in SAP's online magazine *Digitalist*, the monetary cost of a bad hire can range from $25,000 to more than $800,000, depending on a variety of factors, only one of which is what that person earns in salary.[8]

And those monetary costs don't take into account the bigger picture. A poor hire also results in the loss of:

1. Resources

The most immediate and evident loss in resources is money, but you also have to take into account the loss of time and energy. The time spent planning, finding, recruiting, hiring, training, and ramping up that employee, as well as the energy spent on all of these factors, is a significant cost. Worse, you have to start the process all over again at the risk of repeating that mistake unless your hiring process changes.

2. Opportunity

The time, energy, and money wasted on that poor hire wasn't invested wisely elsewhere. The wrong person may never produce any return on investment, and even if they do, it will likely take far longer than it would with the right person in that role.

3. Culture and Momentum

In some cases, a poor hire can also do serious damage to a previously productive team and culture, causing angst, negative energy, and even turnover of your more-productive players. At the very least, the momentum of building, growing, and moving ahead with your team will stagnate.

---

8   Collins, Ava, "The Cost of a Bad Hire and How to Avoid One," *Digitalist*, January 27, 2015, http://www.digitalistmag.com/future-of-work/2015/01/27/the-cost-of-a-bad-hire-and-how-to-avoid-one-02110549.

ARE YOU MAKING THE TOUGH CALLS?

Sales leaders need to regularly and actively assess the makeup of their team. Sales statistics show that the bottom 25 percent of salespeople generate less than 6 percent of the sales. Meanwhile, the top quartile produces 60 percent or more of the sales. If the bottom quartile is dragging your team performance down, then it's time for you to make a tough call as to whether you have the right players on the team. Some may not make the cut.

THE VALUE OF HIRING RIGHT

To avoid these costly mistakes and ensure that your investment will pay off, it's critically important to be sure that you get the right person to fit the position needed. This means hiring slowly and taking the time to thoroughly and carefully bring them onboard. Building your team is not an event—it's a process, and that process needs to be handled as carefully and thoroughly as any other aspect of your business.

Before you start the search for new key players, however, you need to assess the ones you already have. Underperformers will only drag the team down, and it's up to you whether it's worth the effort to "coach them up" according to your performance standards or "coach them out" and bring in team members who are ready and willing to step up to the game.

SALES MANAGER PLAY: THE A-B-C-D TEAM ASSESSMENT

To get, grow, and keep winners on their team, a Sales Manager needs to regularly and actively evaluate the talent on the team to optimize productivity. One clear way to get, grow, and keep winners is to evaluate team members and rank each according to his or her performance. The results can help the Sales Manager assess where he or she needs to focus more time and energy and where some necessary cuts need to be made.

1. Evaluate and rank.

Start by assessing and ranking your team according to the A-B-C-D definitions provided in Chapter 1. To recap, these are:

- **A = Achievers**. They get it done. They nearly always find a way to achieve their goal. They respond to a challenge and make things happen. They somehow find a way to win.

- **B = Be Better**. They're not yet "A" players, but they seriously want to become one. They're always learning, taking action, and striving to be better.

- **C = Content**. Content. Complacent. Satisfied. Most "C" players really don't want to be an "A" player. Sure, they'd like to make more money. But they aren't willing to work hard enough or smart enough to make more.

- **D = Don't Move Much**. Don't sell much. "Dogs on the porch." They will stay there as long as they are allowed to hang out and keep getting fed. Often they'll keep their head low so they don't get noticed. Usually they are really "nice, pleasant people."

2. Deal with underperformers.

Once you've assessed all of your team members, review the bottom quartile of your team and determine what results they're producing.

- Which ones do you truly believe could improve with some additional, focused coaching?

- Which ones are simply not cutting it?

For that bottom 25 percent, the message should be clear: get moving or get out. Healthy competition will either breathe new life into previously poor performers or give them the opportunity to pursue something else.

When it comes to evaluating whether or not those poor performers are worth the additional investment of time, effort, and money, you should consider them in light of the two most important aspects of a productive mindset from Chapter 1:

1. **Are they Coachable?** That is, are they open, teachable, and willing to learn new ideas?

2. **Are they willing to Take Action on ideas?** Do they take action when directed? Do they do their homework and practice before performing? Are they willing to quickly test, implement, and execute new ideas? Are they always looking to improve?

3. Make "A" ranking a goal for every team member.

Now that you know where your team members stand in terms of performance, what can you, as a Sales Manager, do to bring your "B" and "C" performers, as well as those "D" performers that you chose to keep on, up to an "A" player ranking? What can the team do to help these members improve?

The time, effort, and money needed to train, grow, and develop these individuals will be a significant investment, but if you believe in them—if they show those two **all-important strengths of being Coachable and willing to Take Action on ideas**—then investing in the improvement of current team members is far more cost effective than bringing in new blood.

Conversely, keeping poor performers who are unable or unwilling to improve can cost you far more than any hiring and onboarding process.

PLAYBOOK RESOURCES:
SEE SALES MANAGER PLAYBOOK VIDEO, A-B-C Ranking of Salespeople
inSITE-app & http://leveragesalescoach.com/resources

BRINGING IN NEW BLOOD

Before you start posting openings on your website, social networks, and various job sites, take the time to do a careful and thorough profile of the open position. For example:

- What does someone need to do to be effective and excel in this position?

- What does success look like for this role?

- What needs to be done every day in this job?

- What are the critical must-have traits for this role that are nonnegotiable?

At Leverage Sales Coaching, we use a **Profile the Position** tool set that helps employers pinpoint what it takes to excel at a particular job, starting with something we call a Traits List. A completed Traits List will help you create a clear position profile (what *this* job requires to excel) and write a better, more accurate, and more compelling job description and will provide helpful language for creating a stronger job posting. Additionally, the Traits List can be a valuable tool during the interview process, helping you assess the candidates and ensure that they're the right fit—as well as make sure your company is the best fit for them.

In the next section we explain how to use the Traits List, then walk through the **staffing process of recruiting, hiring, onboarding, training and ramp-up, and the thirty-sixty-ninety-day Success Plan**.

Staffing #1: The Traits List

To use the Profile the Position tool, start by choosing five key areas that make up the position you're looking to fill. In most cases, we start with these general areas:

1. Attitude

2. Skills

3. Activities

4. Day-in-the-life

5. Results

Next, choose nine character traits from the following list for each of these five key areas within that position, being sure to rank them from most to least important.

TIP: Your top performers in this role also offer clues for success. Model them to recruit more people like them.

- Personal integrity/intellectual honesty

- Sales skill/people skills/relationship manager

- Vision/mission/goals

- Success patterns/high achiever

- Self-disciplined/sense of urgency

- Good work organization

- Goal oriented/money hungry through value

- Positive outlook and attitude

- High self-esteem

- Industry/company/product knowledge

- Client market-share oriented

- Team player/independent yet supportive

- Understands self-responsibility

- Assertive social style/follow-through

- Continuing-education achievements

- Public-speaking ability/communicator

- Generous with thank-yous

- Professional manner

- Computer literate

A WORD FROM JACK . . .
DEDICATION TO SUCCESS

After I graduated from college with an accounting degree, I went to work for Arthur Andersen, one of the big eight accounting firms of the time. To be hired by one of those big eight was considered a tremendous accolade, and I had offers from seven of them.

I chose Arthur Andersen for two main reasons. I felt a strong indication that Arthur Andersen was going to be interested in me personally and professionally as they put me through five interviews before I was hired.

"We want to make sure that you are the right fit for us," I was told, "and that we're the right fit for you." It was all about finding a way to position me in a company where I would grow. I could see that the people at that company were interested in me as much as I was interested in them. I attribute my success today in business partially on the grounding that I learned at Arthur Andersen.

The second main reason was that they said they had just bought a college in St. Charles, Illinois, near Chicago. They were going to use that as their learning center. I had to go there for three weeks of intensive training before they would let me go out in the field to meet with a client. I was expected to learn the Arthur Andersen systems and processes that would help me be more successful.

I had gone to a terrific college and done quite well in my accounting courses. But in those three weeks at the Arthur Andersen school, I learned more about accounting than in all four years of college. In school I had learned theory. Here, I was learning real-world applications of that theory.

The point that I am making here: If you hope to attract top performers, your attention to personal and professional development will go a long way. I had seven high-powered offers, and what tipped the scale for me were the personal interest and the learning opportunity. You can be sure that your prospective salespeople, if they are hungry for success, will also be looking closely at how much you seem to care about where they are going in their careers. If they see that you are serious, they are far more likely not only to sign up, but to stay on.

PS: I suspect star high school athletes go through a similar process in selecting colleges pursuing them. Model such behavior!

JACK DALY

TOOLS FOR FINDING THE RIGHT-FIT TALENT FOR ANY POSITION

At Leverage Sales Coaching we have created a full Profile the Position tool set designed to coach and help you attract, recruit, and hire the right people. Also, we offer different levels of talent-assessment tools to help you understand the unique talent and strengths of candidates. We can interview candidates to help you select the right talent, if needed.

For information on talent assessments to get the right candidates for the job, contact us at (800) 565-6516, or e-mail dan@leveragesalescoach.com.

Staffing #2: Recruiting

Successfully bringing on new talent is not something that can be done overnight—not without risking the significant cost of a poor hire. From narrowing the field of candidates to the steps taken to ensure that they are fully trained, a deliberate and methodical recruit-to-ramp-up process is key.

- **Recruit, don't absorb.** If one of your Top Producers leaves, avoid absorbing (moving up) less-effective sales talent because it's quicker or because you believe they're more experienced. Instead, ongoing recruiting of Top Producers is the best way to build the strongest sales team.

- **Recruit for skills, hire for attitude.** Recruit top sales performers with the right mindset, attitude, and behavioral drives, especially those willing to do the Key Activities needed to get results.

- **Constantly court talent.** Top Producers typically aren't looking for a job, and if they are, they have plenty of opportunities available to them. To build your team up with the best of the best, keep a working list of Top Producer candidates, and proactively court them so that they know your company is ready for them when they want to make a move.

- **Look beyond your industry.** From our experience, you will have more success and an easier go of teaching a top sales performer your industry than trying to elevate the game of an industry-knowledgeable "C" or "D" player.

- **Consider a finder's fee.** What are those Top Producers worth to your company, should they agree to join your team? Consider paying a finder's fee that will motivate others to find top talent, and provide them with a Traits List of the ideal candidate so they know what to look for.

PLAYBOOK RESOURCES:
SEE SALES MANAGER PLAYBOOK VIDEO, Show Me Your List
inSITE-app & http://leveragesalescoach.com/resources

Staffing #3: Hiring

When the right candidates do start coming in the door, the **Five Threes Process** is an excellent method for helping you discover and learn the inner person. This process consists of multiple interviews within the following variables to help you gather several perspectives:

- Three candidates

- Three interviews

- Three occasions

- Three locations

- Three other people that interview them

Additionally, a **talent-assessment tool** can help you identify the behaviors, motivators, and competencies of your serious candidates.

At Leverage Sales Coaching, we use DiSC talent assessments, employing a simple and accurate survey to assess candidates' observable behavior: how they do what they do and where they fall in the four dimensions that categorize behavior (Dominance, Influence, Steadiness, and Compliance). The resulting talent profile report helps you objectively identify where their strengths and weaknesses exist, how well they match up to the job, and what motivates them. In short, it gives you a clear, objective snapshot of the applicant so that you can quickly determine how well he or she will fit the job requirements.

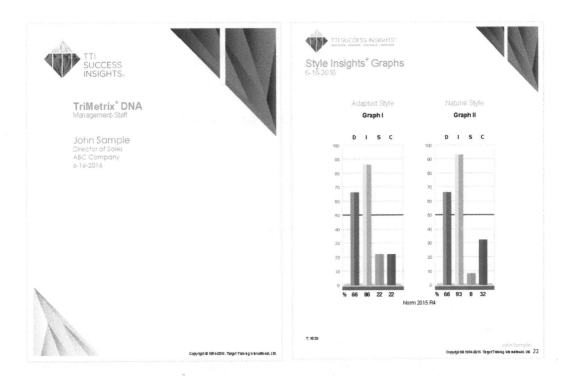

Staffing #4: Onboarding

For those who make it through this careful vetting process and accept the position, be sure to reinforce their good decision to join the team with a celebration on their arrival. Give them a warm introduction to everyone on the team and share how things are done around the company. Have a workspace ready for them, an organization chart so that they know whom to reach out to with questions, and business cards so that they can get started immediately. In effect, throw them a welcome party!

Orientation-Induction Checklist

by Jack Daly

1. Celebration!

2. Make him/her feel welcome and secure. Tour office, introduce to all, and give list of associates with nicknames. Arrange lunch.

3. Explain goals of company, office and unit; who the key team players are.

4. Explain work ground rules.

5. Explain employee benefit plans.

6. Explain position mission and current objectives.

7. Define the work assignment.

8. Present education and training plans—by whom—when. Negotiate the training contract.

9. Present work standards, responsibilities and authorities, reporting systems and productivity expected.

10. Make asking questions easy—where to go for help.

11. Help to be successful on the first day. How?

12. Debrief at end of first day—schedule appointment time.

13. Organize balance of week. Help to be successful—how?

14. Organize balance of month. Help to be successful—how?

15. Set quarterly objectives and quarterly progress reviews. 30-60-90 plan.

16. Hand-deliver calling cards.

Staffing #5: Training and Ramp-Up

Have a training plan ready for your new hires that maps out their first day, first week, and first thirty days.

Staffing #6: Thirty-Sixty-Ninety-Day Success Plan
Sales Manager: Thirty-Sixty-Ninety-Day Ramp-Up Plan with a Salesperson

Here is a list of options for successful hiring and ramping up of a new salesperson. Select what makes sense for you.

- Sales Manager Mindset

  - Develop talent: grow individuals, teams, and *their* ability to produce bigger results.

  - Stick to the basics: (1) "Nonnegotiables"—the must-haves; (2) Hurdles—navigate and/or overcome.

  - Remove obstacles to help them achieve larger results.

1. **Find/Recruit/Hire**

- Hire right-fit "A" players according to the position profile for *this* job.

2. **Onboard**

- Use the Orientation-Induction Checklist.

3. **Ramp-Up**

- Develop a Thirty-Sixty-Ninety-Day Plan and thirteen-week ramp-up plan.

  - Analyze a salesperson's individual needs.

>> NOW: What will deliver immediate, recognizable value and traction for "early success"?

>> SOON: Which of their personal needs are key building blocks that need strengthening to build on from there?

- Define their early sales-success formula.

  □ What are their expectations?

  □ How will they be measured? Provide minimum standards of performance for the first thirty, sixty, and ninety days.

  □ HPAs: High Payoff Activities. Give them a very focused, short list of HPAs to start.

  □ Outline their "day-in-the-life" plan and how they invest their time.

    >> Outline a new-hire calendar.

    >> Week one:

      o Phone calls: Block time window to make calls.

      o F2F meetings: Block time window for meetings.

      o Networking: Block time window for networking.

- **Training & Practice Plan:** Tell-Show-Do-Review

  □ Industry knowledge

  □ Company knowledge / where and whom to go to for answers

  □ Operations knowledge—org chart roles, responsibilities, team functions, work flow, who are the point of contact players

  □ Sales knowledge

    >> Client needs, opportunities, problems

    >> Company general Sales Process and work flow start to finish

- » Company Sales Processes, tools, scripts, activity reporting

- » Certification testing, sales training guide, field training

- ▫ Quicker ramp-up: Model the Masters and mentoring

- Sales Process Scorecard (What & Why/Activities/Effectiveness)

  - ▫ Start individual assessments.

    - » Compare their existing Sales Process to Sales Process Scorecard model.

    - » What and where are their individual strengths?

    - » Identify any weak links in their sales chain (compare to Sales Process Scorecard for the model process).

    - » Identify exactly where to go to work. What will help them get early lift?

    - » Give them one key thing to work on improving

- Goal Achievement Plan

  - ▫ Break down their goals back-to-front—annual/quarterly/monthly/weekly/daily.

  - ▫ **Set thirty-sixty-ninety-day goals** and expectations with them.

    - » Minimum

    - » Realistic

    - » Stretch

  - ▫ Establish key measurements.

    - » How will they be measured? Set clear expectations.

    - » Top three measurements that matter most in first thirty, sixty, and ninety days.

  - ▫ Give them a very focused short list of HPAs to start.

- Early Momentum and Traction

  □ Grow early confidence and success.

    » Phone test

    » Field test

    » Minimum standard of performance

    » Simple objective

  □ Maintain constant contact with their coach on a regular basis.

    » Provide feedback on everything whether good or bad; call after every demo.

      o What worked? What didn't? What needs to improve? What can be best practice?

    » Identify limiting factors.

    » Start with one deal a day, two deals a day, etc.

  □ Know their personal goals/objectives.

  □ Measure and track their progress.

  □ Are they remaining Coachable? Are they taking action on recommended ideas to improve?

PLAYBOOK RESOURCES:
SEE SALES MANAGER PLAYBOOK VIDEO, Jack's 4-Step Recruiting Process
inSITE-app & http://leveragesalescoach.com/resources

SALES TEAM SUCCESS STORY: DIRECTOR OF SALES, NATIONWIDE LOCAL MEDIA CO.

The director of sales for a nationwide local media company heads up one of the company's regional teams. While his company as a whole maintains a 30 percent average retention rate, his sales team, made up of consistent Top Producers, holds an impressive retention rate of 70 percent.

How is he able to keep two times more sales performers on his team than the rest of the Sales Managers in his company?

"By focusing on the top talent that's currently on my team, we've built a huge capacity to *effectively* onboard," he says. "The training capacity we build is why we have faster sales growth in the end."

KNOW YOUR TRAINING CAPACITY

"There are many situations where your existing training capacity needs to be addressed prior to recruiting," he notes. If you hire more than you can competently train, then your results diminish significantly. Through disciplined hiring, you can focus your current talent on helping you develop high payoff with your new talent.

As you hire, keep in mind your capacity to train and launch new hires. You cannot expect to effectively train several people if you find it hard to train and ramp-up a single person. If you lack training capacity, you need to build this aspect of your onboarding process first or risk setting up new hires for failure.

A few ideas for increasing your training capacity include:

- **Make training a discipline and a priority**. As the manager, training should be a high priority in protecting your hiring investment. Block out the time to do it and stick with it.

- **Team training**. Consider how you can train in groups or in sales meetings in order to regularly brush up on skills that the whole team can benefit from.

- **Mentor Best Practices**. Look to your Top Producers to help mentor new hires and train them on Best Practices. This role is often seen as an honor and can be further encouraged with additional compensation for time spent training. For more on Modeling the Masters, see Chapter 3.

DISCIPLINED ONBOARDING

Another key practice that the director of sales attributes to his success is disciplined onboarding. It may seem counterintuitive at first, in that this approach appears to build slower results in the beginning, but in the end, it's much faster at building sales and keeping a consistently high-performing team.

"The sucker's choice," he says, "is to hire fast. If I hire right and spend the time teaching them to produce better on their own, it's so much easier downstream for me to manage and motivate them to perform at consistently higher levels."

Onboarding done in an undisciplined manner results in faster hires and more people selling more quickly, but the result is that you spend a *lot* more time trying to truly train them and get them producing on their own, and keeping them motivated. The ultimate result is lower sales quality and higher turnover rate.

A robust hiring and onboarding process is disciplined. It sticks to the principles that you know are proven to work—your Sales Playbook—and it ensures that these principles and practices are implemented.

How do you create a disciplined onboarding process?

1. **Be demanding of them upfront**. If they're the right people for your team, they'll want the challenge and will respond positively to it.

2. **Set clear expectations immediately**. Once they've been trained on the lay of the land and have a basic understanding of your Sales Process, don't coddle them. For him, this means giving them a nine-minute presentation on their first day that they need to memorize within their first two weeks on the job. If they don't have it down cold by then, then their services are no longer needed.

"Either they will or they will not step up. Take this opportunity to find out who they are early on; it saves a lot of hassle down the road," the director of sales says.

3. **Earn the territory.** Another point he stresses with new hires from the start is that they aren't just going to be handed their first sales. They need to earn them.

   "You have to prove that you're capable of producing in that territory according to my expectations, or you're not the right fit for the job," he says. "'There's a big opportunity here,' I tell them, 'but you have to take it. It won't just be given to you. But if you do show me you can do it, I have more opportunities I can give you.'"

   The best salespeople want a challenge that is worth pursuing. Find out what excites them, what makes them hungry, and feed them!

4. **Build personal trust.** At the same time you're challenging them, make sure that new hires know that you're on their side and that they can believe in you. Work *for* them, look out for them, and the loyalty you engender will only drive them to achieve more.

5. **Motivation.** When you onboard new talent correctly, you shouldn't need to motivate them down the road. Instead, your conversations will more likely focus on keeping a proper work/life balance.

HIRE SLOW TO GROW FAST

Highly focused and effective hiring and onboarding enhances the whole game of sales managing. If you get this part wrong, you wind up with poor sales and high turnover. Get it right—hire slow and onboard well—and you'll grow faster than you ever expected!

All of the previous items are key components of the Sales Manager's Playbook and need to be addressed accordingly.

CHAPTER 11

TIME MANAGEMENT

 **CHAPTER GAME PLAN**

The life of a Sales Manager is a busy one, and the job of growing salespeople is a full-time, critical, and demanding responsibility.

To do this effectively requires dedicated attention to the Three Vital Areas:

1. PEOPLE: Team development
2. PROCESSES: Management processes
3. PRACTICES: Training and development

These Three Vital Areas encompass a dozen elements essential to producing and nurturing a high-performance sales team. We listed those in Chapter 8 and showed how the total time **each month comes to 136 hours**, which means that time management is essential. Sales Managers have no time to spare! They must focus on the High Payoff Activities—the HPAs that will build the team's **Quality** even as it grows in **Quantity**.

The big question is: How much time will you devote to these activities, and where will you find the time? How will you make sure these crucial activities are accomplished?

To answer these questions, we've created a tool we call the Sales Manager's Key Activities Calendar. This tool will help you manage this workload in such a manner that your HPAs can be tracked and accomplished consistently, letting you know what needs to be done, when it should be done, and how you will get it done so that you can becoming a far **stronger developer of People, Processes, and Practices**.

SALES MANAGER KEY ACTIVITIES CALENDAR

Sales Manager Key Activities	Frequency Per Month

1. People, Processes, and Practices Development

- Sales team stack-rank assessment

- Sales Process Steps defined, proven

- Key Activities *really matter*, drive results and Best Practices

- Success guide: Objection Responses/Best Questions/Differentiator sales-ready Value Proposition

2. Culture & Team-Building Activities   1x system per month

- Recognition

- Communication

- Personal and professional development

- Empowerment

3. Goal Achievement/Key Activities Inspection and Accountability

- Scorecard dashboard   reports 1x/week

- Weekly pre-call planning   1x/week per person

- Sales team stack-rank assessment   1x/quarter

4. **Team-Training Meetings & Role Practice**

   - Sales Process/Key Activities scorecard   1x/quarter per person

   - Key Activities & Best Practices   1x/month

   - Objection Responses/Best Questions   1x/month

5. **Pipeline, 1:1 Meetings, Touch Plan, Field Calls**

   - 1:1 Meetings: progress reviews/career plan   1x/month

   - Pipeline Management: inspect the baskets   reports 1x/week

   - Touch System inspection   inspect 1x/month

   - Field calls   1x/seller/month (or min. EOM)

6. **Recruiting Activities**

   - Always be looking   daily (position is profiled/know what's required)

   - Touches to target list: ideal candidates   1x/week or minimum 1x/mo.

This Sales Manager Key Activities Calendar not only promotes success but also reduces stress. It eases your mind to know that you have a plan in place and a specific schedule to accomplish what you need to do in the course of a year, a month, a week, and a day. By gauging how much time each of these essential activities will take in advance, you can schedule them, find a place for the things that matter most, and focus accordingly.

This will also help you stay on track so that important matters do not get pushed aside. For example, recruiting new talent will always be a necessity, and by regularly scheduling time for that, it's far more likely it will get done.

You know that these things are necessary to attaining success—scheduling them is the way to make sure they happen.

Remember that **your job is to build the team, to grow the talent**. You will need to customize your attention to each individual, understanding what might be limiting him or her and finding ways to overcome it. You need to devote the necessary hours to accomplish that. It is a full-time job. It requires the courage, the discipline, and the commitment to actually schedule these activities on your calendar and then make sure they get done, no matter what urgent matter of the moment tries to call you away. Easy to say, hard to do.

We have often found Sales Managers who are also dedicating up to 70 percent of their time to being a salesperson—one of the Three Sins of Sales Management. If you're serving in a salesperson capacity as well as managing, take another look at the list of Sales Manager Key Activities and decide which ones you'll sacrifice so that you can continue to play the salesperson role.

It's pretty hard to do, right? If 70 percent of your time is sales and 10 percent is necessary administrative tasks, then that means you're only spending 20 percent of your time managing your sales team—not nearly enough time to focus on success, let alone growth.

Change comes from the top. The top officers of the company need to recognize the essential role of the Sales Manager. They often keep that person selling because they do not want to give up the revenue that he or she produces. But good Sales Managers multiply that revenue. When they are allowed to do their job properly and develop the talent, they enhance profits far greater than any one person can do.

Is that an investment that the company is willing to make? Are the top leaders willing to let go of the manager's personal production and turn that person into a developer of talent? If they do, and if the Sales Manager takes to heart the essential tasks to grow the team and gets them on the success calendar, the bottom line will swell.

Note: In 100 percent of our clients who have moved away from the Three Sins of Sales Management, the feedback is "I sure wish we had done this sooner!"

GAME ON! ONLY THE BEST GET COACHED

People are overwhelmed.

It's the biggest challenge facing Sales Managers and salespeople. Those who come to our training sessions are already working almost from before the sun comes up to well after it's gone down, and then they hear us talk about the systems, processes, and activities that they should be incorporating into their workload if they truly wish to attain success.

Consider, again, that the Sales Manager should be spending at least four hours a month with each salesperson out in the field on training calls. For a manager supervising a staff of ten, just that one activity will require forty hours a month—and this Playbook is filled with similar valuable actions that likewise call for the devotion of time and energy.

We're not going to find any more hours in a week. Each of us gets the same number of hours every week (168 to be exact), and ideally we need some of those to sleep, eat, and maybe even relax a little and enjoy life.

Where is the extra time going to come from to attend to our sales career? From organization, from coordination, and from prioritization. Take a moment to look at the activities on your calendar and then ask yourself:

- *How many hours would it take to get each task accomplished effectively?*

- *Which activities are my highest priorities?*

- *Which activities offer the highest payoff—my HPAs?*

Then coordinate your calendar with your Playbook and start scheduling as much and as far in advance as you can.

Success is not something you can compromise on. Take the time to identify the things that you have learned here that you believe will be the most beneficial. Write them all down on an Action Plan and then **identify your top three priorities**.

You may have fifty valuable action items on your list, but narrow them down to the top three that you will commit yourself to accomplishing. Then, put a timeline on when you will have those three things done. It doesn't matter if it's thirty days, sixty days, or ninety days; the important thing is that a deadline has been established and that you work time into your schedule to make sure they're accomplished on time.

To hold yourself to it, sign your name to that timeline and give it to whoever holds you accountable, asking them to check back with you as your deadlines approach. Tell them you want them to make sure that you are actually keeping your commitment. Once those three action items are incorporated into the normal behavior patterns of your organization, then move on to the next three.

You will never get more hours in the day than twenty-four. You will never get more hours in the week than 168. Therefore, you must make some concrete decisions. Establish priorities. Would it be better to put in place the next item on your list than to continue doing whatever else is consuming so much of your time?

We assure you that the more you can include elements of your custom Playbook into your schedule, the better you and your team will perform. When you work on the higher-payoff activities and you observe the results that they bring, you no doubt will want to open up more time for them, not less.

This advice goes for both the Sales Manager and for the salesperson. Salespeople who implement the systems and processes that we have described, and who become more proactive than reactive, will find a significant boost in their sales, revenue, and income. That's quite an incentive to find even more time for those High Payoff Activities!

We have seen salespeople begin to operate as if they were their own company once they have begun to abide by their Playbook. Even though they are working on behalf of an employer, they are engaging personal assistants and finding them so beneficial that they got one exclusively for themselves. And why stop there? Some have even brought on a second assistant, then a third and fourth, to the point where they are now finding themselves with a lot more time to do more enjoyable things. They are working less, making more, and driving more revenue into the company. Such is the value of the Playbook.

Remember, though, that you can build the greatest Playbook in the world, but if nobody uses it, it just does not matter. **You need to get traction on ideas**. That's why we urge you to pick a few of the best ideas that you have found in this book, and find that traction. What are the priorities that will have the biggest impact on you, the team, and the company? How will they influence where you are going with your goals and vision?

Grab your gear, rehearse your processes, and start practicing them. Focus on the activities that will bring you the most value, the highest payoff. To make money, you need to be more than busy—you need to produce. We are confident that if you take to heart what you have learned in this book, you will find yourself producing better than you ever could have imagined.

ALWAYS COMPETE.

As you progress through your sporting life . . .
Always Compete.
If you want to go for it . . .
Always Compete.

PETE CARROLL

PART III

ACTION PLAN:
FOLLOW-UP AND RESOURCES

PRIORITIES & ACTION

Five Steps to Take Right Away

Thank you for reading *The Sales Playbook for Hyper Sales Growth*. Jack talks about the importance of being an action taker on ideas. Here are five actions to take to get your Playbook moving to produce more.

1. **Have the owners/executives, management, and sales team read the Sales Playbook book.** Help everyone better understand that the purpose of the Playbook is to help customize your Best Practices in the important areas of People, Processes, and Practices into a plan for action. And to consider what improvements will help your company increase sales performance.

2. **Hold a Playbook Priorities meeting.** Meet with a core group of six to eight of your key contributors from the owner/executive, management, and sales team areas to come to this meeting. Ask them to prepare their inputs on the **My Sales Team Performance Diagnostic** to help identify their top priority areas

that would help the company get more traction and improve sales performance. Download the free **My Sales Team Performance Diagnostic** provided in the Resources section. You can choose to distribute the diagnostic tool to your group prior to the meeting so that they can prepare their ratings and ideas for priorities in advance.

PLAYBOOK RESOURCES:
SEE SALES PLAYBOOK, My Sales Team Performance Diagnostic
inSITE-app & http://leveragesalescoach.com/resources

3. **Appoint a Playbook quarterback to lead building and implementation.** Appoint an effective project leader who will stay on task to lead the Playbook process, organize the effort and people, and make progress in building the Playbook according to the decided priorities.

4. **Decide the resources you need to build, improve, train, and implement.** Building and implementing a customized Sales Playbook requires several steps in a focused, efficient plan to produce a quicker, yet ongoing payoff. You will need to organize the priorities and gather up the related processes/tools/practices and Intel that currently exists. Then build your first component do the initial training, and test it. Note what works and doesn't, and refine and improve it. Finalize it, roll it out team wide, and train and practice it in-house. Now systemize it as a management process for ongoing training, practicing, and monitoring to increase performance.

5. **Use the Sales Playbook processes, tools, templates, and examples provided in the Resources section.** These tools are provided in this book and online to help your team speed up the development and implementation of your Playbook. Be sure to take full advantage of them!

Options to help you accelerate your Playbook results:

Some companies have the talent, time, and training capabilities they need to build and use their Playbook. Even if it's just one Playbook priority developed at a time, commit to being consistent at building, practicing, and implementing. If your company lacks the talent, time, training, or capability to implement—or if you just want to speed it up—contact Leverage Sales Coaching at (800) 565–6516, or dan@leveragesalescoach.com. We're here to help discuss your situation and to map out the options for your best plan to get it done.

Certified Coaches: If you need help to build, train, or implement your priority processes and tools in a customized Sales Playbook, we have certified coaches in North America and Australia to help you. They have the experience, expertise, and know-how to help you build and implement quicker and avoid mistakes and slow-downs. Certified sales coaches utilize our Leverage Sales Coaching Master Track of proven systems, processes, tools, templates, and models that accelerate sales growth in fifteen key areas of sales and sales management. Schedule a free thirty-minute strategy call to discuss your situation at (800) 565–6516.

World-Class Training: Jack Daly offers numerous training options. See the Resources section for more.

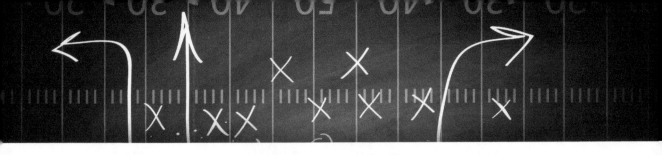

RESOURCES

Using the inSITE-app to get PLAYBOOK RESOURCES:

Remember all of the examples, sales tools, templates, and videos here are available by downloading the free inSITE-app in the Apple or Google Play Stores!

Please register your FREE account at http://leveragesalescoach.com/resources. Simply click "Register for Playbook Resources" and create a FREE account to access the inSITE-app to get PLAYBOOK RESOURCES on your mobile device or computer.

My Sales Team Performance Diagnostic

Use this to: Evaluate: Rate to find your strengths and weaknesses.
Prioritize: What do we need to work on improving first?

Sales Team Performance Diagnostic: Sales & Sales Management	10 high

1. **Prospecting - New Biz Dev**: We are generating enough new business to meet our growth goals.

_____

2. **Closing Sales**: We are closing our share or better of opportunities. Not missing too many.

_____

3. **Differentiate - Selling Value**: We are good at communicating and differentiating our unique value. We avoid discounting and low-priced competitors pretty well. We can differentiate to increase new customer engagement.

_____

4. **Goals & Results**: We are achieving or beating our sales goals consistently. Forecasting is pretty predictable and reliable. We identify and regularly focus on our high payoff target list (Top 10).

_____

5. **Sales Skills – Training - Role Practicing**: The sales team is customer-focused, asks questions, and listens. They identify High Value Needs and present our solutions well. They handle Objections effectively. We regularly train & practice with sales team & individuals to keep their skills sharp.

_____

6. **Customer Retention** We retain our customers at a high rate and avoid too much attrition.

_____

7. **Sales Mgmt**. Our sales management is effective at leading the team with high motivation and sufficient activity.

_____

8. **Sales strategy & game plan** We have a clear and confident sales strategy that directs our sales game plan we need to win.

_____

9. **Sales Processes**: We have an effective sales process. Easy to train & ramp-up sellers with 1) clearly defined Steps of the process 2) HPAs for each step (High Payoff Activities) 3) and Best Sales Practices. We focus on the right client targets. We manage our sales pipeline well to close deals.

_____

10. **People - Talent - Recruiting**: We have a solid team of producers. We are able to attract strong talent when we need to upgrade.

_____

TOTAL (100 possible)

_____

LINKS
in the
SALES
CHAIN

Where does *YOUR* sales chain break?

Find the weak links & fix them.

Work smarter. Earn more.

1. **Prospecting**

2. **Qualifying**

3. **Appointment Setting**

4. **Presenting**

5. **Objections Management**

6. **Closing**

7. **Follow-Up / Through**

The Profession of Sales is for Sales Professionals

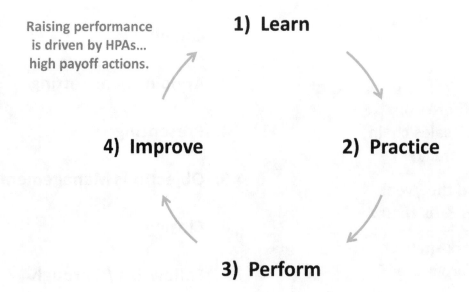

1) Learn

Raising performance
is driven by HPAs...
high payoff actions.

4) Improve

2) Practice

3) Perform

My Sales HPAs Checklist

Key Area	My Sales HPAs	An important HPA	I'm Performing well	I'm OK at this	I need to Learn or Improve
Sales Plan	Territory Mgmt/Planning	☐	☐	☐	☐
	Prep / Planning / Strategy	☐	☐	☐	☐
	Profit Analysis	☐	☐	☐	☐
	Organization-Action Plans-Prioritizing	☐	☐	☐	☐
	Key Account Planning & Growth	☐	☐	☐	☐
	Goal Pursuit / Achievement	☐	☐	☐	☐
	Manager Communication	☐	☐	☐	☐
	Win / Loss Review	☐	☐	☐	☐
Preparation	Best Questions Practicing	☐	☐	☐	☐
	Innovating Ideas that Sell	☐	☐	☐	☐
Prospecting	Target List Planning	☐	☐	☐	☐
	Ask Questions & Effective Listening	☐	☐	☐	☐
	Prospecting / Door-Opening	☐	☐	☐	☐
	Networking – Ext. & Internal	☐	☐	☐	☐
	Calling Cold & Warm	☐	☐	☐	☐
	Developing COI Channel Partners	☐	☐	☐	☐
	Networking Events & Social Media	☐	☐	☐	☐
	Conferences / Trade Shows	☐	☐	☐	☐
Qualifying	Qualifying to Fit Criteria / Identify HVNs	☐	☐	☐	☐
Presenting	Presenting Solutions to HVNs	☐	☐	☐	☐
	Objection Mgmt/Tough Questions	☐	☐	☐	☐
	Demos / Sampling	☐	☐	☐	☐
	Cross-Selling/Upselling	☐	☐	☐	☐
	Selling to Consensus Buy-in	☐	☐	☐	☐
	Selling Value/Pricing Strategy	☐	☐	☐	☐
	Problem Solving/Creativity	☐	☐	☐	☐
	Managing Customer Expectations	☐	☐	☐	☐
Closing	Closing / Ask for the Business	☐	☐	☐	☐
	Price Negotiations	☐	☐	☐	☐
Pipeline Mgmt	Pipeline Mgmt. / CRM Reporting	☐	☐	☐	☐
	Touch System to Differentiate	☐	☐	☐	☐
Follow-up	Follow-up / Follow-thru	☐	☐	☐	☐
Messaging	Create Perception of Value / Differentiate	☐	☐	☐	☐
Training	Continuous Learning / Practicing	☐	☐	☐	☐
	Mentoring	☐	☐	☐	☐
	Model the Masters	☐	☐	☐	☐
	Role Practicing	☐	☐	☐	☐
	Ride-Alongs with Manager	☐	☐	☐	☐
Time Mgmt	Time & Prioritization Focus	☐	☐	☐	☐

The Profession of Sales is for Sales Professionals

Raising performance is driven by HPAs... high payoff actions.

1) Learn

2) Practice

3) Perform

4) Improve

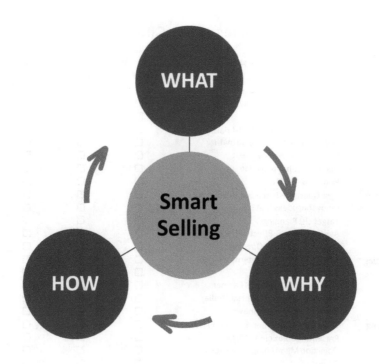

THREE high payoff things done by Top Producers

Top Producers make more money, because they find a way to get it done. They achieve their goals when others don't. **WHY? Because <u>they do best sales practices *consistently*</u>.** They are open and willing to learn what works. They take action. And they have the discipline to do it consistently by committing to follow systems & processes that increase their success.

WHAT & WHY

Do you understand <u>WHAT</u> to do? AND... <u>*WHY*</u> to do it?

1) <u>QUANTITY</u> of Activities

2) <u>QUALITY</u> of Activities

3) <u>CONSISTENCY</u>

ACTION

<u>Amount</u>
of
Activities?

EFFECTIVENESS

<u>How well</u>
is it
done?

SYSTEMS &
PROCESSES

<u>Consistency</u>
of activities in a
reliable way?

Rank the Sales Team

A – Achievers

B – Be Better

C – Content

D – Don't Move much!

> Where does the Sales Manager invest their time?

Personality Styles

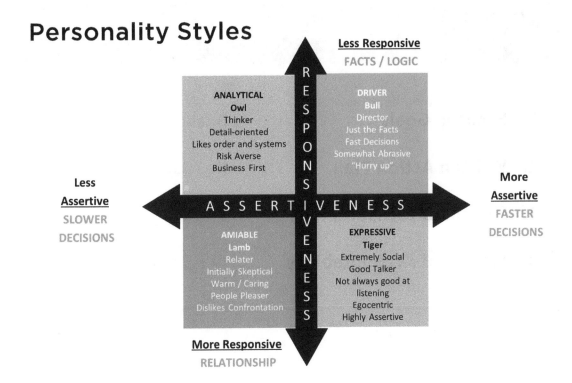

Goal Achievement Plan

1. **Focused Goals** — Backward Thinking

2. **Written Action Plan** — Key Activities

3. **System of Measurement** — Tracking Performance

4. **System of Accountability** — Progress Reports

Goal Achievement Plan Overview

The Goal Achievement Plan (GAP) is an underlying foundation to the very purpose of a successful sales organization. If you are serious about achieving your goals, then you should want to create a serious plan to make it happen. We know that "Winners keep score!"

The crux of a Goal Achievement Plan is to consistently perform the high payoff activities on the high payoff target accounts to drive bigger results. Below are the key elements needed to create a GAP that works.

Goal Achievement Plan	
1. Focused Goals	Backward Thinking
2. Written Action Plan	Key Activities
3. System of Measurement	Tracking Performance
4. System of Accountability	Progress Reports

Goal Achievement Plan

- 1) **Goals in Writing**   **Backward Thinking**
  - o Break down your goals "back to front" (Annually → Quarterly → Monthly → Weekly → Daily)
  - o Using your specific Key Measurements. Some examples below
    - ▪ # Existing_____Sold (accounts, units, etc)
    - ▪ # New_____Sold (accounts, units, etc)
    - ▪ Revenue $ per_____(period)
    - ▪ Average $ per_____(sale $, margin, etc for your key measurements)

- 2) **Written Plan**   **Key Activities**
  - o What Key ACTIVITIES *really matter* to drive results?
    - ▪ # Prospecting calls to target accounts → # Qualified leads
    - ▪ # Appointments set → # Presentations to key decision makers
    - ▪ # Deals won → # Relationships advancing
    - ▪ # Referral partners developing
    - ▪ Marketing visibility: # Networking events; # Trade Shows, etc.
    - ▪ Other? _____

- 3) **System of Measurement**   **Tracking Performance**
  - o How you are pacing toward your goal?
  - o Use your CRM, pipeline reporting, pacing report or other system to track your progress & pacing toward your goal

- 4) **System of Accountability**   **Progress Reports**
  - o What adjustments do you need to make?
  - o Look for ways to adjust activities, targets or effectiveness to be sure to stay on track

 **Goal Achievement Plan Summary**

Goal Achievement Plan driven by Backward Thinking

Below are several keys to implement an effective Goal Achievement Plan using Jack Daly's "backward thinking." The end result is to develop an effective action plan to know what you need to achieve your goals.

Principles/Concept:

- **The "funnel" concept** of "begin with your end $$ needed" (e.g. $1,000,000 revenue)

- **Sales Process Steps & Key Activities**: Then backward think/reverse engineer the activity plan. Break down the amount of Key Measurements and Key Activities required at each step.

- **Three related factors affect the amount of activity you need to achieve goal:**

  - 1) <u>High Payoff Targets</u> = The right <u>best-fit targets</u> must be the focus

  - 2) <u>Key Activities</u> = <u>Amount of Activity</u> required to be sure to hit your goal?

  - 3) <u>Conversion Rate</u> at each step is determined by <u>how effective</u> you are at each step?

  - Achieving your goal requires having enough leads & best-fit target opportunities in the front end of the funnel that are sufficient to reach your goal.

  - Your Conversion Rate at each step helps determine if you have sufficient target opportunities in the front end or if you need to get more.

Top 10 Best-Fit Account Rating Steps

The steps below will help you identify your **Best-Fit Target Accounts** for your highest payoff activities.

 **Goal Achievement Plan Summary**

Identify your Top 10 high payoff accounts for Existing and New Accounts:

1. Begin with your broad list of all Existing accounts and New target accounts.
2. Use the ratings steps below to identify your Top Account targets. It's recommended doing this in an Excel spreadsheet so that it can be easily sortable.
3. Identify the Best-Fit Targets using the criteria below or choose your own. Determine the most productive Top 10 Accounts to pursue and grow.

Best-Fit Account Ratings Tool used to focus your high pay-off activities on the best key account targets

Purpose: Be more objective about identifying the best target accounts to grow your business. Create a system and process that helps you target better to work smarter.

Rate your list of Prospects and Customers according to the following:

VOLUME OF BUSINESS account is doing <u>in the marketplace</u> (not with you)

- **A**   X-Large $_____/ yr or more   (<u>set your own rating thresholds</u>)
- **B**   Large $_____/ yr
- **C**   Med $_____/ yr
- **D**   Small $_____/ yr

YOUR **SHARE** OF CUSTOMER

- **1**   Does most/all buying thru your company
- **2**   Does some buying thru your company
- **3**   Does no/little buying thru your company
- **4**   Good potential as a Referral source

Best-Fit Account Rating for Top 10 Targets:

- **A2 & A3:**   Focus greatest mktg/sales effort
- **B2 & B3:**   Focus strong mktg/sales effort
- **C2 & C3:**   Focus medium mktg/sales effort
- **A1, B1 & C1:**   Maintain good relations & ensure good contacts and service

Top 10 Accounts Activities Goal:

1. Use Best-Fit Account Rating to identify the best targets for focused sales & touch program effort.
2. Sellers schedule follow-up communication plan based on progress and Best-Fit Account Rating.

Top 10 List Forms

 **LEVERAGE** SALES COACHING **Goal Achievement Plan Summary**

PROSPECTS Best-Fit Target List:

Focus precedes success. What accounts deserve your biggest focus in order to greatly increase your income?

	PROSPECTS: Top 10 Best-Fit Target List				
	List your best prospect targets according to your ratings & sales potential. What will each account be worth when successful?				
Target #	Company	Best-Fit Acct Rating	Account's Total Purchase Vol./Yr.	Your Current Purchase Vol./Yr.	Your Target Purchase Vol./Yr-1
1			$	$	$
2			$	$	$
3			$	$	$
4			$	$	$
5			$	$	$
6			$	$	$
7			$	$	$
8			$	$	$
9			$	$	$
10			$	$	$

 **LEVERAGE** SALES COACHING **Goal Achievement Plan Summary**

CUSTOMERS Best-Fit Target List:

Focus precedes success. What accounts deserve your biggest focus in order to greatly increase your income?

CUSTOMERS: Top 10 Best-Fit Target List					
List your best customer targets according to your ratings & sales potential. What will each account be worth when successful?					
Target #	Company	Best-Fit Acct Rating	Account's Total Purchase Vol./Yr.	Your Current Purchase Vol./Yr.	Your Target Purchase Vol./Yr-1
1			$	$	$
2			$	$	$
3			$	$	$
4			$	$	$
5			$	$	$
6			$	$	$
7			$	$	$
8			$	$	$
9			$	$	$
10			$	$	$

 **Goal Achievement Plan Summary**

CLIENTS Best-Fit Target List:

Focus precedes success. What accounts deserve your biggest focus in order to greatly increase your income?

Target #	Company	Best-Fit Acct Rating	Account's Total Purchase Vol./Yr.	Your Current Purchase Vol./Yr.	Your Target Purchase Vol./Yr-1
CLIENTS: Top 10 Best-Fit Target List					
List your best client targets according to your ratings & sales potential. What will each account be worth when successful?					
1			$	$	$
2			$	$	$
3			$	$	$
4			$	$	$
5			$	$	$
6			$	$	$
7			$	$	$
8			$	$	$
9			$	$	$
10			$	$	$

The Funnel – Goal Achievement Plan – ANNUAL

Conversion Rate (approx.)
- 20%
- 50%
- 40%
- 80%
- 63%
- 56%
- 90%

Best-Fit OPPORTUNITIES
1. Prospecting / Target / Intell
2. Qualifying / Needs / Best-Fit
3. Appmt Set / Dec-Mkr
4. Present / HV Needs
5. Obj Mgmt
6. Close/AFB
7. Follow-Up

$1,000,000

5,000 Calls
- $10M (500 Fits)
- $4M (200 Needs)
- $3.2M (160 Solutions)
- $2M (100 Proposals)
- $1.1M (56 Agreed)
- $1M (50x - $20K Confirmed)

Backward Thinking

Goals Back-to-Front

Begin with end $$ needed

The Funnel – Goal Achievement Plan – ACTIVITIES

Conversion Rate (approx.)
- 20%
- 50%
- 40%
- 80%
- 63%
- 56%
- 90%

Level of Effectiveness

Best-Fit OPPORTUNITIES
1. Prospecting / Target / Intell
2. Qualifying / Needs / Best-Fit
3. Appmt Set / Dec-Mkr
4. Present / HV Needs
5. Obj Mgmt
6. Close/AFB
7. Follow-Up

$1,000,000

Activity Level required for goal

100 Calls per wk
- 20 Leads / week
- 10 Qualified / week
- 4 Appmts / week
- 3.2 Presents / week
- 2.0 Ready to Buy / week
- 1 Close/Agreed / week
- 1 Confirmed Sale / week

Key Measurements & Minimum Standards

Sales Process-Scorecard Example

Below are examples of HPAs (High Payoff Activities) that really matter to drive results in each step of a sales process. Note the following attributes of the HPA descriptions:

- **Succinct, Clear, Useable:** "Bite-size" description that's still clear enough to know exactly what to do
- **Specific:** Specific actions to be taken and key questions or reminders of best sales practices
- **Quantifiable:** Wherever possible, add an amount of activity to establish Min Stds for sellers

SALES STEPS & HPAs	Tools & Training
Step 1: Prospecting << KPI: # CONTACTS >>	
Target Prospect List Prep & Planning: Prep weekly Top 10 List for prospects, customers, clients from Target List based on Pre-Qualifying Checklist	• Master Target List • Top 10 List • Pre-Qualifying Checklist
Networking/Trade Shows: Goal = 8 or more pre-qualified leads; Give cards to sales asst.; Complete a trade show recap; 24-hr follow-up touch on leads	• Networking Best Practices
Social networking: Post blog update & insights post at least 1x per week	• Social media marketing
Calling-Warm/Cold: Min 5 hours blocked/week for directors and above, inside sales calling your top 20 list	• Calling Best Practices • Top 10 List TODAY • Pre-Qualifying Checklist • 10 Tips Better Voicemails
Leads Tracking & Follow-Up: 24 hr or less follow-up, track in CRM	• CRM
Step 2: Qualifying Phone Call/Meeting << KPI: # QUALIFIED >>	
Advance prep work on target: Identify Decision-makers & key influencers	
Qualifying Checklist: Questions List to determine deeper Qualifying criteria; Current buying program; Questions list; Consultative selling training	• Qualifying Checklist • Questions list • Consultative selling training
Step 3: Appmt Setting << KPI: # APPMTS that STICK >>	
Appointment setting: "Calendar handy?"; Suggest specific time/date; Ensure right people will be there; Outline agenda for meeting-1; Meet/exceed Appmt activity Success Goals each month	• Appmt Setting Best Practices • Success Goals
Opportunity Brief: Create and review Opportunity Brief with Mgr	• Opportunity Brief
Meeting Reminder/Confirm: Send reminder & confirm 24 hrs in advance	
Step 4: Needs Analysis: Mutual-Fit	
Role Practice Tough Questions: Anticipate prospect's tough questions. Who will answer (if team selling)?	• Role practice training
Needs Analysis meeting: Get prospect talking; Understand their needs & priorities; Probing questions to learn business objectives & core issues; Identify HVNs; Reason to proceed/Solution awareness/End results/Value we deliver	• Qualifying Checklist • Questions list • Consultative selling training

Step 5: Presentation << KPI: # PRESENTATIONS >>	
Presentation Prep meeting: Focus on HVNs (High value needs) = Know their 'end zone' (what matters most to client)	
Create Presentation: Focus on THEIR needs and smart solutions, discuss measurable value, relevant success examples	• Presentation templates
Role Practice: Practice Q&A and buyer's tough questions	• Role practice cheat sheet
Solution Presentation: Customer-focused presentation, interactive questions, Focus on THEIR reasons/HVNs	• Presentation notes cheat sheet
Follow-up: Recap next steps who-what-when for all, Send calendar to all	• Calendar invitation
Step 6: Closing / Won or Lost << KPI: # WINS >>	
Negotiate with Buyer/Mgr: Negotiate terms, discuss & confirm	
Closing: Recap solution plan that meets their needs, terms, and timeline	
Agreement Signature: Get signature or follow up to secure signature	
Submit signed order & process it: Alert Mgr, fulfillment or operational team	
Win/Loss ratio: 50% or higher?	
Success Review: What worked? What didn't? What can we learn? What needs to be improved?	• Success Review tool
Step 7: Follow-Up / Follow-Through	
Follow-up/Follow Through: Recap actions; Who is doing what by when? Calendar follow-up actions and follow-through	
KEY ACTIVITIES	
Total Score	

Sales Key Activities Dashboard

Regional Sales Manager		Rudy									
Week Start Date		02/15/16									

LEVERAGE SALES COACHING

	Name	KEY ACTIVITIES - LEADING KPIs					KEY RESULTS - LAGGING KPIs				
		# Contacts (min 50)	# Qualifd (min 25)	# Appmts (min 10)	# Presents (min 6)	# Wins (min 3)	# Units Sold A	B	C	Total # Units Sold	Amount Sold
1	Chris	55	30	13	8	5	22	36	25	83	$33,200
2	Matt	52	27	12	8	5	20	32	30	82	$32,800
3	Kent	44	24	10	7	5	18	29	28	75	$30,000
4	Paul	42	23	10	6	3	20	26	21	67	$26,800
5	Michelle	40	20	9	5	3	18	29	19	66	$26,400
6	Ed	38	18	8	5	3	15	22	18	55	$22,000
7	Frank	35	17	9	5	2	14	24	25	63	$25,200
8	Ray	33	15	7	3	2	12	19	20	51	$20,400
9	Robin	31	14	6	3	1	15	18	16	49	$19,600
10	Robert	28	18	7	4	2	14	22	17	53	$21,200
Team Totals		398	206	91	54	31	168	257	219	644	$257,600
		80%	82%	91%	90%	103%	84%	129%	110%	107%	$400

Inspect the Baskets

- Top 10 Prospects – Customers – Clients?

- What ways have you touched them?

- What frequency?

- What can you do to advance them?

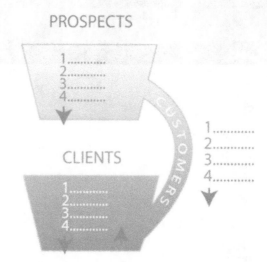

PROSPECTS

CUSTOMERS

CLIENTS

Proactive Pipeline Mgmt. – Touch System
Inspect the Baskets

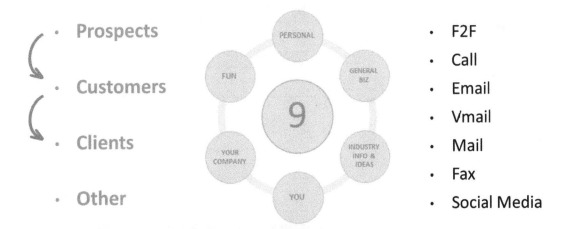

- Prospects
- Customers
- Clients

- Other

- F2F
- Call
- Email
- Vmail
- Mail
- Fax
- Social Media

Touch System:

- **Top 10 focus in each Basket**

- **Money Bag – immediate & personalized to Differentiate**

- **Other Touches made regularly**

  - **Other Influencers affecting the buy**

- **What high payoff touches can you make to advance your pipeline?**

Proactive Pipeline Mgmt. – Touch System
Inspect the Baskets

- Prospects
- Customers
- Clients

- Other

- F2F
- Call
- Email
- Vmail
- Mail
- Fax
- Social Media

Weekly Pre-Call Planner:

Big picture Quarterly view

- • Plan the "big rocks"

- **4-Week View**

  - • Territory Planning

- **2-Week Focus**

  - • Pre-Call Planning your key accounts

Weekly Pre-Call Planner Review: WEST Territory ONGOING						
4-Week View/2-Week Focus	JANUARY					FEBRUARY
	Dec 29 - Jan 4	Jan 5 - 11	Jan 12-18	Jan 19 - 25	Jan 26 - Feb 1	Feb 2 - 8
KEVIN MADISON	2-Week Focus		4-Week View		Longer View →	
Key Product-1 Presentations / Activities						
Key Product-2 Presentations / Activities						
Key Product-3 Presentations / Activities						
Promotional Activities & Support						
Prospecting / Lead-Gen Activities						
Special Activities / Projects						

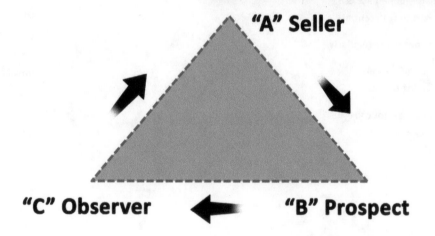

ROLE PRACTICE

Purpose: Practice, uncover & collaborate best sales practices.

Discuss:

1. What was done well?
2. What can improve?
3. What can you use as Best Practice?

"A" Seller

"C" Observer ← "B" Prospect

Why Your Company?
Create Value that Differentiates Worksheet

"If you don't have a competitive advantage, don't compete."

Jack Welch, Former GE CEO

Why Your Company? The Problem: *It all sounds like everyone else*!

- Quality, Competitive, Friendly
- Good Customer Service, Responsive, Knowledgeable
- Trust, Convenient, Lots of Choice
- ME! Results, Save You Money

The key question: **What are _you_ offering that your _competitors aren't or can't_?**

- The best answers are the ones that are <u>sustainable</u> and <u>tough for competitors to duplicate</u> the benefits.

Why Your Company? The Opportunity

- Show buyers how you are **unique, different and better**!
- "Dazzle them with details." What do you or should you be offering to truly differentiate?

_____

_____

_____

Examples from **Creating Competitive Advantage** by Jaynie Smith

- We guarantee that your order will be confirmed and shipped within 3 hours of placement. Your calls will be returned within 20 minutes; our technicians will be on site the next day.
- Over 90% of our business comes from referrals.
- Last year, less than ½ of 1% of our customers returned one of our products.
- Our customer retention rate is 95%, twice that of our nearest competitor.
- After switching to our product line, our customers reported an average 25% boost in manufacturing productivity.

_____

_____

_____

Areas often overlooked or to be considered

- Terms, Materials, Delivery
- Guarantees, Inventory Turns
- Training, Information

Look for things *not claimed by the competition*. Start your list here.

_____

_____

_____

Brainstorm Exercise

1. What would **your competitors say** are their unique "Why their company" points?
2. What would you say to this question: ***"What's so special about your product/service?"***
3. What **values add/extras**, beyond the basic product/services, do you provide? Spell it out.

_____

_____

_____

Additional Guidelines

- Strengths are important *but they are NOT differentiators*.
- If you *have the most options* for your customers, *say so*.
- *Show* customers how much you *save them*.
- What are you *measuring* (and not measuring) today in your company *that could give you differentiation*?
- *Review* your marketing and sales materials, as well as your website.
- What are you doing to *ensure that you will have a new list each year*?

_____

_____

_____

Personality Styles:

- **Be more effective with more people**

- **Identify the buyer's style and adjust accordingly**

- **Two Questions:**

  1) Are they MORE or LESS assertive?

  2) How do they tend to make

     decisions using LOGIC

     or EMOTION?

     (Facts or Feelings?)

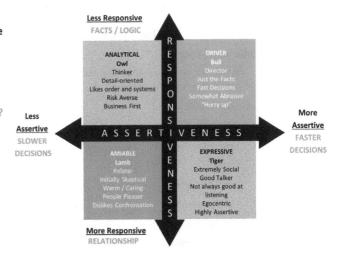

Pre-Call Planning Worksheet

3 Questions MUST BE asked before every call!

1. **What do we _KNOW_?**

   - INFO RESOURCES: What info do we already know or have access to better sell/grow this account?

   - Internal sources

   - Internet research

   - Their website/collateral

   - Vendors

   - Their Competition

   - Their customers

   - Your personal network

   - Their employees

   - Their sales dept.

2. **What do we _NEED TO KNOW_?**

   - What info do we need to learn to progress this sale?

   - Decision-Makers & Influencers

   - Decision making process

   - Business & Personal Objectives that drive the deal

   - HVNs: Highest Value Needs prioritized

   - Timeframe / Deadline

   - Budgets

   - Political agendas

3. **What do we need to _GET THEM TALKING ABOUT_?**

   - What do we need to learn to progress this sale?

   - Socrates → Collaborative discussion

   - They have the Answers, the Reasons, the Motivations for THEIR Buying Process

   - Need to Ask-Questions-And-Listen to learn it

Ask yourself this Question before every call!

What is the purpose of _THIS_ call?

Never make a call WITHOUT a specific purpose!

Best Questions Guide
EXAMPLES

A Best Questions Guide has the most power and works best <u>WHEN it's</u> <u>collaborated and built with inputs from the entire sales team</u>. This has proven to increase results for companies that focus on building it. Below are sample excerpts from companies in a variety of industries.

Once a Question Guide is completed, training is essential to its successful implementation:

1) Prepare them for the answers they may hear.
2) Promote and reward the memorization of the questions.
3) Design prospecting calls using them.
4) Role practice in a variety of situations and styles.
5) Field coach using the guide before & after calls.
6) Coach them to develop the habits of pre-call preparation using the Question Guide as the focus on the "<u>Purpose of *THIS* Call</u>."

<u>Example of Pre-Call Preparation</u>

- What is the *<u>purpose of THIS call</u>*?

- What do we *<u>KNOW</u>*?

- What do we *<u>NEED TO KNOW</u>*?

- What do we *<u>need to GET THEM TALKING ABOUT</u>*?

RELATIONSHIP BUILDING

Excerpts from a company in the advertising industry

HOBBIES – OTHER LEISURE ACTIVITIES:

- What extracurricular activities do you enjoy outside of work?
  - What is your optimal work-life balance?
- How do you unwind after a long, tough day?
- What is your favorite sport?
  - Favorite team?
  - Do you golf? Where?
- What are your other interests outside of work?
  - Do you like to travel, and if so, where do you go?
  - What's your favorite type of music?

BUSINESS ACCOMPLISHMENTS:

- What accomplishments are you most proud of?
  - What kind of recognition have you received?

LAY OF THE LAND

Excerpts from a company in the contract packaging industry

VALUE ADDED / GIFT ITEM OVERVIEW:

- What seasons do you target?
  - Have you tried other holidays and discontinued them?
  - How do you evaluate how successful your programs are?
- What is your annual budget for these programs?
  - What are your goals for this type of marketing?
- What stores are you currently doing business with?
  - What other outlets are you pursuing?
  - When do you normally design products for the upcoming season?
  - What is your sourcing process?

PAIN

Excerpts from a company in the commercial plumbing industry

FINANCIAL:

- What has been the impact in the past when you have chosen a sub contractor on as the primary reason to award a job?
- How has a plumbing contractor or any sub contractors inability to meet a scheduled deadline affected you?
- What effects have the sub-prime mortgage industry had on your company?
- What experience have you encountered working with sub contractors that were not financially stable?

Objections Guide:
Best Responses to your Top Objections

An Objection Response Guide works best <u>WHEN it's collaborated and involves the entire sales team.</u> It is dynamic! Commit to constantly improve it by listening to the responses of the top performers.

Objection Responses Foundation

There's hardly anything that goes on in a sales call that couldn't be anticipated before one's arrival. So it's wise to prepare and practice for the objections and tough questions that you know you will need to deal with!

The primary reason your customer does not buy is his or her FEAR of making a bad decision.

Why do we get Objections?

- People **don't like change**
- People **don't trust you or your solution**
- Previous **bad experience/bad reputation**
- **Shortfall in developing HVNs (High Value Needs)**

Managing Objections Guidelines

1. Managing Objections is selling and good communication: "Seek first to understand, then to be understood."
2. Selling is easy if there is a true need.
3. Qualify any objection so the focus is on the primary reason preventing the prospect from moving ahead.
4. "No" does not mean "No, I don't like you", but "No, I'm not comfortable with going ahead with a decision yet."
5. Think of objections as the details that need to be worked out.
6. Once you have effectively answered an objection, continue your presentation and...ask for the business!

Special Note:
One size does not fit all! Generalized objection responses rarely are specific enough to be effective. Every company needs to customize their Objection Guide to their specific business and industry to optimize the winning!

Actions to take:
Identify the top 3 to 5 most common, and difficult objections and start there. Go around the room and get everyone's best objection responses to each, one at a time. Capture those responses, improve them. Then circulate those best responses and practice them in-house regularly!

How many Objections?

Many people think there are dozens or hundreds of objections. The reality is there are very few. Brainstorm your top 5 or 10. Define the best responses and practice them!

Types of Objections out there:

- *PRICE:*
    - *Your price is too high.* / I need a better price.

- **COMPETITION:**
    - *We are using a competitor. / We only use (certified; approved; etc..) vendors. /* You do not have enough experience.

- **COMPANY ISSUES**
    - BAD EXPERIENCE with this solution or your company. / The last time we used your company, the service was terrible. / Your way of doing business is too cumbersome.

- **TIME**
    - *I'm too busy right now. / I don't have time. / It's not the right time.*

- *SATISFIED:*
    - *I don't need your service. / I'm happy with my current relationship/provider. / We are using a competitor. / We do that inside our company.*

- **FINANCIAL CONSTRAINTS**
    - *We have no budget*

- **STALL/ INDIFFERENCE/BRUSH-OFF**
    - *Let me think about it. / Decision making put off 'til later. / Send me some information.*

- **WRONG PERSON/NOT DECISION-MAKER:**
    - *I don't know the answer. / I don't make this decision.*

Below are some example Objection Responses.

EXAMPLES: 3 Objections and Responses

STALL

Buyer: *I like what we discussed, but let me think about it. / Put off decision making until later.*

- **Note: A classic stall. Any response that stops the sale from moving forward is <u>a decision not to make a decision</u>.** The best sales people won't leave until they know WHY the prospect can't make a decision (or is unable to).

<u>**Qualify their level of Interest**</u>:

- *(Seller Q1:) On a scale of 1 to 10 where 10 is high... where's your level of interest?*

  - Their answer: 5 or 6 = Not interested; 7 or 8 =   Maybe; 9 = Very interested

- *(Seller Q2:) What would it take to get you to a "10"?*

  - Their answer: 9 =   You're real close. They may need you to address a concern or make a minor concession. (You've QUALIFIED the GENUINE PROSPECTS)

  - Their answer: 7 or 8 = You have the real opportunity to close a lot more genuine prospects.

    - They like what you've discussed... but they believe there's still ___(ISSUE)___ and they don't want to ___(ACT TOO SOON / STILL UNCOMFORTABLE / UNANSWERED QUESTIONS)___.

  - The key is, now you know what's in the way and you can better deal with it. (You've learned what SPECIFIC CONCERN is holding back a genuine prospect)

  - Their answer: 5 or 6 = You're miles apart (unless they're being cagey). If they can't tell you what it'll take—mark them for a "call back" or put them in your touch system and move on. (You've DIS-QUALIFIED the NON-BUYERS)

PRICE

Buyer: *Your price is too high/higher than I'm paying. I need a better price. It's more than I can afford.*

Clarify the Objection–

- **Our price is too high? Why do you say that?**

- Get clear on what they're comparing you to, then deal with it.

Framing the True Cost

- We agree. **I wouldn't expect you to buy from me if we are a truly higher cost for your company.**

- But savvy buyers know that it's important to **consider ALL the cost factors**—not just the initial cost/pound.

- They look at all the factors that go into the mix on costs and a good working supplier relationship.

  - **Cost of irregular Quality**

  - **Cost of inconsistent product**

  - **Cost of lack of Control of supply chain**

- That's exactly why savvy buyers know that it's important to consider ALL the cost factors—not just the initial cost/pound. They look at all the factors that go into the mix on costs and a good working supplier relationship.

Your True Costs – Do you know how much you're really paying?

- Ask deeper questions to find out what they know OR point out "hidden" costs.

- Difference between TOP LINE PRICE and BOTTOM LINE PRICE.

- **How price, sales & bottom line profit tie together (Hidden cost)** – It's not the price you pay that matters most... isn't it the price & profit margin that becomes your bottom line gain that matters most? Would you agree?

- **Sales Cost of Lower Quality, weaker service and other factors** – How much in sales and profit could you be losing due to...

  - Consistent quality product? Service? Response time? Knowledge and advice?

    - (Cost of irregular Quality, Cost of inconsistent product, Cost of lack of Control of supply chain)

  - Give success stories/case studies that illustrates the point. Examples of how much sales and profit can be lost buying lower quality product that is lower price on the supply side.

SATISFIED

Buyer: *I don't need your service. I'm happy with my current relationship/provider. We are using a competitor. We do that inside our company.*

You're dealing with a "satisfied" objection—one of the most challenging to overcome.

If you're getting this early in the conversation, often they're just hoping you'll go away. They don't see enough reason to continue or don't want to go to the effort.

If it's after you've had some good Q&A dialog, it still could be a brush-off or be more legitimate after they've considered your value proposition.

Either way you need to get them talking and get more info. You can easily challenge their "all-OK" assertion with questions like…

- **"So you're happy with your_____…**

    - **Current pricing** that is at or below   %?;

    - **Level of customer service, attention and care** to make sure you're fully maximizing all the support you need for your operation to run smoothly, and avoid slowdowns?

    - **Level of innovation** to locate new ideas that match-up well to your needs as they change? (You're looking for an opening of "I'm really not that satisfied")

- The better you probe to uncover their needs, opportunities or problems that they're experiencing… the better you expose new needs and opportunities for your solutions.

At Leverage Sales Coach, we coach sales managers to train their teams to sell more effectively using powerful sales tools like a customized Objections Response Guide. This guide is most powerful when it is *developed with and through your team in a process to develop their buy-in*.

Sellers and sales managers produce more when they train and practice using clear, focused selling tools. Practice using them in-house or you're practicing on your customers!

Dan Larson, Leverage Sales Coach

Best Questions & Active Listening:

- **Do you prepare and ask effective Questions?**

- **Do you ask deeper, probing questions to learn the underlying reasons?**

- **Do you listen actively as much or more than you talk?**

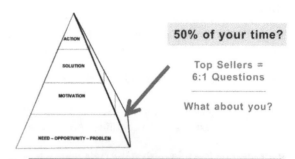

50% of your time?

Top Sellers =
6:1 Questions

What about you?

Victory Goes to Those Best Prepared

Do your Homework – Deeper / Taking control!

- Best questions to <u>uncover THEIR Needs</u>? Surface hidden issues?
- Best questions to <u>uncover THEIR Problems</u>? Unexpected problems?
- Best questions to <u>uncover THEIR Opportunities</u>? Possibilities?
- When it comes to decisions like this, how are they decided?
- Would you like to know our points of difference?
- Is there anything else prohibiting you from going ahead?
- What question should I be asking that I'm not asking?

Objection Responses:

- **Have you prepared best responses to your top 5 toughest objections & questions?**
  - **ROI Calculator**
- **Are you practiced?**
- **How effectively do you manage them and close successfully?**

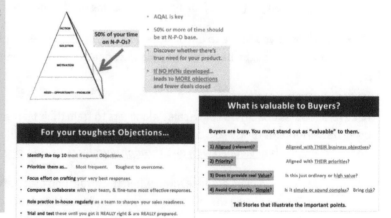

50% of your time on N-P-Os?

- AQAL is key
- 50% or more of time should be at N-P-O base.
- Discover whether there's true need for your product.
- If NO HVNs developed... leads to MORE objections and fewer deals closed

For your toughest Objections...

- Identify the top 10 most frequent Objections.
- Prioritize them as... Most frequent. Toughest to overcome.
- Focus effort on crafting your very best responses.
- Compare & collaborate with your team, & fine-tune most effective responses.
- Role practice in-house regularly as a team to sharpen your sales readiness.
- Trial and test these until you got it REALLY right & are REALLY prepared.
- Ready for a customer to throw objections at you because you'll nail it.
- What would that do for your selling confidence, effectiveness and results?

What is valuable to Buyers?

Buyers are busy. You must stand out as "valuable" to them.

- 1) Aligned (relevant)?   Aligned with THEIR business objectives?
- 2) Priority?   Aligned with THEIR priorities?
- 3) Does it provide real Value?   Is this just ordinary or high value?
- 4) Avoid Complexity. Simple?   Is it simple or sound complex? Bring risk?

Tell Stories that illustrate the important points.

Success Stories Guide

- **Categorize Success Stories by common situations & problems**

- **Match relevant stories to prospects**

- **Sell results and outcomes**

- **'Paint the picture' – make memorable**

- **Collect them & share with team**

- **Practice them, be sales-ready**

Build your
Success Stories
Guide:

- **Keep a notebook**

- **Capture your stories**

- **Use them with buyers in similar situations**

Role Practice

Role Practice:

- **Deliberate practice on specifics**

- **1) Set-up Purpose & Situation**

- **2) Seller Presentation**

- **3) Observer Feedback**

  - 1) What was done well?

  - 2) What can improve?

  - 3) What can you use as a Best Practice?

  - 4) Discussion – What did we learn?

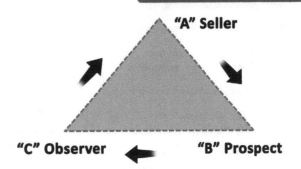

ROLE
PRACTICE

Purpose: Practice, uncover & collaborate best sales practices.
Discuss:
1. What was done well?
2. What can improve?
3. What can you use as Best Practice?

"A" Seller

"C" Observer   "B" Prospect

Sales-Ready Messaging

EXAMPLE: Why Leverage Sales Coaching?

The only coaching & sales development company that wrote
the book with Jack Daly on creating a Hyper Sales Growth Playbook

- **Deliverable Results:**
  - A manufacturing client grew their results by 108% in 32 months. Their sales process became 40% more time-efficient so they could close more business more effectively in much less time
  - We helped a distributor client sell-through 71% of their slow-moving inventory. They cut their fixed overhead cost by $3.5 million per year & realized a huge boost in profits
  - We helped another client change one sales closing process that increased their close rate from 20% to 85% in the first 30 days. It remained over 80% closing for years. They got paid 4x better for doing the same amount of work

- **Guarantee:** We guarantee you'll grow results with 2 commitments from you. 1) **Be Coachable** – open, teachable and willing to accept new ideas 2) You and your team **Take Action** on ideas consistently to get the work done, implement, and execute

- **Customized Playbook:** We help you develop a Hyper Sales Growth Sales Playbook that gets your team focused on their HPAs (High Payoff Activities) to drive reliably bigger results. Train, practice and improve while using the best in People, Processes and Practices. Customized to your industry, company and culture

- **Experience & Know-How:** We've been working closely with Jack Daly since 2003. Our experienced coaches know how to implement these hyper sales growth ideas to get your team producing more

- **Implement Quicker:** We help you Build, Coach and Manage proven sales growth systems and processes quicker and better. Choose top priorities for greatest impact. Speed up building using templates, coaching help and know-how. We help the Sales Manager and sales team Train & Practice to change behavior to grow & scale results

- **Delivery:** Sales development coaching is done onsite or online to increase effectiveness and efficiency

- **Action:** Get your Sales Managers and sales team focused on consistently taking action on their HPAs. We are always agenda-driven and focused on driving change and improvement

- **Terms & Options:** Easy to start. We offer customized solutions to create the right-fit coaching and training plan for your needs

We help you implement better and faster.

SALES MANAGER MULTIPLIER EFFECT

Model the Masters / Mentoring

- Know your *personal strengths* (what you can offer someone)

- Know *your weak spots* (help needed)

- Look for resources on your team to "trade strengths" or mentor with

- Observe intently who you can learn from

- Role practice what is learned. Collaborate often

- Practice deeply: 1) Stretch your self Make mistakes 2) Correct immediately 3) Fix it and repeat 4) Anchor in the correction

LINKS in the SALES CHAIN

Where does *YOUR* sales chain break?

Find the weak links & fix them.

Work smarter. Earn more.

1. Prospecting

2. Qualifying

3. Appointment Setting

4. Presenting

5. Objections Management

6. Closing

7. Follow-Up / Through

Annual Goal Worksheet (Backward Thinking / Goals Back-to-Front Plan) LEVERAGE
SALES COACHING

	Name:		Dated updated:		1/1/2016

GOAL LEVELS		Minimum	Realistic	Stretch
		Minimum results I commit to this period no matter what the conditions.	What I realistically expect to produce this period.	Results I expect this period, if favorable, better than expected conditions.
Annual Goal (example)		$750,000	$1,000,000	$1,300,000
Quarterly (Consider seasonality or variables)	Q1			
	Q2			
	Q3			
	Q4			
	Total	$0	$0	$0
Monthly (Consider seasonality or variables)	1			
	2			
	3			
	4			
	5			
	6			
	7			
	8			
	9			
	10			
	11			
	12			
	Total	$0	$0	$0

Weekly
The minimum I need to produce every week to achieve my goal.

Daily
The minimum I need to produce every day to achieve my goal.

My High-Payoff Top Targets

My Key Activities
that really matter most to drive results

SMART Selling Role Practice: A-B-C Method

A-B-C Roles   Responsibilities

- A = **Seller** – goes through key steps of presentation (condensed for time)

- B = **Prospect** – prospect plays desired role for type of FOCUS practice (below)

- C = **Observer** – make notes of observations
  - Strengths and Weaker areas to improve

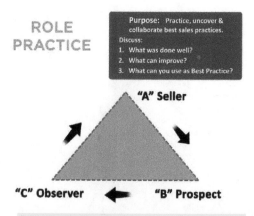

Steps:

- **15 minutes total**   (time may vary but keep it focused on ONE main area to practice)

  - 1 min set-up/agree on situation. GOAL is a Realistic buyer/seller situation; Constructive learning experience to help everyone be more effective

  - 5 min to present / role practice

  - 4 min for Observer feedback

  - 5 min Discussion

- **1) Set-up Purpose & Situation**

  - Type of Selling Practice to FOCUS on   _____
    - What do you want to work on? General? Questions? Objections? Closing? etc.

  - Call type – 1st call, Follow-up, Service call, etc.   _____

  - Situation
    - Type of account? – Relevant to selling situation?   _____

- **2) Seller Presentation**

- **3) Observer Feedback**
  - 1) What was done well?
  - 2) What can improve?
  - 3) What can you use as a Best Practice?

- **4) Discussion – What did we learn?**

- **5) Repeat 2 more times rotating A-B-C roles. Total time approximately 45 min.**

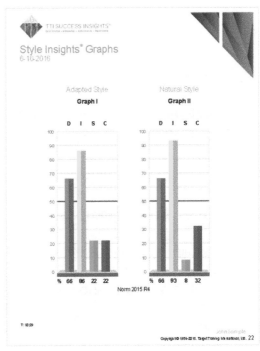

Orientation-Induction Checklist
by Jack Daly

1. Celebration!

2. Make him/her feel welcome and secure. Tour office, introduce to all, and give list of associates with nicknames. Arrange lunch.

3. Explain goals of company, office and unit; who the key team players are.

4. Explain work ground rules.

5. Explain employee benefit plans.

6. Explain position mission and current objectives.

7. Define the work assignment.

8. Present education and training plans—by whom—when. Negotiate the training contract.

9. Present work standards, responsibilities and authorities, reporting systems and productivity expected.

10. Make asking questions easy—where to go for help.

11. Help to be successful on the first day. How?

12. Debrief at end of first day—schedule appointment time.

13. Organize balance of week. Help to be successful—how?

14. Organize balance of month. Help to be successful—how?

15. Set quarterly objectives and quarterly progress reviews. 30-60-90 plan.

16. Hand-deliver calling cards.

My Sales Management HPAs Checklist

Key Area	My Sales Mgmt HPAs	An important HPA	I'm Performing well	I'm OK at this	I need to Learn or Improve
Team Development	Ranking of Sales Staff	☐	☐	☐	☐
	Recruiting & Upgrading Talent	☐	☐	☐	☐
	Culture & Team-Building	☐	☐	☐	☐
Mgmt Process	Sales Strategy Improvement	☐	☐	☐	☐
	Sales Org. Planning, Strategy & Org	☐	☐	☐	☐
	Sales Game Plan Building & Execution	☐	☐	☐	☐
	Prioritization / Focus	☐	☐	☐	☐
	Territory Strategy/Planning	☐	☐	☐	☐
	Goal Achievement & Key Activities Tracking	☐	☐	☐	☐
	Minimum Standards of Performance	☐	☐	☐	☐
	Inspect Expectations/Accountability	☐	☐	☐	☐
	Sales Process Build, Train, Practice & Perform	☐	☐	☐	☐
	Use of CRM & Reporting Tools	☐	☐	☐	☐
	Pipeline Mgmt – Inspect the Baskets	☐	☐	☐	☐
	Touch System Inspection	☐	☐	☐	☐
	Follow-Up & Follow-Through	☐	☐	☐	☐
	Sales Data Tracking & Interpretation	☐	☐	☐	☐
	Profit Analysis	☐	☐	☐	☐
Training & Development	Sales Mgmt Skills Development	☐	☐	☐	☐
	Sales Success Guide Building & Training	☐	☐	☐	☐
	Effective Sales Meetings	☐	☐	☐	☐
	Sales Process Build, Train, Practice & Perform	☐	☐	☐	☐
	Role Practicing Leadership	☐	☐	☐	☐
	1:1 Development & Progress Reviews	☐	☐	☐	☐
	Field Coaching Calls to TGD Mentoring	☐	☐	☐	☐
	Empowerment & Leader Development	☐	☐	☐	☐
	Career Path Planning & Communication	☐	☐	☐	☐
	Effective Communication – Team & Upper Mgmt	☐	☐	☐	☐
	Continuous Learning	☐	☐	☐	☐

The Profession of Sales is for Sales Professionals

Raising performance is driven by HPAs... high payoff actions.

1) Learn

4) Improve

2) Practice

3) Perform

FOR MORE INFORMATION:

Leverage Sales Coaching: Call Dan Larson (800) 565-6516

For help with your Sales Playbook or for coaching and sales development needs, we help you get sales right—the right people, the right systems, and the right leadership to help grow results by Jack Daly's design. We deliver a customized Playbook and coaching plan focused on achieving your sales growth goals, as well as assessment and strategy, skills development, a prioritized action game plan, and accountability to get it done.

E-mail dan@leveragesalescoach.com or visit www.leveragesalescoach.com and click Free Coaching Session.

Jack Daly Speaking: Call Jennifer Geiger (888) 298-6868

Jack delivers explosive customized keynotes, general session presentations, workshops, seminars, and training sessions that inspire audiences to take action in the areas of sales, sales management, corporate culture, customer loyalty, and personal motivation.

E-mail jennifer@jackdaly.net or visit www.jackdaly.net.

Jack Daly Workshops: Call Gabriel Clift (855) 733-7378

Jack's sales workshops, sales-management programs, and performance seminars are ideal for owners, executives, and sales personnel looking to grow sales profitably and increase competitiveness. Available on a per-seat enrollment basis.

E-mail gabriel@jackdaly.net or visit www.jackdaly.net.

Jack Daly Training Tools: www.jackdaly.net/content/dvd-and-cd-tools

A digital library that features Jack Daly's business acumen is available for purchase. The comprehensive collection features lessons on corporate culture, sales management, sales skills, and growing a business, among others. Each of these topics is available in either an audio CD or DVD format. Get motivated with Jack!

Jack Daly Online University: www.jackdalysalesu.com/

The Jack Daly Sales U curriculum was designed to provide entrepreneurs and CEOs, Sales Managers, and sales professionals the tools, knowledge, and application to successfully sell in today's hypercompetitive business environment. Jack Daly pulls back the curtain and leaves no stone unturned. When you complete the curriculum, you will have the tools and knowledge to grow your sales and management team in Quantity and Quality and effectively build a culture that attracts "A" players.

Jack Daly Free Newsletter Signup: www.jackdaly.net/content/newsletter-sign-up/

Sign up to get valuable sales ideas that Jack Daly's clients use to grow their business and increase profitability. Start thinking, acting, and selling more effectively today!

SALES GROWTH RESOURCES

www.jackdaly.net/sales-services/

Jack Daly brings a wealth of experience and can help companies with the growth of their top line and bottom line in a significant fashion. Additionally, he has assembled a team of "Beyond Jack" sales growth resources, which he has personally vetted regarding their capabilities.

Visit the link for a listing of sales services and sales growth resources we can assist you with. Just let us know how we can help, and we will make it happen!

Coaching to grow: Change behaviors to change results.
Customize your Playbook. People. Process. Practices.

Build it. Use it.

Three important drivers to implement a powerful Sales Playbook.

OUR SALES
PLAYBOOK

Work smarter | Earn more

① Build it

- **Build** this "tool" to replicate success. Best practices for Sales & Sales Mgmt.
- Systems, processes & tools to train, replicate & scale success

② Coach it

- **Coaching** to change mindset, attitude & behaviors
- **Training** and **practicing** using the Playbook
- Focus on HPAs (high payoff activities) using best sales practices on best targets

③ Manage it

- **Coaching** Sales Managers focus to train, grow & develop a team to perform
- Grow the team in Quality & Quantity to scale the results

- Guaranteed to grow results.
- Get coaching experience, know-how, clear strategy, and expert help to build & implement quicker.
- Contact us. Get a free sales growth call to help you strategize your Playbook.

(800) 565-6516   leveragesalescoach.com

We help you implement better and faster.

LEVERAGE SALES COACHING

GET THE RIGHT TALENT IN THE RIGHT SEATS
Talent assessments: Recruit, hire, manage & grow better

INCREASED Sales Training and Effectiveness

BETTER COMMUNICATION

IMPROVED PRODUCTIVITY

ELIMINATION of Bad Hires

LEVERAGE SALES COACHING

A TTI Success Insights Value Added Associate

Gain:
- Better communication
- Eliminate bad hires
- Increase employee retention
- Improve productivity
- Better job fit & workplace engagement
- Increase sales training & effectiveness
- Improve management effectiveness
- Develop high potential employees
- Reduce destructive stress
- Full assessment. Behaviors, Motivators and Competencies

(800) 565-6516

leveragesalescoach.com

We help you implement better & faster

Printed in the USA
CPSIA information can be obtained
at www.ICGtesting.com
LVHW082034241123
764766LV00001B/1